PHOTOGRAPHIS 83

PHOTOGRAPHIS 83

The International Annual of Advertising and
Editorial Photography

Das internationale Jahrbuch der Werbephotographie
und der redaktionellen Photographie

Le répertoire international de la photographie
publicitaire et rédactionnelle

Edited by: / Herausgegeben von: / Réalisé par:

Walter Herdeg

Graphis Press Corp., Dufourstr. 107, Zurich (Switzerland)

GRAPHIS PUBLICATIONS

GRAPHIS, International bi-monthly journal of graphic art and applied art
GRAPHIS ANNUAL, The international annual of advertising and editorial graphics
GRAPHIS POSTERS, The international annual of poster art
GRAPHIS PACKAGING VOL. 3, An international survey of package design
CHILDREN'S BOOK ILLUSTRATION VOL. 3, VOL. 4, An international survey of children's book illustration
GRAPHIS DIAGRAMS, The graphic visualization of abstract data
FILM + TV GRAPHICS 2, An international survey of the art of film animation
ARCHIGRAPHIA, Architectural and environmental graphics

GRAPHIS-PUBLIKATIONEN

GRAPHIS, Die internationale Zweimonatsschrift für Graphik und angewandte Kunst
GRAPHIS ANNUAL, Das internationale Jahrbuch der Werbegraphik und der redaktionellen Graphik
GRAPHIS POSTERS, Das internationale Jahrbuch der Plakatkunst
GRAPHIS PACKUNGEN BAND 3, Internationales Handbuch der Packungsgestaltung
KINDERBUCH-ILLUSTRATION BAND 3, BAND 4, Eine internationale Übersicht über die Kinderbuch-Illustration
GRAPHIS DIAGRAMS, Die graphische Visualisierung abstrakter Gegebenheiten
FILM + TV GRAPHICS 2, Ein internationaler Überblick über die Kunst des Animationsfilms
ARCHIGRAPHIA, Architektur- und Umweltgraphik

PUBLICATIONS GRAPHIS

GRAPHIS, La revue bimestrielle internationale d'arts graphiques et d'arts appliqués
GRAPHIS ANNUAL, Le répertoire international de l'art publicitaire et l'art illustratif
GRAPHIS POSTERS, Le répertoire international de l'art de l'affiche
GRAPHIS EMBALLAGES VOL. 3, Répertoire international des formes de l'emballage
ILLUSTRATIONS DE LIVRES D'ENFANTS VOL. 3, VOL. 4, Un aperçu international des illustrations de livres d'enfants
GRAPHIS DIAGRAMS, La visualisation graphique de données abstraites
FILM + TV GRAPHICS 2, Un panorama international de l'art du film d'animation
ARCHIGRAPHIA, La création graphique appliquée à l'architecture et à l'environnement

Distributors / Auslieferung / Distribution:

USA: HASTINGS HOUSE, PUBLISHERS, INC., 10 East 40th Street, New York, N.Y. 10016, [ISBN 0-8038-5897-3]
CANADA: HURTIG PUBLISHERS, 10560-105 Street, Edmonton, Alberta T5H 2W7, tel. (403) 426-2469
FRANCE: GRAPHIS DISTRIBUTION, Milon-la-Chapelle, F-78470 St-Rémy-lès-Chevreuse, tél. 052-13-26
ITALIA: INTER-ORBIS, Via Lorenteggio, 31/1, I-20146 Milano, tel. 422 57 46
SPAIN: COMERCIAL ATHENEUM, S.A., Consejo de Ciento, 130-136, Barcelona 15, tel. 223 14 51-3
AMERICA LATINA, AUSTRALIA, JAPAN AND OTHER ASIAN COUNTRIES, AFRICA:
FLEETBOOKS S.A., c/o Feffer & Simons, Inc., 100 Park Avenue, New York, N.Y. 10017, tel. (212) 686-0888

All other countries / Alle anderen Länder / Tout autres pays:

GRAPHIS PRESS CORP., 107 Dufourstrasse, CH-8008 Zurich (Switzerland)

PUBLICATION No. 170 (ISBN 3-85709-283-1)

Contents

Inhalt

Sommaire

Abbreviations   Abkürzungen   Abréviations

Argentina	ARG	Argentinien	ARG	Afrique du Sud	SAF
Australia	AUS	Australien	AUS	Allemagne occidentale	GER
Austria	AUT	Belgien	BEL	Argentine	ARG
Belgium	BEL	Brasilien	BRA	Australie	AUS
Brazil	BRA	Dänemark	DEN	Autriche	AUT
Canada	CAN	Deutschland (BRD)	GER	Belgique	BEL
Denmark	DEN	Finnland	FIN	Brésil	BRA
Finland	FIN	Frankreich	FRA	Canada	CAN
France	FRA	Grossbritannien	GBR	Danemark	DEN
Germany (West)	GER	Hongkong	HKG	Espagne	SPA
Great Britain	GBR	Indien	IND	Etats-Unis	USA
Hong Kong	HKG	Italien	ITA	Finlande	FIN
India	IND	Japan	JPN	France	FRA
Italy	ITA	Kanada	CAN	Grande-Bretagne	GBR
Japan	JPN	Niederlande	NLD	Hongkong	HKG
Netherlands	NLD	Norwegen	NOR	Inde	IND
Norway	NOR	Österreich	AUT	Italie	ITA
South Africa	SAF	Schweiz	SWI	Japon	JPN
Soviet Union	USR	Sowjetunion	USR	Norvège	NOR
Spain	SPA	Spanien	SPA	Pays-Bas	NLD
Switzerland	SWI	Südafrika	SAF	Suisse	SWI
Thailand	THA	Thailand	THA	Thailande	THA
USA	USA	USA	USA	Union Soviétique	USR

Cover Design / Umschlag / Couverture: Siegbert Kercher

We once more wish to thank all our contributors, whether their work has been reproduced in this volume or whether they have not been lucky this year. It is their cooperation— whether directly recompensed or not—that enables us to compile this rich international survey of modern photography, and we hope we can continue to count on their support. The invitation to submit work for the next volume will be despatched in the near future.

An dieser Stelle möchten wir wiederum allen Einsendern herzlich danken, ob sie nun berücksichtigt werden konnten oder vielleicht dieses Mal leider nicht vertreten sind. Dank ihrer Mitarbeit haben sie es uns ermöglicht, diese vielfältige, internationale Übersicht auf dem Gebiet der Photographie zusammenzustellen, und wir hoffen, auch weiterhin auf sie zählen zu dürfen. In Kürze wird bereits die Einladung für den nächsten Band verschickt.

Nous aimerions remercier ici très chaleureusement tous nos correspondants pour les envois qu'ils nous ont fait tenir, qu'ils aient pu être publiés cette fois-ci ou qu'ils n'aient à notre grand regret pas pu trouver place dans ce volume. C'est grâce à la collaboration de tous ces correspondants que nous avons pu composer ce panorama diversifié de l'art photographique international, et nous espérons bien pouvoir compter aussi à l'avenir sur leur précieuse contribution. Nous leur ferons bientôt parvenir l'appel d'envois pour le prochain volume.

SIEGBERT KERCHER took the shot "Reflections" that appears on this year's cover. He was born in the vicinity of Stuttgart in 1942. After completing his training in photography and laboratory technique he spent three years abroad before opening his own studio in Hanover. A second studio in Hamburg has since been added. His favourite subject is the still life: examples of his work will be found in PHOTOGRAPHIS 1979, 1981 and 1982 as well as in the present volume.

SIEGBERT KERCHER ist der Photograph der Aufnahme «Reflexionen» auf dem Umschlag der diesjährigen Ausgabe. Er wurde 1942 in einem Ort bei Stuttgart geboren, und nach Abschluss seiner Ausbildung als Photolaborant und Photograph verbrachte er drei Jahre im Ausland, bevor er 1975 ein eigenes Photostudio in Hannover eröffnete. Inzwischen ist ein zweites Studio in Hamburg hinzugekommen. Sein bevorzugtes Arbeitsgebiet sind Stilleben – verschiedene Beispiele seiner Arbeiten wurden schon den PHOTOGRAPHIS-Ausgaben von 1979, 1981, 1982 sowie auch im vorliegenden Band vorgestellt.

C'est SIEGBERT KERCHER qui a réalisé la photo «Réflexions» qui orne notre couverture. Né en 1942 dans une localité près de Stuttgart, au bénéfice d'un apprentissage de laborantin photo et de photographe, il a passé trois années à l'étranger avant d'ouvrir un studio de photographie à Hanovre, auquel est venu s'ajouter depuis une second studio à Hambourg. Son thème favori, ce sont les natures mortes. Ses travaux ont été présentés dans les volumes de PHOTOGRAPHIS pour les années 1979, 1981, 1982 et dans la présente édition.

Henry Wolf

Preface

HENRY WOLF, born in Vienna in 1925, emigrated to the United States in 1941. From 1952 onwards he worked there as art director of various magazines and agencies, in 1966 became partner in a new agency (Trahey/Wolf Advertising) and in 1971 founded and became President of Henry Wolf Productions (photography, film, design). He also teaches at the Cooper Union in New York and has exercised various functions in organizations such as the AIGA, the Art Directors Club of New York and the Aspen Design Conference. The honours and awards he has received for his work are too numerous to mention here, but he was nominated Art Director of the Year no less than five years in succession.

Every generation in history has viewed itself (with some pride mixed in with the general sense of doom) to be on the brink of disaster, at the end of the road, the pressure gauge at 99.

A look back in time reveals a golden view of better days, of a more sensible and leisurely existence and a life of tradition and order. Looking forward produces bizarre prognostications that are either too conservative or so outrageous that they never come into being. Jules Verne's predictions of circling the world in 80 days were far exceeded by reality within little more than half a century. On the other hand, exhibits at the 1939 World's Fair envisioned a New York of 1975 with automobiles travelling on multilevel aerial ramps suspended between glass towers and pedestrian malls on the ground. In reality, present-day New York is essentially as it was in 1939, only a little dirtier and generally less pleasant.

The past is predictably lovely, the present puzzling and the future impossible to predict. And so it is with photography.

The days of Daguerre, Atget, Stieglitz and Baron de Meyer are forever gone and their work is considered masterful partly because of the feelings of nostalgia their images conjure up. There is a sense of loss in knowing things have changed and mostly not for the better. The future looks foggy and threatening and speculations about where we are going could be as wrong as the two examples cited earlier. One thing is sure, however: we are not at dead end and continuing change is not only possible but certain. Actually Jules Verne was very far out in his scenario and yet reality trumped him. The World's Fair prophecy turned out to be wrong (even though it was more timid) because it focused on a bad example. Breakthroughs will occur, but we cannot foresee in what areas. The atomic bomb was not one of the eventualities considered by military strategists of the years between the wars. And who, writing on photography in 1940, would have dared to imagine the Polaroid Camera?

Maybe we shall in a not-too-distant future have a way of "seeing" photographs in three dimensions—a real addition to the photographic vocabulary just as colour was after decades of black-and-white. I will not speculate further after denouncing this activity as futile, just hint that there are possibilities in the area of technology.

The artistic province is quite another matter. Here it is not a question of adding new inventions to a repertory of tools but of drawing on different sources, most of them already in existence. Images can be said to consist of two parts: Content and Style. Content is a constant in this equation—it can be described accurately with few words. The caption accompanying a photograph does not need to change with time. In the photographs taken at Pearl Harbor on 7 December 1941 content is everything and style quite unimportant. No one "directed" that event; the recording photographer's main responsibility was to get as sharp a picture as possible and not to be blown up in the process. At the other end of this scale, I think of a photograph Lartigue gave me some years ago of a very young girl and a dog on a beach. Here style is everything. The event is banal, the girl was, I think, a cousin of the artist. The style of dress, the placement of the dog, the diffused light combine to make what could have been just another snapshot into a haunting image.

Content is immovable and doesn't filter through the personality of the artist as much as style. Style is hard to define, always in an airy state of transition and very dependent on fashion. It is through style that the artist becomes visible in his work because he adds to the content of the image his own obsessions, his own past, his own ambivalence. In short, he adds himself. A photographer who doesn't care about fashion should not work for *Vogue.* An artist who likes little girls should have the good sense to write about them and photograph them as did

Lewis Carroll. *Alice in Wonderland* is an enduring work because it is the disclosure of an obsession.

When I worked at *Harper's Bazaar* many young photographers came to see me. It was difficult to pick the ones I should like to work with and I devised a simple imaginary test: If I took their portfolios and spread out all their photographs on the floor and mixed them up well with the work of five other photographers, could I retrieve better than two thirds of a body of work and put it back in the proper folder? If I could, then the work had enough of a personal stamp to be worth considering: what made the pictures recognizable was also what made them unique and therefore interesting. Students often ask me how this uniqueness can be acquired and put into the work. Unfortunately the most common method is to look at the work of other photographers. This mostly encourages a sort of hero worship which results in direct imitation. To become personal and thereby unique, you have to first know who you are and then exploit this knowledge. It takes an amount of courage to let your own background enter into your work because it involves a private knowledge being shared with the public at large. It is a form of undressing in front of an audience. Another possible step toward a personal style is to integrate new sources into your way of seeing. I have always liked surrealism in art and it has played a large part in my method of addressing visual problems.

There is also the importance of physical background. The story line of *War and Peace* could not stand being transposed into present day Chicago. It needs the ballrooms, the uniforms, the Russian winters, the devoted servants, the horses. One of the great changes in the look of photography was brought about by a revolutionary idea: the elimination of background. Sometime in the 1930s someone—I believe it may have been the great innovator Martin Munkacsi—did away with Art Deco columns and replaced them with white paper. Easily portable, it covered up a myriad of table lamps and etched glass doors.

Inspiration for a personal style should not come directly from the work of another artist in the same medium. A painter cannot copy another painter and have a chance at greatness, but he could be inspired by Chinese calligraphy or his parents' stories of the Russian ghetto.

Sources are infinite and every artist is unique. It is enough to be autobiographical to make a new beginning.

Henry Wolf

Vorwort

HENRY WOLF, 1925 in Wien geboren, emigrierte 1941 in die Vereinigten Staaten. Dort arbeitete er ab 1952 als Art Director für verschiedene Zeitschriften und Agenturen, ab 1966 als Partner einer eigenen Agentur (Trahey/Wolf Advertising), und schliesslich als Präsident der Henry Wolf Productions (Photographie, Film, Design), die er 1971 gründete. Daneben unterrichtet er an New Yorks Cooper Union, bei Organisationen wie der AIGA, dem New York Art Directors Club und der Aspen Design Conference übte und übt er verschiedene Funktionen aus. Die hohen Auszeichnungen, die er für seine Arbeiten erhielt, sind zu zahlreich, um hier einzeln aufgezählt werden zu können – u. a. wurde er in fünf aufeinanderfolgenden Jahren vom New York Art Directors Club als Art Director des Jahres nominiert.

Jede Generation in der Geschichte hat sich (mit gewissem Stolz, vermischt mit der allgemeinen Untergangsstimmung) am Rande der Katastrophe gesehen, am Ende der Strasse, kurz vor der Explosion.

Der Blick zurück dagegen lässt alles im goldenen Licht erscheinen, schönere Tage einer sinnvolleren und freieren Existenz und eines Lebens in Tradition und Ordnung. Der Blick in die Zukunft führt zu bizarren Voraussagen, die entweder zu konservativ sind oder so extrem, dass sie nie eintreffen. Jules Vernes Vorhersage einer Weltumfahrung in 80 Tagen wurde nach wenig mehr als einem halben Jahrhundert durch die Wirklichkeit bei weitem übertroffen. In der Zukunftsvision der Aussteller der Expo 1939 hingegen entstand ein Bild der Stadt New York von 1975, worin sich die Autos auf zwischen Glastürmen aufgehängten Rampen auf verschiedenen Ebenen in der Luft bewegen, während es unten auf der Erde nur noch Fussgängerzonen gibt. In Wirklichkeit ist das heutige New York im wesentlichen so wie es 1939 war, nur ein bisschen schmutziger und allgemein weniger angenehm.

Die Vergangenheit erscheint zwangsläufig schön, die Gegenwart verwirrend und die Zukunft unmöglich vorherzusagen. Und so ist es mit der Photographie. Die Zeiten von Daguerre, Atget, Stieglitz und Baron de Meyer sind für immer vorbei. Ihre Arbeit wird als meisterhaft angesehen, zum Teil wegen des Nostalgiegefühls, das ihre Bilder heraufbeschwören. Es liegt ein Gefühl des Verlustes in dem Wissen, dass sich die Dinge geändert haben, und meistens nicht zum Besseren. Die Zukunft erscheint verschwommen und bedrohlich; Spekulationen über das Wohin könnten sich als ebenso falsch erweisen, wie die beiden genannten Beispiele. Eines ist jedoch sicher: wir sind nicht in einer Sackgasse, und ein ständiger Wechsel ist nicht nur möglich sondern sicher. Jules Vernes Voraussage war für seine Zeit sehr gewagt, und trotzdem übertraf die Wirklichkeit sie noch. Die Prophezeiung der Weltausstellung erwies sich als falsch (obgleich sie zurückhaltender war), weil der Gegenstand schlecht gewählt war. Durchbrüche wird es geben, aber wir können nicht voraussehen, auf welchem Gebiet. Die Atombombe gehörte nicht zu den Möglichkeiten, welche die militärischen Strategen der Jahre zwischen den Kriegen in Betracht gezogen haben. Und welcher Journalist hätte 1940 an die Polaroid-Kamera zu glauben gewagt?

Vielleicht haben wir in nicht allzu ferner Zukunft die Möglichkeit, Photographien dreidimensional zu «sehen» – eine echte Neuheit im photographischen Vokabular, so wie es die Farbe nach Jahrzehnten der Schwarzweiss-Photographie war. Ich werde mich nicht weiter in Spekulationen ergehen, nachdem ich sie als nutzlos bezeichnet habe; es ist nur ein kleiner Hinweis, dass auf dem Gebiet der Technologie einiges möglich ist.

Mit der künstlerischen Seite verhält es sich anders. Hier geht es nicht darum, den vorhandenen Mitteln neue Erfindungen hinzuzufügen, sondern um die Ausschöpfung anderer Quellen, von denen die meisten bereits existieren. Man kann sagen, dass Bilder aus zwei Komponenten bestehen: Inhalt und Stil. Inhalt ist eine Konstante in dieser Gleichung – sie kann mit wenigen Worten genau beschrieben werden. Die Legende zu einer Photographie muss nicht unbedingt mit den Jahren an Gültigkeit verlieren. In den Aufnahmen von Pearl Harbor am 7. Dezember 1941 ist alles Inhalt, der Stil ist ziemlich unwichtig. Niemand arrangierte das Geschehen; die Hauptverantwortung des Photographen war ein so scharfes Photo wie möglich zu machen und dabei nicht selbst in die Luft gejagt zu werden. Am anderen Ende dieser Skala denke ich an die Photographie eines sehr jungen Mädchens und eines Hundes am Strand, die mir Lartigue vor einigen Jahren gab. Das Geschehen ist banal, das Mädchen war, glaube ich, eine Cousine des Künstlers. Der Stil des Kleides, die Plazierung des Hundes, das diffuse Licht machten diese Aufnahme, die sonst ein Schnappschuss gewesen wäre, zu einem unvergesslichen Bild.

Inhalt ist unveränderbar und lässt nicht so viel von der Persönlichkeit des Photographen erkennen wie Stil. Stil ist schwer zu definieren, er ist immer in luftiger Schwebe und sehr abhängig von der Mode. Durch Stil wird der Künstler in seiner Arbeit sichtbar, weil er dem Inhalt des Bildes seine eigene Besessenheit, seine eigene Vergangenheit und seine eigene Widersprüchlichkeit hinzufügt. Kurz, er fügt sich selbst hinzu. Ein Photograph, der sich nichts aus Mode macht, sollte nicht für *Vogue* arbeiten. Ein Künstler, der kleine Mädchen mag, sollte über sie schreiben und sie photographieren, wie es Lewis Carroll tat. *Alice im Wunderland* ist ein unsterbliches Werk, weil es die Enthüllung einer Besessenheit ist.

Als ich für *Harper's Bazaar* arbeitete, suchten mich viele junge Photographen auf. Es war schwer, jene herauszupicken, mit denen ich gerne gearbeitet hätte, und so entwickelte ich ein einfaches theoretisches Testverfahren: Wenn ich ihre Mappen nahm und alle ihre Photos auf dem Boden ausbreitete und mit Aufnahmen von fünf anderen Photographen vermischte, war ich dann in der Lage, mehr als zwei Drittel ihrer Arbeiten in die richtige Mappe zurückzusortieren? Falls ich dies konnte, dann war der persönliche Stempel auf diesen Arbeiten ausgeprägt genug, und sie waren es wert, angesehen zu werden: was diese Arbeiten kennzeichnete, machte sie auch einmalig und deshalb interessant. Schüler fragen mich oft, wie diese Einmaligkeit erreicht und in der Arbeit wiedergegeben werden kann. Leider ist die allgemein übliche Methode, sich Arbeiten anderer Photographen anzusehen. Dies fördert eine Art Heldenverehrung, was in direkter Nachahmung resultiert. Um Individualität zu bekommen und dadurch einmalig zu werden, muss man erst wissen, wer man ist und diese Erkenntnis dann ausschöpfen. Es braucht eine Portion Mut, der eigenen Persönlichkeit Eingang in die Arbeit zu gewähren, weil dadurch eine persönliche Erkenntnis mit einer grösseren Öffentlichkeit geteilt wird. Es ist eine Art seelischer Striptease vor einem Publikum. Ein anderer Weg zu einem persönlichen Stil ist die Einbeziehung neuer Quellen in die eigene Art des Sehens. Ich habe den Surrealismus in der Kunst immer geschätzt, und er spielte immer eine grosse Rolle in meiner Handhabung visueller Aufgaben.

Der technische Hintergrund ist ebenfalls wichtig. Die Geschichte von *Krieg und Frieden* liesse sich nicht in das heutige Chicago verlegen. Sie braucht die Ballsäle, die Uniformen, die russischen Winter, die ergebenen Dienstboten, die Pferde. Eine der grossen Veränderungen in der Photographie wurde durch eine revolutionäre Idee verursacht: die Eliminierung des Hintergrundes. Irgendwann in den dreissiger Jahren hat jemand – ich glaube, es könnte der grosse Innovator Martin Munkacsi gewesen sein – die Art-Déco-Säulen verschwinden lassen und sie durch weisses Papier ersetzt. Leicht zu transportieren, verdeckte es unzählige Tischlampen und geätzte Glastüren.

Inspiration für einen persönlichen Stil sollte nicht direkt aus der Arbeit eines anderen Künstlers des gleichen Mediums kommen. Ein Maler kann nicht einen anderen Maler kopieren und dadurch Grösse erlangen, aber er könnte durch chinesische Kalligraphie inspiriert werden oder durch die Erzählungen seiner Eltern über russische Ghettos.

Quellen sind unendlich vorhanden, und jeder Künstler ist einmalig. Es genügt, autobiographisch zu werden, um einen neuen Anfang zu machen.

Henry Wolf

Préface

HENRY WOLF, né à Vienne en 1925, émigre en 1941 aux
Etats-Unis. On l'y trouve dès 1952 directeur artistique de
divers magazines et agences; en 1966, il codirige sa propre
agence, Trahey/Wolf Advertising; en 1971, il fonde les Henry
Wolf Productions (photo, cinéma, design), dont il devient
président. Simultanément il enseigne à la Cooper Union de
New York et exerce diverses fonctions dans des organisations
telles que l'AIGA, l'Art Directors Club newyorkais et l'Aspen
Design Conference. Le nombre des grands prix qui lui ont été
décernés pour ses travaux défie l'énumération – il a entre
autres été nommé cinq fois de suite directeur artistique de
l'année par le New York Art Directors Club.

Chaque génération de l'Histoire s'est déjà vue, avec un sentiment mitigé d'orgueil et
d'appréhension, à deux doigts du désastre, au bout du chemin, sur le point de sombrer dans
la déflagration finale.

S'arrachant à la contemplation de l'avenir, le regard qui se porte sur le passé révèle un
tableau invariablement plus réconfortant: des jours heureux et ensoleillés, une vie plus
placide, plus chargée de sens, ancrée dans l'ordre et dans la tradition. Porter son regard vers
l'avenir, c'est aboutir à des pronostics bizarroïdes où s'affirme un conservatisme excessif ou
alors une vision tellement progressiste des choses qu'elle risque bien de ne jamais se réaliser.
Les prévisions de Jules Verne concernant le tour du monde en 80 jours ont été dépassées de
loin en l'espace de 60 ans. A l'Exposition de New York de 1939, la circulation de 1975 était
envisagée sous forme d'autoroutes multi-étages suspendues entre des gratte-ciel vitrés, les
piétons étant relégués au sol. Près d'un demi-siècle plus tard, rien n'a changé à New York, si
ce n'est que la ville est devenue encore plus sale et encore moins agréable.

Il est prévisible que le passé soit enchanteur, le présent déconcertant et l'avenir impossible à
prévoir. Il en est de même en photographie.

L'époque de Daguerre, d'Atget, de Stieglitz et du baron de Meyer est à jamais révolue. Leurs
travaux sont jugés magistraux en partie en raison de la nostalgie que suscitent leurs images.
Nous éprouvons un sentiment de perte en voyant les choses changer, et guère pour le mieux.
L'avenir nous paraît confus et menaçant. A quoi bon se livrer à des spéculations sur un futur
possible, alors que les deux exemples cités sont là pour nous en rappeler la vanité? Une
chose est certaine cependant: nous ne sommes pas dans une impasse, et le monde va
continuer à se transformer – cela, c'est non seulement possible, mais certain. Jules Verne
était fort en avance sur son temps. La réalité lui a pourtant damé le pion. Les prédictions
faites à l'Expo de 39 se sont avérées fausses (quoiqu'elles fussent plus timides que celles du
grand Nantais) parce qu'axées sur un objet inadéquat. Il y aura des percées, mais nous ne
savons pas dans quels domaines. La bombe atomique n'a pas fait partie des considérations
stratégiques prospectives de l'entre-deux-guerres. Et qui, écrivant un rapport sur les
perspectives de la photographie en 1940, aurait pu imaginer les polaroïds?

Peut-être aurons-nous dans un avenir assez proche la possibilité de «voir» une photographie
en trois dimensions – ce qui constituerait un enrichissement du vocabulaire photographique
comparable à la découverte de la couleur après des décennies de noir et blanc. Mais
arrêtons-là les spéculations, dont j'ai dit qu'elles étaient futiles, et retenons simplement que
la technologie nous réserve encore mainte possibilité d'action.

Le domaine purement artistique, c'est bien autre chose. Là, il ne s'agit pas d'ajouter de
nouvelles inventions à un arsenal déjà bien fourni, mais de s'inspirer d'une multiplicité de
sources, connues pour la plupart. Une image peut être dissociée en deux éléments, le
contenu et le style. Au sein de l'équation «image», le contenu se voit affecter une valeur de
constante et peut se décrire correctement en quelques mots. La légende qui accompagne
une photo n'est pas soumise au passage du temps. Dans les clichés pris à Pearl Harbor le
7 décembre 1941, le contenu prime absolument, tandis que le style n'a pratiquement pas
d'importance. Aucun directeur artistique n'était là pour surveiller la mise en scène. La
responsabilité essentielle du photographe consistait à prendre une photo aussi nette que
possible tout en évitant les balles et les bombes. A l'autre bout de la chaîne, on trouve par
exemple une photo que Lartigue m'a donnée il y a quelques années. On y voit une fillette et
un chien sur une plage. Le sujet est banal; la fillette était, si je m'en souviens bien, une
cousine de l'artiste. C'est le style de la robe, la position du chien, la lumière diffuse qui font
d'un simple instantané une image qui ne vous lâche plus.

Le contenu est immuable; la personnalité de l'artiste ne s'y glisse pas comme elle le fait du
style. Ce dernier est malaisé à définir, il est constamment et aériennement transitoire et très

soumis aux aléas de la mode. C'est grâce au style que l'artiste devient visible dans son œuvre; c'est qu'il ajoute au contenu de l'image ses propres obsessions, son propre passé, sa propre ambivalence. Bref, il s'y ajoute lui-même, en entier. Un photographe qui ne se soucie guère de la mode ne devrait pas travailler pour *Vogue*. Un artiste qui aime les petites filles devrait avoir assez de bon sens pour les mettre en récits et en photos à la manière de Lewis Carroll. *Alice au pays des merveilles* est une œuvre pérenne parce que révélatrice d'une obsession.

Quand je travaillais pour *Harper's Bazaar*, un grand nombre de jeunes photographes venaient me voir. Ce n'était pas facile de choisir parmi eux ceux avec qui je désirais travailler; aussi ai-je mis au point un test imaginaire très simple: j'éparpillais sur le sol le contenu de leurs portefeuilles photo et y mélangeais les photos de cinq autres artistes, puis je m'évertuais à tout remettre dans le portefeuille idoine. Si j'arrivais à reconstituer plus des trois quarts du portefeuille d'un artiste déterminé, j'y voyais la preuve d'un cachet assez personnel pour mériter d'être pris en considération. L'identification des photos était d'autant plus facile qu'elles avaient un caractère unique et, partant, intéressant. Mes étudiants me demandent souvent comment obtenir cette unicité de l'œuvre. Malheureusement, le moyen le plus commun pour y parvenir est encore l'examen des réalisations d'autres photographes. Je dis malheureusement parce qu'il en résulte une sorte de culte des héros avec pour corollaire inévitable une sotte tendance à l'imitation. Pour devenir personnel et donc unique en son genre, il faut d'abord savoir qui on est, puis tirer profit de ce savoir. Il faut pas mal de courage pour laisser ses propres antécédents s'immiscer dans l'œuvre qu'on crée, parce que cela signifie partager avec le grand public une connaissance de soi réservée au seul individu. Cela revient en somme à se déshabiller sur scène. Une autre approche possible pour l'acquisition d'un style personnel consiste à intégrer des sources nouvelles dans sa façon de voir. J'ai toujours aimé le surréalisme en art, et il joue depuis longtemps un rôle important dans la méthode que j'emploie pour résoudre un problème visuel.

Reste l'importance du décor matériel. Le scénario de *Guerre et Paix* ne résisterait pas à une transposition dans le Chicago d'aujourd'hui. Il y faut de salles de bal, des uniformes, des hivers russes, des serviteurs zélés, des chevaux. L'un des grands changements intervenus dans l'aspect de la photographie est né d'une idée révolutionnaire: l'élimination du décor, de l'arrière-plan. Quelque part dans les années 30, quelqu'un – ce pourrait bien être le grand innovateur Martin Munkacsi – s'est avisé d'escamoter les colonnes d'art déco et de les remplacer par du papier blanc. Facile à transporter, ce matériau servit à recouvrir d'innombrables lampes de table et portes vitrées aux fines gravures.

On ne devrait pas puiser l'inspiration source d'un style personnel directement dans l'œuvre d'un autre artiste relevant du même média. Un peintre ne peut pas copier un autre peintre et espérer se tailler un rôle de premier plan, mais il peut par exemple trouver sa source d'inspiration dans la calligraphie chinoise ou dans les récits du ghetto russe que lui firent ses parents.

Les sources sont infinies, et chaque artiste est unique. Il suffit d'être autobiographique pour relancer sa créativité.

Index to Photographers
Verzeichnis der Photographen
Index des Photographes

Index to Designers
Verzeichnis der Gestalter
Index des Maquettistes

Index to Art Directors
Verzeichnis der künstlerischen Leiter
Index des Directeurs Artistiques

Index to Agencies and Studios
Verzeichnis der Agenturen und Studios
Index des Agences et Studios

Index to Publishers
Verzeichnis der Verleger
Index des Editeurs

Index to Advertisers
Verzeichnis der Auftraggeber
Index des Clients

■ We regret that an error occurred in the credits for the two photographs taken from an invitation to an exhibition of the photographer Regina Relang shown in Figs. 235, 236 on page 102 of PHOTOGRAPHIS 82. The photographer was Regina Relang and not Stefan Böhle.

■ In der letzten Ausgabe von PHOTOGRAPHIS zeigten wir auf Seite 102 unter den Abbildungsnummern 235, 236 Aufnahmen der Photographin Regina Relang. Unter den Künstlerangaben wurden diese Aufnahmen versehentlich Stefan Böhle, dem Photographen von Abb. 233, 234, zugeschrieben, während in den Legenden der Name der Photographin richtig erwähnt ist.

■ Dans la dernière édition de PHOTOGRAPHIS nous avions reproduit à la page 102, figs. 235, 236, deux photos d'une carte d'invitation à une exposition de la photographe Regina Relang. Malheureusement une erreur s'est glissée dans la liste des photographes, maquettistes, directeurs artistiques et studios: Regina Relang a réalisé ces photos, et non pas Stefan Böhle.

■ Entry instructions may be requested by anyone interested in submitting samples of exceptional graphics or photography for possible inclusion in our annuals. No fees involved. Closing dates for entries:
GRAPHIS ANNUAL (advertising and editorial art and design): 31 January
PHOTOGRAPHIS (advertising and editorial photography): 30 June
GRAPHIS POSTERS (an annual of poster art): 30 June
Write to: Graphis Press Corp., Dufourstrasse 107, 8008 Zurich, Switzerland

■ Einsendebedingungen können von jedermann angefordert werden, der uns Beispiele hervorragender Photographie oder Graphik zur Auswahl für unsere Jahrbücher unterbreiten möchte. Es werden keine Gebühren erhoben.
Einsendetermine:
GRAPHIS ANNUAL (Werbe- und redaktionelle Graphik): 31. Januar
PHOTOGRAPHIS (Werbe- und redaktionelle Photographie): 30. Juni
GRAPHIS POSTERS (ein Jahrbuch der Plakatkunst): 30. Juni
Adresse: Graphis Verlag AG, Dufourstrasse 107, 8008 Zürich, Schweiz

■ Tout intéressé à la soumission de travaux photographiques et graphiques recevra les informations nécessaires sur demande. Sans charge de participation.
Dates limites:
GRAPHIS ANNUAL (art graphique publicitaire et rédactionnel): 31 janvier
PHOTOGRAPHIS (photographie publicitaire et rédactionnelle): 30 juin
GRAPHIS POSTERS (annuaire sur l'art de l'affiche): 30 juin
S'adresser à: Editions Graphis SA, Dufourstrasse 107, 8008 Zurich, Suisse

Editor and Art Director: Walter Herdeg
Assistant Editor: Stanley Mason
Project Manager: Heinke Jenssen
Designers: Marino Bianchera, Martin Byland, Ulrich Kemmner
Art Assistants: Willy Müller, Walter Zuber

1

Magazine Advertisements

Newspaper Advertisements

Zeitschriften-Inserate

Zeitungs-Inserate

Annonces de revues

Annonces de presse

PHOTOGRAPHER / PHOTOGRAPH:

1, 2 Joop Greypink
3, 5 K. P. Ohlenforst
4 Dennis Manarchy
6 Masamitsu Shibano

DESIGNER / GESTALTER / MAQUETTISTE:

3 Kurt Schumacher
4 William Zabowski
5 Carlo Opolka
6 Osamu Hibino

ART DIRECTOR / DIRECTEUR ARTISTIQUE:

1, 2 Dieter Muntz
3 Kurt Schumacher
4 William Zabowski
5 Carlo Opolka
6 Osamu Hibino

AGENCY / AGENTUR / AGENCE – STUDIO:

1–3, 5 Intermarco Farner
4 Martin/Williams Advertising
6 Create Sam

1, 2 "Drinking like God in France." Examples from a SOPEXA advertising campaign, an organization for the promotion of French agricultural products such as champagne and wine. In full colour. (GER)
3 Full-page magazine advertisement for *Berentzen* apple liqueur. Bright red apple, golden liqueur on a white ground. (GER)
4 Full-page magazine advertisement for an *ADM Foods* sweetener processed from sweet corn. The slogan refers to the company's successful conquest of the market for this product. Photograph turning from hoary grey into a livid grey. (USA)
5 From an advertising campaign for *Maggi* soups. In full colour. (GER)
6 Double-spread advertisement for *Peak*, a Japanese whisky. (JPN)

1, 2 Beispiele aus einer Anzeigenkampagne von SOPEXA, Förderungsgemeinschaft für französische Landwirtschaftserzeugnisse, hier für Champagner und Weine aus Frankreich. In Farbe. (GER)
3 Ganzseitiges Zeitschrifteninserat für *Berentzen*-Apfelkorn. Leuchtend roter Apfel, goldgelber Korn auf weissem Grund. (GER)
4 «Wir brauchten nicht lange, um Eindruck zu machen.» Ganzseitiges Zeitschrifteninserat für aus Mais gewonnenen Süssstoff von *ADM Foods*, die hier auf die erfolgreiche Eroberung des Marktes hinweisen. Aufnahme von Eisgrau in Blaugrau übergehend. (USA)
5 Aus einer Werbekampagne für Dosensuppen von *Maggi*. In Farbe. (GER)
6 Doppelseitige Anzeige für japanischen Whisky der Marke *Peak*. (JPN)

Der Korn macht ihn kernig.

BERENTZEN APPEL, DER KERNIG-KORNIGE VOM LANDE.

3

1, 2 Exemples tirés d'une campagne d'annonces de la SOPEXA, un organisme spécialisé dans la promotion des produits agricoles français – ici du vin et du champagne. En couleurs. (GER)
3 Annonce de magazine pleine page pour l'eau-de-vie de pommes *Berentzen*. Pomme rouge vif, eau-de-vie jaune or sur fond blanc. (GER)
4 «On n'a pas mis longtemps pour faire impression.» Annonce de magazine pleine page pour un édulcorant à base de maïs produit par *ADM Foods*, à haute teneur en fructose et qui s'est rapidement imposé sur le marché. Photo dégradée du gris glacé au gris bleu. (USA)
5 Pour une campagne en faveur des potages *Maggi* en boîtes. En couleur. (GER)
6 Annonce double page pour le whisky japonais *Peak*. (JPN)

これ、ふだん着で飲むウイスキー PEAK ピーク
玉泉堂酒造株式会社

6

7

8

9   10

PHOTOGRAPHER / PHOTOGRAPH:

7, 8   Jurriaan Eindkoven / Chris Lewis
9, 10   Jim Marvy / Kerry Peterson
11, 12   Martin Thompson
13   Steve Steigman
14   Thomas Cugini

DESIGNER / GESTALTER / MAQUETTISTE:

9, 10   John Porter
13   Mark Hughes

ART DIRECTOR / DIRECTEUR ARTISTIQUE:

7, 8   Morton Kirschner
9, 10   John Porter
11, 12   Ron Brown
13   Mark Hughes
14   A. Heidelberger

AGENCY / AGENTUR / AGENCE – STUDIO:

7, 8   KVH/GGK
9, 10   Marsteller, Inc.
11, 12   Abbott Mead Vickers/SMS Ltd.
13   Doyle Dane Bernbach
14   Klöti Werbeagentur

11

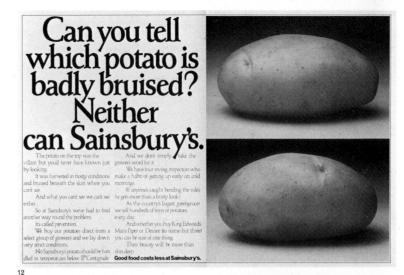

12

13

14

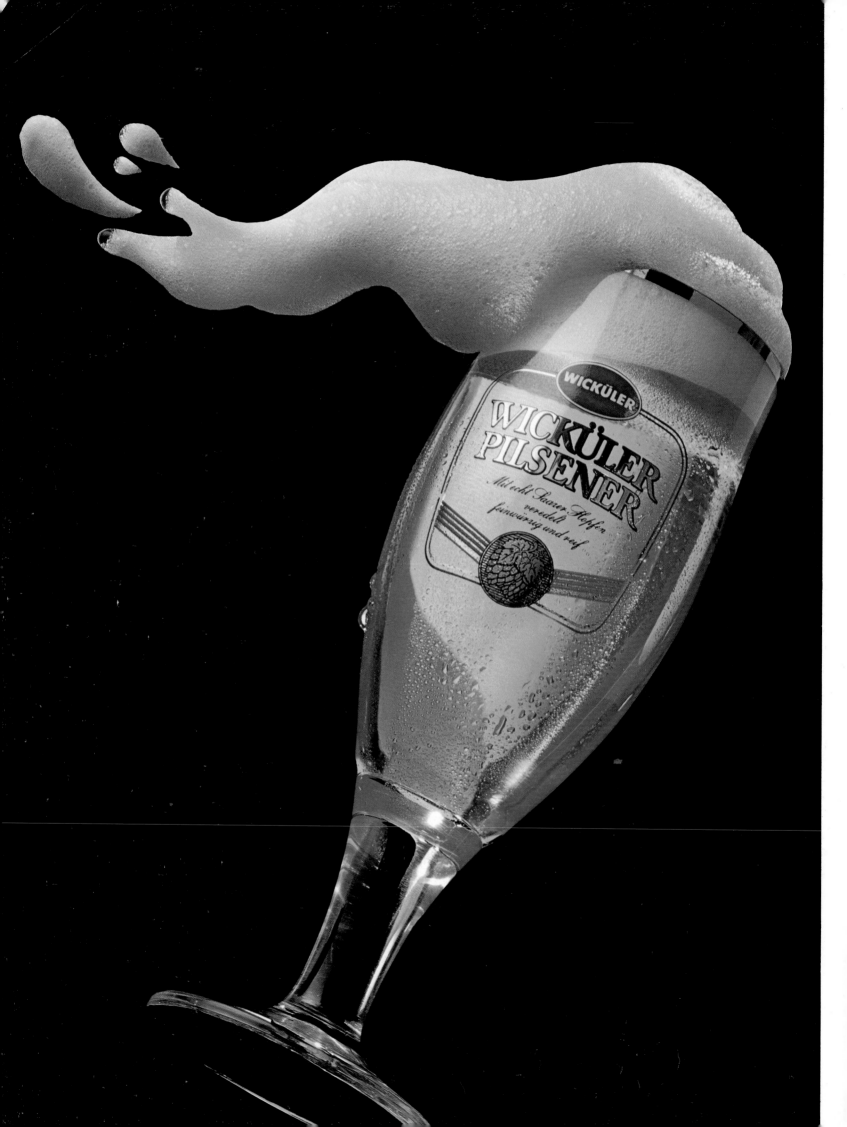

Und jetzt ein Wicküler

16

PHOTOGRAPHER / PHOTOGRAPH / PHOTOGRAPHE:

15, 16 K. P. Ohlenforst
17 Larry Robins

DESIGNER / GESTALTER / MAQUETTISTE:

15, 16 Ingo Bätzel
17 Mark Hughes

ART DIRECTOR / DIRECTEUR ARTISTIQUE:

15, 16 Ingo Bätzel
17 Mark Hughes

AGENCY / AGENTUR / AGENCE – STUDIO:

15, 16 Imparc GmbH & Co.
17 Doyle Dane Bernbach

15, 16 Detail of the photograph and complete full-page trade journal advertisement for *Wicküler* beer. (GER)
17 Trade journal advertisement for Columbian coffee. The theme is the comprehensive advertising campaign on television for this coffee which has completely exhausted Juan and his four-legged friend, the stars of the TV spots. (USA)

15, 16 Detail der Aufnahme und vollständiges, ganzseitiges Fachzeitschriften-Inserat für *Wicküler*-Bier. (GER)
17 «Ruhm hat seinen Preis.» Fachzeitschriften-Inserat für Kaffee aus Kolumbien. Das Thema ist die umfangreiche Fernseh-Werbekampagne für diesen Kaffee, die Juan und seinen vierbeinigen Freund, die Stars der Spots, vollkommen erschöpft hat. (USA)

15, 16 Détail de la photo et annonce complète, pleine page, pour la bière *Wicküler* (revues professionnelles). (GER)
17 «La rançon de la gloire.» Annonce de revue professionnelle pour le café de Colombie, qui a fait l'objet d'une campagne télévisée tellement intense que les vedettes des spots, Juan et son ami le cheval, sont complètement épuisés. (USA)

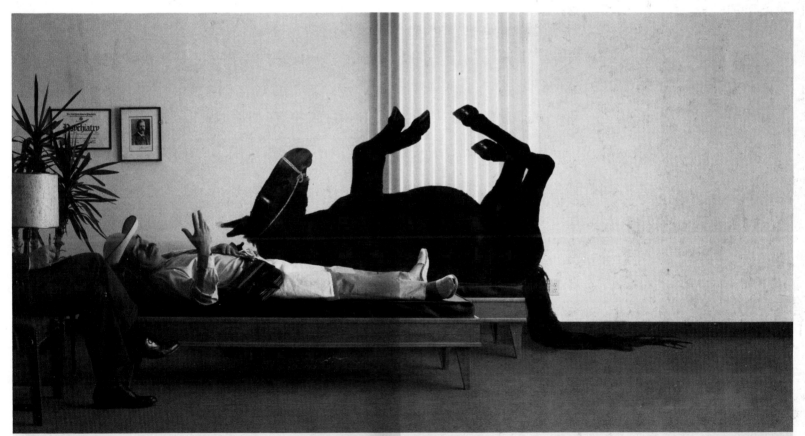

Fame has its price.

"Doctor, it's gotten to the point where people are constantly asking for my autograph. I can't even eat my chorizos in peace."
These words recently came from the fatigued form of Juan Valdez. Along with his partner he's starting to feel the pressure of success.
The cause of it all, of course, is their huge television exposure for Colombian Coffee. In fact this year alone, Juan and his friend will be seen almost 2 billion times in American living rooms.

Frankly they've proven to be successful spokesmen. A recent survey indicates that most Americans now believe that Colombian Coffee is the best in the world. Which, unfortunately for Juan, makes him even more popular.
What this means to you is that if you're not offering a 100% Colombian Coffee brand, it's time to start. Every day you delay you're losing potential profits.
And if you let that happen you'll end up like Juan. Spilling the beans to a psychiatrist.

The National Federation of Coffee Growers of Colombia, 140 East 57th Street, New York, N.Y. 10022

100% Colombian Coffee

17

Plum crazy.

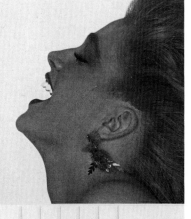

18

Creamy is dreamy.

19

PHOTOGRAPHER / PHOTOGRAPH / PHOTOGRAPHE:

18 Alex Chatelain
19 Barry Lategan
21–24 Hans Hansen/Manfred Kamp
25, 26 Uwe Ommer

DESIGNER / GESTALTER / MAQUETTISTE:

21–24 Detlef Krüger/Manfred Kamp
25, 26 Michel Pahin

ART DIRECTOR / DIRECTEUR ARTISTIQUE:

18, 19 Jon Parkinson
21–24 Jürgen Heymen
25, 26 J. M. Imoucha

AGENCY / AGENTUR / AGENCE – STUDIO:

18, 19 Waring & La Rosa
21–24 GGK
25, 26 R&D Campbell-Ewald

20

Das Ei liebt den Zucker.

21

Die Kirsche liebt den Zucker.

22

Die Erbse lieb t den Zucker.

23

Der Kaffee liebt den Zucker.

24

18, 19 From a series of full-colour advertisements for new nail varnishes by *Cutex*. (USA)
20 Double-spread magazine advertisement for *Cruzan* rum. Mainly in shades of blue. (USA)
21–24 Double-spread advertisements from a comprehensive cooperative campaign for sugar. (GER)
25 Example from an advertising campaign for the *Charles Jourdan* shoe collection for the autumn-winter season 1982/83. In full colour. (FRA)
26 Another *Charles Jourdan* advertisement, here for the autumn-winter 1982/83 leather fashions. (FRA)

18, 19 Aus einer Serie von farbigen Anzeigen für neue Nagellack-Modefarben von *Cutex*. (USA)
20 Doppelseitiges Zeitschrifteninserat für *Cruzan*-Rum. Vorwiegend Blautöne. (USA)
21–24 Doppelseitige Inserate aus einer umfangreichen Zucker-Gemeinschaftswerbung der Wirtschaftlichen Vereinigung Zucker e.V. (GER)
25 Beispiel aus einer Anzeigenkampagne für die Schuhkollektion von *Charles Jourdan* für Herbst/Winter 1982/83. In Farbe. (FRA)
26 Eine weitere Anzeige für *Charles Jourdan*, hier für Ledermode im Herbst/Winter 1982/83. (FRA)

18, 19 D'une série d'annonces pour les nouveaux coloris du vernis à ongles *Cutex*. Couleur. (USA)
20 Annonce de magazine double page pour le rhum *Cruzan*. Tons bleus prédominants. (USA)
21–24 Annonces double page d'une importante campagne en faveur du sucre. «L'œf (la cerise, le petit pois, le café) aime le sucre.» (GER)
25 Exemple d'annonce figurant dans une campagne pour les chaussures *Jourdan*. Couleur. (FRA)
26 Une autre annonce pour *Charles Jourdan*, ici pour la mode du cuir 1982/83. (FRA)

Advertisements / Anzeigen / Annonces

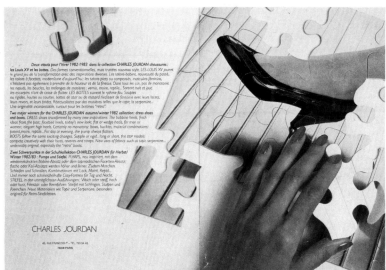

25

26

27 Magazine advertisement for *Frette* bed-linen. In soft shades of beige and brown. (ITA)
28 Black-and-white newspaper advertisement for the *Bloomingdale's* store's "Yes" collection. (USA)
29, 32–34 Complete full-page newspaper advertisement and black-and-white photographs from an advertising campaign by the New York department store *Bloomingdale's* for perfume and cosmetic products made by well-known international manufacturers. (USA)
30, 31 Photograph and complete advertisement from a campaign for *Rocola* shirts. Tanned skin, clothing in black, white shirt. (GBR)

27 Zeitschrifteninserat für *Frette*-Bettwäsche. In sanften Beige- und Brauntönen. (ITA)
28 Zeitungsinserat in Schwarzweiss für die «Yes»-Kollektion des Kaufhauses *Bloomingdale's*. (USA)
29, 32–34 Vollständiges, ganzseitiges Zeitungsinserat und Aufnahmen in Schwarzweiss aus einer Werbekampagne des New Yorker Kaufhauses *Bloomingdale's* für Parfums und Kosmetik international bekannter Hersteller. (USA)
30, 31 «Das *Rocola*-Hemd. Je näher man kommt, um so besser sieht es aus.» Beispiel aus einer Werbekampagne für *Rocola*-Hemden. Haut in warmem Braun, Kleidung schwarz, Hemd weiss.(GBR)

27 Annonce de magazine pour le linge de maison *Frette*. Tons doux beiges et bruns. (ITA)
28 Annonce de journal noir-blanc pour la collection «Yes» du grand magasin *Bloomingdale's*. (USA)
29, 32–34 Annonce de journal pleine page complète et photos noir et blanc pour une campagne publicitaire du grand magasin newyorkais *Bloomingdale's* en faveur des parfums et produits cosmétiques de maisons spécialisées connues au plan international. (USA)
30, 31 «La chemise *Rocola*. Plus on s'en approche, meilleure allure elle a.» Campagne en faveur des chemises *Rocola*. Brun chaud de la peau, vêtements noirs, chemise blanche. (GBR)

PHOTOGRAPHER / PHOTOGRAPH / PHOTOGRAPHE:

27 David Hamilton
28 Gordon Munro
29 Jamie Amrine
30 Richard Prescott
32–34 Shig Ikeda

DESIGNER / GESTALTER / MAQUETTISTE:

28, 29 Fred J. DeVito
30 Peter Rose
32–34 Charles Banuchi

Advertisements / Anzeigen / Annonces

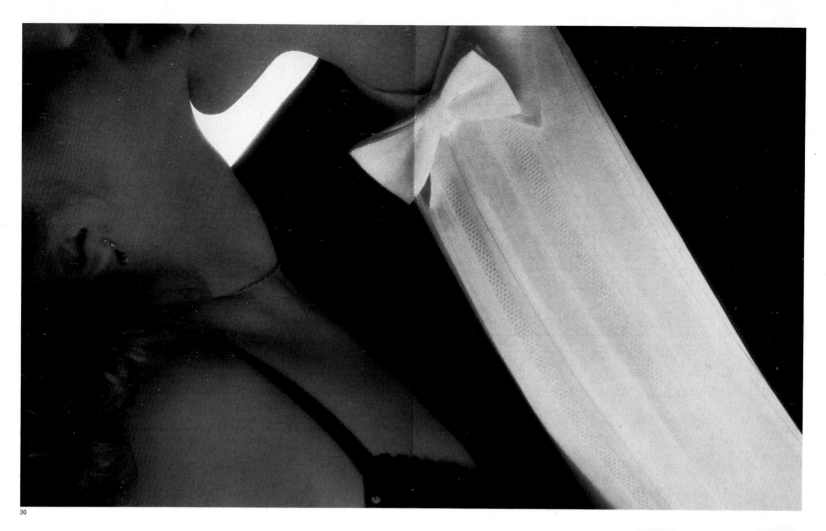

30

ART DIRECTOR / DIRECTEUR ARTISTIQUE:

27 Mauro Mortaroli
28, 29 Fred J. DeVito
30 Peter Rose
32–34 John C. Jay

AGENCY / AGENTUR / AGENCE – STUDIO:

27 Altra
28, 29, 32–34 Bloomingdale's
30 GBA

The Rocola shirt. The close r you get the better it looks.

31

32

33

34

35

35–37 Full-page photographs from a magazine campaign for *Lois* jeans and jackets based on the slogan "*Lois* jeans for people who never get old". Figs. 35 and 37 with combinations of dark blue and white; Fig. 36 with dark clothing contrasting with a light yellow background. The photographer worked with light effects in all these photographs. (GER)
38, 38a Double-spread advertisement and detail of the photograph for the Hilton International chain of hotels, referring to its cosmopolitan characteristics. (USA)

35–37 Ganzseitige Aufnahmen aus einer Zeitschriftenkampagne für *Lois*-Jeans und Jacken unter dem Motto «*Lois*-Jeans für Typen, die nie alt werden». Abb. 35 und 37 mit Kombinationen von Dunkelblau und Weiss, Abb. 36 mit dunkler Kleidung im Kontrast zu einem hellgelben Hintergrund. Bei allen Aufnahmen arbeitete der Photograph mit Lichteffekten. (GER)
38, 38a Doppelseitige Anzeige und Detail der Aufnahme für die Hotel-Kette Hilton International, «wo die Welt zu Hause ist». (USA)

35–37 Photos pleine page figurant dans une campagne de magazines pour les jeans et vestes *Lois* sous le slogan «Des jeans *Lois* pour les gens qui ne vieillissent jamais». Les fig. 35 et 37 combinent le bleu foncé et le blanc, la fig. 36 fait contraster les vêtements sombres et le fond jaune clair. Tout ces photos ont été réalisées avec des effets de lumière. (GER)
38, 38a Annonce double page et détail de la photo réalisée pour la chaîne d'hôtels Hilton International, «où le monde est chez soi». (USA)

PHOTOGRAPHER / PHOTOGRAPH / PHOTOGRAPHE:

35–37 Nick Jarvis
38, 38a Phil Marco

ART DIRECTOR / DIRECTEUR ARTISTIQUE:

35–37 Wolfgang Schulz
38, 38a Laura Vergano

AGENCY / AGENTUR / AGENCE – STUDIO:

35–37 Troost Campbell-Ewald
38, 38a Lord, Geller, Federico, Einstein, Inc.

36

37

Advertisements
Anzeigen
Annonces

39

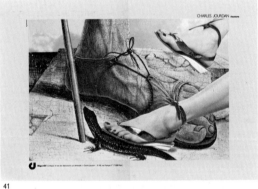

41

PHOTOGRAPHER / PHOTOGRAPH / PHOTOGRAPHE:

39–41 D. Engelhard
42 Detlef Trefz
43 Hank Londoner

DESIGNER / GESTALTER / MAQUETTISTE:

39–41 Roman Cieslewicz
43 Aric Frons

ART DIRECTOR / DIRECTEUR ARTISTIQUE:

39–41 Frank Salier
43 Aric Frons

AGENCY / AGENTUR / AGENCE – STUDIO:

39–41 R&D Ketchum
42 Studio Vogue
43 Harvard, Peskin & Edrick Inc.

39–41 Photo-montages and complete double-spread advertisement for *Charles Jourdan* shoes. The producer, Roman Cieslewicz, employed excerpts from classical works for this campaign, here from one of Giorgione's works and from Dürer's "Four Apostles". (FRA)
42 Full-page advertisement for the 1982 "Alexander" collection of the Parisian cloth manufacturer *Ducrocq*. (FRA)
43 Double-spread magazine advertisement for *Jordache* jeans. Title in reddish brown, jeans in dark blue. (USA)

39–41 Photomontagen und doppelseitige Anzeige für Schuhe von *Charles Jourdan*. Der Gestalter, Roman Cieslewicz, verwendete für diese Kampagne Ausschnitte aus klassischen Werken, hier aus einem Werk von Giorgione und Dürers «Vier Apostel». (FRA)
42 Ganzseitige Anzeige für die «Alexander»-Kollektion 1982 des Pariser Stoffherstellers *Ducrocq*. (FRA)
43 Doppelseitiges Zeitschrifteninserat für *Jordache*-Jeans. Titel in Rotbraun, Jeans in Dunkelblau. (USA)

39–41 Photomontage et annonce double page complète pour les chaussures *Charles Jourdan*. Le concepteur, Roman Cieslewicz, a utilisé pour cette campagne des détails de tableaux classiques, ici un Giorgione et un Dürer («Quatre Apôtres»). (FRA)
42 Annonce pleine page pour la collection «Alexandre» 1982 du fabricant de tissus parisien *Ducrocq*. (FRA)
43 Annonce de magazine double page pour les jeans *Jordache*. Titre brun roux, jeans bleu foncé. (USA)

40

42

43

39

44

44 Magazine advertisement in actual size for the French *François Villon* shoes sold in Japan. (JPN)
45 Magazine advertisement for *Round-The-Clock* panty-hose. Sandy colours and brown shades. (USA)
46 "I feel good in my skin." Example from an advertising campaign for *Dermo-Mild* washing lotion and soap. Photograph in soft brown shades, lettering relating to the product colour. (GER)
47 Full-page advertisement for *Bill Bass* perfume by *Revlon*. Colours from light grey to dark grey, yellow bottle contents. (USA)
48 Example from a multi-page advertising campaign with various full-colour photographs for *Rolex* watches. (FRA)

44 Zeitschriftenanzeige in Originalgrösse für französische Schuhe der Marke *François Villon* in Japan. (JPN)
45 «Zu elegant zum Ausziehen.» Zeitschriftenanzeige für *Round-The-Clock*-Strumpfhosen. Sandfarben und Brauntöne. (USA)
46 Beispiel aus einer Anzeigenkampagne für *Dermo-Mild*-Waschlotion und -Seife. Aufnahme in sanften Brauntönen, der Beschriftung bzw. der Farbgebung des Produktes entsprechend. (GER)
47 Ganzseitiges Inserat für *Bill-Bass*-Parfum von *Revlon*. Farben von Hellgrau bis Schwarzgrau, Flascheninhalt gelb. (USA)
48 Beispiel aus einer mehrseitigen Werbekampagne mit verschiedenen Farbaufnahmen für *Rolex*-Uhren. (FRA)

44 Annonce de magazine au format original pour les chaussures françaises *François Villon* au Japon. (JPN)
45 «Trop élégants pour qu'on les enlève.» Annonce de magazine pour les collants *Round-The-Clock*. Sable, divers bruns. (USA)
46 Exemple d'une campagne d'annonces pour la lotion de lavage et le savon *Dermo-Mild*. Photo aux tons bruns assortis. (GER)
47 Annonce pleine page pour le parfum *Bill Bass* de la maison *Revlon*. Teintes allant du gris clair au gris noir, contenu du flacon jaune. (USA)
48 Exemple tiré d'une campagne publicitaire illustrée de diverses photos couleur, en faveur des montres *Rolex*. (FRA)

Too Elegant To Take Off.   Round-The-Clock.

Sheer Radiance.
Silky, splendid pantyhose.
In softest Ultra Sheer. And a
control top of smoothing shimmer.
There are 17 spring shades,
so you can bury yourself in
color. Ask for #147. At $4.

45

ICH FÜHL MICH WOHL IN MEINER HAUT

Eine zarte und gepflegte Haut macht es jeder Frau ein bißchen
leichter, mit sich und der Welt in Einklang zu leben. Doch viele
Frauen sind mit ihrer Haut nicht glücklich: ist sie empfindlich,
rötet sie sich sehr leicht und spannt unangenehm. Besonders
nach dem Waschen. Das liegt daran, daß Seife, auch die
mildeste, den natürlichen Schutzmantel der Haut angreift und
sie darauf gereizt reagieren kann.
Dermomild ist keine Seife, sondern ein alkalifreies Waschkosmetikum, abgestimmt auf die verschiedenen Hauttypen.
Das Ihre Haut ganz sanft und behutsam reinigt, sie pflegt,
schützt und bewahrt. Was viele dermatologische Tests eindeutig
bewiesen haben.
Dermomild gibt es für empfindliche, trockene oder fettige Haut.
Als Lotion und als Savonette-Stück. Sie erhalten es in Apotheken
und in guten Fachgeschäften.
Dermomild. Damit Sie sich in Ihrer Haut wohl fühlen. Jeden Tag
aufs neue.

DERMOMILD. DAS WASCHKOSMETIKUM
FÜR EMPFINDLICHE HAUT.

46

Own an original Blass.
Bill Blass Fragrance.

Very original in perfume,
cologne, spray cologne.

Bill Blass

47

48

Advertisements
Anzeigen
Annonces

THE MOST EXTRAVAGANT SHOES, BOOTS, AND ACCESSORIES IN MANHATTAN
440 PARK AVENUE NEW YORK, NY 10022 (212) 755-4197

SUSAN**BENNIS**WARREN**EDWARDS**

49

Modewochen in München.
Beine von Bi.

Bi

Strümpfe und Strumpfhosen. Für Beine, die mit der Mode gehen. Ab 7 den.

51

Advertisements
Anzeigen
Annonces

PHOTOGRAPHER / PHOTOGRAPH:	DESIGNER / GESTALTER / MAQUETTISTE:
49, 50 John Pilgreen	49, 50 Stan Eisenman
51 Jost Wildbolz	51 Manfred Gerden
52 S. Kercher	52 Werner Würdinger
53 Masanobu Fukuda	53 Masunobu Okamoto
54 Nora Scarlett	54 Gene Federico

THE MOST EXTRAVAGANT SHOES, BOOTS, AND ACCESSORIES IN MANHATTAN
440 PARK AVENUE NEW YORK, NY 10022 (212) 755-4197

SUSAN**BENNIS**WARREN**EDWARDS**

50

Wie glaubhaft ist ein Kosmetik-Institut, das die gleiche Kosmetik anbietet wie der Einzelhandel um die Ecke.

ROSA GRAF

52

53

AGENCY / AGENTUR / AGENCE – STUDIO:

49, 50 Eisenman & Enock Inc.
51 Wiesmeier
52 Gottschling & Würdinger
53 Daiko Advertising
54 Lord, Geller, Federico, Einstein, Inc.

ART DIRECTOR / DIRECTEUR ARTISTIQUE:

49,50 Stan Eisenman/Dennis Dollens
51 Rudolf Wiesmeier
52 Werner Würdinger
53 Satoshi Mihara
54 Gene Federico

49, 50 Full-page advertisements for *Susan Bennis* and *Warren Edwards*. The obliquely placed photographs are typical for the general advertising concept of this design team. (USA)
51 "Fashion weeks in Munich. Legs by *Bi*." From a campaign for *Bi* stockings and panty-hose. (GER)
52 "How credible is a cosmetics institute that offers the same cosmetics as the retailer around the corner?" Trade journal advertisement for *Rosa-Graf* cosmetics, with emphasis on exclusivity. (GER)
53 Magazine advertisement for *Roger-Vivier* shoes from Paris. (JPN)
54 Newspaper advertisement for *Reva* handbags. Full-colour photograph with a black "R". (USA)

49, 50 «Die ausgefallensten Schuhe, Stiefel und Accessoires in Manhattan.» Ganzseitige Anzeigen für *Susan Bennis* und *Warren Edwards*. Die schräggestellten Aufnahmen sind typisch für die gesamte Werbung dieses Design-Teams. (USA)
51 Beispiel aus einer Zeitschriften-Kampagne für *Bi*-Strümpfe und Strumpfhosen. (GER)
52 Fachzeitschriften-Anzeige für *Rosa-Graf*-Kosmetik, die ausschliesslich Kosmetikinstituten angeboten wird. Hier soll dieser Kunde von den Vorteilen der Exklusivität überzeugt werden. (GER)
53 Zeitschriften-Anzeige für *Roger-Vivier*-Schuhe aus Paris. (JPN)
54 Zeitungswerbung für *Reva*-Handtaschen. Mehrfarbige Aufnahme mit schwarzem «R». (USA)

49, 50 «Les chaussures, bottes et accessoires les plus insolites de Manhattan.» Annonces pleine page pour *Susan Bennis* et *Warren Edwards*. Les photos prises de travers sont typiques du style publicitaire de cette équipe de design. (USA)
51 Exemple tiré d'une campagne de magazines pour les bas et collants *Bi*. (GER)
52 Annonce de revue professionnelle pour les cosmétiques *Rosa Graf* exclusivement distribués à travers les instituts de cosmétique. On met ici en vedette les avantages de cette formule. (GER)
53 Annonce de magazine pour les chaussures *Roger Vivier* de Paris. (JPN)
54 Annonce de journal pour les sacs à main *Reva*. Photo polychrome, «R» en noir. (USA)

54

55

56

PHOTOGRAPHER / PHOTOGRAPH:

55, 56 Wilas Bhende
57, 58 Lois Greenfield
59 Günther Misof
60 Ingolf Thiel

DESIGNER / GESTALTER / MAQUETTISTE:

55, 56 Rasik Patel
57, 58 Frank Young
59 Klaus Gerwin

ART DIRECTOR / DIRECTEUR ARTISTIQUE:

55, 56 Shri A. G. Krishnamurthy
57, 58 Regina Ovesey
59 Klaus Gerwin
60 Uli Weber

AGENCY / AGENTUR / AGENCE – STUDIO:

55, 56 Mudra Communications Pvt. Ltd.
57, 58 Ovesey & Co., Inc.
60 Leonhardt & Kern

57

44

DER STRUMPF-MARKT IST IM UMBRUCH

JETZT BRAUCHEN SIE DEN RICHTIGEN PARTNER

falke

59

55, 56 Photograph and complete double-spread advertisement from a campaign for *Vimal* saris made of 100% polyester. (IND)
57, 58 Examples from a series of double-spread advertisements for ballet outfits and sports clothing by *Capezio*. (USA)
59 Trade journal advertisement for *Falke* stockings. Full-colour photograph with red-white trademark. (GER)
60 Advertisement from a series based on the theme of "people of today" for *Mustang* jeans. This photograph shows Kitty McLaine, one of the last lassoo performers. (GER)

55, 56 «Eine Frau drückt sich in vielen Sprachen aus. *Vimal* ist eine davon.» Aufnahme und vollständige, doppelseitige Anzeige aus einer Kampagne für *Vimal*-Saris. (IND)
57, 58 Beispiele aus einer Serie von doppelseitigen Anzeigen für Ballett- und Sportbekleidung von *Capezio*. (USA)
59 Fachzeitschriften-Inserat für *Falke*-Strümpfe. Mehrfarbige Aufnahme mit rot-weissem Markenzeichen. (GER)
60 Inserat aus einer Kampagne für *Mustang*-Jeans unter dem Motto «Leute von heute», hier mit Kitty McLaine, einer der wenigen Lassodreherinnen, die es noch gibt. (GER)

55, 56 «Une femme s'exprime en beaucoup de langues. *Vimal* est l'une d'entre elles.» Photo et annonce double page complète d'une campagne pour les saris *Vimal*. (IND)
57, 58 Exemples d'annonces double page dans une série pour les costumes de ballet et les tenues de sport *Capezio*. (USA)
59 Annonce de magazine spécialisé pour les bas *Falke*. Photo polychrome, marque déposée rouge et blanc. (GER)
60 Annonce extraite d'une campagne en faveur des jeans *Mustang* intitulée «Les gens d'aujourd'hui», ici avec Kitty McLaine, l'une des dernières artistes au lasso. (GER)

YOU'RE A STAR IN CAPEZIO

Capezio's been dancing since 1887

58

Leute von heute, von sich selbst fotografiert. Diesmal: Kitty McLaine, eine der ganz wenigen Lassodreherinnen, die es noch gibt. Ihren Ehering (siehe Foto), Schmetterling, Texas-Skip, Sonnenfischer, Überroller, Mary-Go-Around, Flip-Flop – und wie die Lassofiguren sonst noch heißen – zeigt sie auf der ganzen Welt. Kitty McLaine macht, was sie will. Und sie trägt, was ihr paßt: Jeans-Shorts von Mustang.

MUSTANG

60

45

61 Example from a campaign with full-page, full-colour magazine advertisements for *Penalty* football boots. Mainly in shades of black, white and yellow. (BRA)

62 Magazine advertisement for *Danskin* swimsuits that are so smart they could be worn to go dancing. Here an exotic model in black with a colourful dragon. (USA)

63, 64, 66 Examples from an advertising campaign with double spreads and single-page newspaper advertisements for *Dior*. Here for bathing fashions (Fig. 63), accessories (Fig. 64) as well as men's fashions and jewellery (Fig. 66). Full-colour photographs. (USA)

65 Double-spread advertisement from an advertising campaign printed in magazines for *Christian Dior* clothes and jewellery. (See also figs. 67–70). In full colour. (USA)

61 Beispiel aus einer Kampagne mit ganzseitigen, farbigen Zeitschriften-Anzeigen für *Penalty*-Fussballschuhe (Penalty = Elfmeter). Vorwiegend schwarz, weiss und gelb. (BRA)

62 «*Danskin* – nicht nur zum Tanzen.» Zeitschriften-Anzeige für *Danskin*-Badeanzüge; hier ein exotisches Modell in Schwarz mit buntem Drachen. (USA)

63, 64, 66 Beispiele aus einer Werbekampagne mit doppel- und einseitigen Zeitungs-Anzeigen unter dem Motto «Ihr *Dior*». Hier für Bademode (Abb. 63), Accessoires (Abb. 64) sowie Herrenmode und Schmuck (Abb. 66). Farbaufnahmen. (USA)

65 Doppelseitige, mehrfarbige Anzeige aus einer Zeitschriften-Kampagne für Kleidung und Schmuck von *Christian Dior*. (Siehe auch Abb. 67–70.) (USA)

61 Exemple-type d'une campagne d'annonces de magazines pleine page en couleur pour les chaussures de football *Penalty*. Tons prédominants: noir, blanc, jaune. (BRA)

62 «*Danskin* – pas seulement pour la danse.» Annonce de magazine pour les maillots de bain *Danskin*, ici pour un modèle exotique en noir décoré d'un dragon multicolore. (USA)

63, 64, 66 Exemples tirés d'une campagne d'annonces de journaux pleine page et double page intitulée «Votre *Dior*», ici pour les modes de plage (fig. 63), les accessoires (fig. 64), la mode messieurs et les bijoux (fig. 66). En couleurs. (USA)

65 Annonce double page en polychromie dans une campagne de magazines pour les vêtements et les bijoux créés par *Christian Dior*. (Cf. aussi les fig. 67–70). (USA)

61

62

63

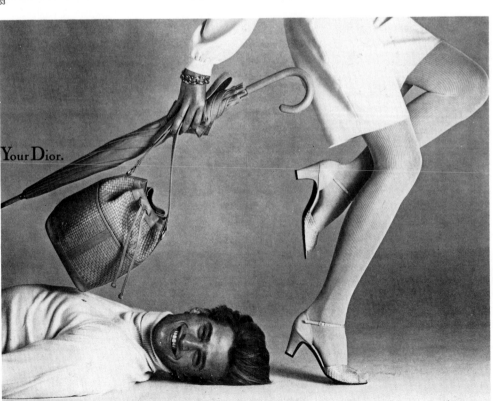

64

They loved armadillos, the American flag, and they disliked all their friends equally.

Dior Women's Sportswear
Women's Jewelry, Men's Dress Shirts, Neckwear, Accessories and Formal Wear.
Christian Dior

65

Your Dior.

66

PHOTOGRAPHER / PHOTOGRAPH / PHOTOGRAPHE:

61 Dú Ribeiro
62 Cosimo
63–66 Richard Avedon

DESIGNER / GESTALTER / MAQUETTISTE:

61 Zezito Marques da Costa/Javier Talavera
63, 64, 66 Gene Federico

ART DIRECTOR / DIRECTEUR ARTISTIQUE:

61 Javier Talavera
62 Mark Shap
63, 64, 66 Gene Federico
65 Richard Avedon

AGENCY / AGENTUR / AGENCE – STUDIO:

61 Marques da Costa Propaganda Ltda.
62 Ogilvy & Mather
65 Lansdowne

Advertisements
Anzeigen
Annonces

67

69

68

PHOTOGRAPHER / PHOTOGRAPH / PHOTOGRAPHE:

67–70 Richard Avedon

ART DIRECTOR / DIRECTEUR ARTISTIQUE:

67–70 Richard Avedon

AGENCY / AGENTUR / AGENCE – STUDIO:

67–70 Lansdowne

67–70 Full-page magazine advertisements and one of the full-colour photographs from an advertising campaign for *Dior*, in which the "Diors" trio is employed throughout. Fig. 67 advertises a ruby-red dressing-gown for men, women's underwear (here in black), jewellery, stockings as well as shirts (here in white). The main theme in Fig. 68 is *Dior*'s glasses; in Figs. 69 and 70 the accent is on women's handbags, stockings and shoes. Another example from this campaign is shown in Fig. 65. (USA)

67–70 Ganzseitige Zeitschriften-Inserate und eine der Farbaufnahmen aus einer Werbekampagne für *Dior*, für die immer dasselbe Trio, die «Diors», gebraucht wurde. In Abb. 67 geht es sowohl um einen weinroten Herren-Hausmantel, Damenwäsche (hier in Schwarz), Schmuck, Strümpfe als auch um Oberhemden (hier in Weiss). Das Hauptthema in Abb. 68 ist die Brille von *Dior*; in Abb. 69, 70 geht es vor allem um Damen-Taschen, Strümpfe und Schuhe. Ein weiteres Beispiel aus dieser Kampagne wird in Abb. 65 gezeigt. (USA)

67–70 Annonces de magazines pleine page, ainsi que l'une des photos publicitaires qui les illustrent. Cette campagne pour *Dior* met toujours en scène le même trio, les «Diors». La fig. 67 concerne une robe de chambre bordeaux pour hommes, de la lingerie fine pour dames (ici en noir), des bijoux, des bas, des chemises (ici en blanc). La fig. 68 est centrée sur les lunettes *Dior*, les fig. 69, 70 sur les sacs à main pour dames, les bas et les chaussures. La fig. 65 provient de la même campagne. (USA)

70

71

72

73   74

UMBERTO GINOCCHIETTI

DISTRIBUTION INTERNATIONAL FINELS PARIS TEL 2256000

75

71, 72 Photograph and complete double-spread advertisement for fashions by *Umberto Ginocchietti*. (ITA)
73, 74 Example from an advertising campaign for *Nina Ricci*, here the photograph and the complete advertisement. (MEX)
75 Another advertisement for *Umberto Ginocchietti*. (ITA)
76 Full-page advertisement for *Chayto*, jewellers situated in Geneva. Photograph in full colour. (SWI)
77 First things first, then … Double-spread magazine advertisement for *Vassarette* ladies' underwear. The model is shown in white, and the chair in black. (USA)

71, 72 Aufnahme und vollständiges, doppelseitiges Inserat für Mode von *Umberto Ginocchietti*. (ITA)
73, 74 Beispiel aus einer Werbekampagne für *Nina Ricci*, hier die Aufnahme und das vollständige Inserat. (MEX)
75 Eine weitere Anzeige für *Umberto Ginocchietti*. In Farbe. (ITA)
76 Ganzseitiges Inserat aus einer Werbekampagne des Juweliers *Chayto* in Genf. Farbaufnahme. (SWI)
77 «Zuerst *Vassarette* … was danach kommt, ist Ihnen überlassen.» Doppelseitige Zeitschriften-Anzeige für *Vassarette*-Damenwäsche. Modell in Weiss, Sessel in Schwarz. (USA)

71, 72 Photo et annonce double page complète pour les créations de mode d'*Umberto Ginocchietti*. (ITA)
73, 74 Exemple des annonces figurant dans une campagne *Nina Ricci*, avec la photo qui l'illustre. (MEX)
75 Une autre annonce couleur pour *Umberto Ginocchietti*. (ITA)
76 Annonce pleine page tirée d'une campagne réalisée pour le bijoutier *Chayto* de Genève. Photo couleur. (SWI)
77 «D'abord *Vassarette*... ce qui suivra dépend de vous.» Annonce de magazine double page pour la lingerie féminine de *Vassarette*. Modèle en blanc, chaise en noir. (USA)

CHAYTO

31, QUAI DES BERGUES, 1201 GENEVE

76

first the Vassarette...

...what goes on after that is up to you.

77

51

78, 79 Safety and security thanks to precise information sought quickly for every investment situation. Full-page, black-and-white advertisement for *Paine Webber*, an investment firm. (USA)
80, 81 Double-spread advertisement from a campaign for the *Club Méditerranée*, advising prospective holidaymakers to flee the winter. Both photographs are mainly in green. (FRA)
82–84 Photograph and complete double-spread advertisement from a gastronomical advertising campaign extolling the virtues of the Hilton chain of hotels. (USA)

78, 79 «Das Wichtigste ist, die Dinge richtig anzupacken. Ganz gleich, welches Spiel Sie spielen.» Ganzseitige Schwarzweiss-Anzeige für eine Anlageberatungs-Firma. (USA)
80, 81 Doppelseitige Anzeigen aus einer Kampagne für den *Club Méditerranée*, der hier empfiehlt, dem Winter zu entfliehen. Beide Aufnahmen vorwiegend grün. (FRA)
82–84 Photo und vollständige, doppelseitige Inserate aus einer gastronomischen Werbekampagne für die Hilton-Hotelkette: «Wo die Welt zu Hause ist.» (USA)

78, 79 «L'important, c'est de prendre les choses par le bon bout. Quel que soit le jeu auquel vous jouiez.» Annonce pleine page, noir et blanc, pour un conseiller en investissements. (USA)
80, 81 Annonces double page tirées d'une campagne du *Club Méditerranée* qui appelle à l'évasion hors des frimas de l'hiver. C'est le vert qui domine dans ces deux photos. (FRA)
82–84 Photo et annonces double page complètes. Campagne gastronomique pour la chaîne des hôtels Hilton: «Où le monde est chez soi.» (USA)

PHOTOGRAPHER / PHOTOGRAPH / PHOTOGRAPHE:

78, 79 Sean Egan
80, 81 Gilles Bensimon
82–84 Charles Gold

DESIGNER / GESTALTER / MAQUETTISTE:

78, 79 David Nathanson
82–84 Laura Vergano

Advertisements / Anzeigen / Annonces

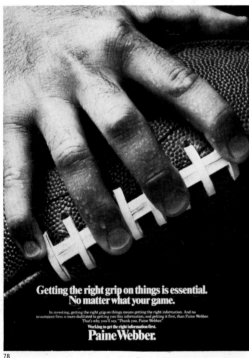

78

80

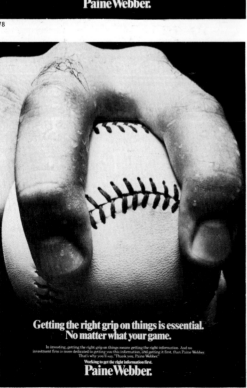

79

79   81

82

HILTON INTERNATIONAL

The sun is barely up and our chef in Athens is already combing the markets for the freshest basil and the ripest tomatoes. By noon our kitchen at the Cavalieri Hilton International in Rome is alive with chopping and the fragrance of simmering sauces. While the last rays of sunlight linger over the Quai du Mont Blanc beside our hotel in Geneva, we're busy serving up this morning's catch. And in Milan, our guests are savoring risotto, rich with cheese from nearby Gorgonzola. Even as you enjoy your brandy on Park Lane in London, or dance late into the night, we're preparing for tomorrow all over the world. For reservations today, call your travel agent or Hilton Reservation Service.

WHERE THE WORLD IS AT HOME™

83

ART DIRECTOR / DIRECTEUR ARTISTIQUE:

78, 79 David Nathanson
80, 81 Bernard Gerbier
82–84 Laura Vergano

AGENCY / AGENTUR / AGENCE – STUDIO:

78, 79 Doyle, Dane, Bernbach
80, 81 Synergie
82–84 Lord, Geller, Federico, Einstein

84

53

First up.

Progressive Farmer.® Month after month, year after year, it's the information source more Southern farmers pick first. Has been since 1886.

At Progressive, we've always been first with the farmer, because the farmer's always been first with us.

We've led him from behind the mule and plow to the high production farm technology of today. We've introduced him to every major advancement in Southern agriculture that's happened in this century.

And we've explained it all with in-depth articles of unfailing accuracy and consistent credibility. Reporting he has come to respect – and expect – in every Progressive issue.

That's why he prefers Progressive two to one over other farm publications. And pays the highest subscription rate in the industry to get it.

Progressive Farmer. We're up first in the field, because we make every issue something to crow about.

Progressive Farmer. We wrote the book on the South.

85

Shop talk.

The farmer. The farmer's wife. When it comes to buying an $80,000 tractor, who decides?

If you think it's the farmer, you're only half right. He may make the purchase. But they both do the shopping.

At Progressive, we've always recognized the wife's importance to the Southern family farm. Especially her evolution as a full-fledged business partner.

So we offer clear, concise articles about farm equipment and supplies, farm management, bookkeeping, marketing – and more – to help both partners make sound business decisions together.

Plus cooking, gardening, sewing and other features for the housewife role she never saw up.

That's why they prefer Progressive two to one over other farm publications. And pay the highest subscription rate in the industry to get it.

Progressive Farmer. We talk shop with her so she can talk turkey with him.

Progressive Farmer. We wrote the book on the South.

86

**Advertisements
Anzeigen
Annonces**

PHOTOGRAPHER / PHOTOGRAPH / PHOTOGRAPHE:

85, 86 Phillip Vullo
87 Clive Arrowsmith
88 Eric Michelson
89 Gordon Munro Studio
90 Michel Meunier

DESIGNER / GESTALTER / MAQUETTISTE:

88 Eric Michelson
90 Fabrice Goux

ART DIRECTOR / DIRECTEUR ARTISTIQUE:

85, 86 Jim Condit
87 Alan Walde
89 Marc Balet
90 Michel Delacroix

AGENCY / AGENTUR / AGENCE – STUDIO:

85, 86 Fletcher Mayo Assoc. Inc.
87 Collett Dickenson Pearce & Partners Ltd.
89 Epstein Raboy Advertising, Inc.
90 Mandarine

Mary's Brave Face.
Brave Faces from Quant. New eyes, cheeks, lips and nails for the civilised savage.

87

54

A drop of Paris LANVIN

88

Issey Miyake at

BARNEY'S, NEW YORK

The Shops for Issey Miyake, Giorgio Armani, Missoni, Sonia Rykiel, Basile, Gianfranco Ferré, Zoran, Shamask are in the Women's Duplex. Shop by shop by shop, our collections are the best of theirs.

Seventh Avenue and Seventeenth Street. Open 9:30 am to 9:30 pm. Free parking. We welcome the American Express card, your Barney's card and other major charge cards.

89

Bio-Météo de Stendhal:
jour après jour, votre peau
se met au beau.

90

85, 86 Double-spread advertisements from a campaign for the *Progressive Farmer* magazine. (USA)
87 Double-spread magazine advertisement for new *Mary Quant* make-up colours. (GBR)
88 Advertisement for a *Lanvin* men's perfume. (USA)
89 Black-and-white newspaper advertisement for *Barney's*, a New York store. (USA)
90 Double-spread advertisement for *Stendhal* cosmetics. The model's clothes in red and black, relating to the trademark of this line of cosmetics. (FRA)

85, 86 Doppelseitige Inserate aus einer Kampagne in Fachorganen für eine Zeitschrift mit dem Titel *Progressive Farmer* («Der fortschrittliche Landwirt»). (USA)
87 Doppelseitiges Zeitschrifteninserat für neue Make-up-Farben von *Mary Quant*. (GBR)
88 «Ein Tropfen von Paris.» Anzeige für ein Herrenparfum von *Lanvin*. (USA)
89 Zeitungsanzeige eines New Yorker Bekleidungsgeschäftes. In Schwarzweiss. (USA)
90 Doppelseitige Anzeige für *Stendhal*-Kosmetik. Die Kleidung des Modells in Rot und Schwarz, dem Markenzeichen der Kosmetiklinie entsprechend. (FRA)

85, 86 Annonces double page réalisées pour des revues professionnelles. Campagne en faveur d'un magazine destiné au monde agricole, *Progressive Farmer* (Le Fermier moderne). (USA)
87 Annonce de magazine double page pour de nouveaux coloris de maquillage *Mary Quant*. (GBR)
88 «Une goutte de Paris.» Annonce pour un parfum hommes de *Lanvin*. (USA)
89 Annonce de journal pour un magasin de confection newyorkais. En noir et blanc. (USA)
90 Annonce double page pour les cosmétiques *Stendhal*. Les vêtements rouges et noirs du modèle correspondent aux couleurs de la marque de cette gamme de produits. (FRA)

92

91

93

94

96

95

DESIGNER / GESTALTER / MAQUETTISTE:

94–96 Susan Casey
97, 98 Axel Gottschall

ART DIRECTOR / DIRECTEUR ARTISTIQUE:

91–93 Sandra Mazzuchelli / Gino Ciccognani
94–96 Susan Casey
97, 98 Axel Gottschall

AGENCY / AGENTUR / AGENCE – STUDIO:

91–93 Armando Testa S. p. A.
94–96 Lord, Geller, Federico, Einstein
97, 98 Gottschall, Martens & Blume

91–93 Advertising for *Milde Sorte* cigarettes, brought to consumers' attention by means of an advertising campaign for sports clothes. Complete advertisements and one of the full-colour photographs. (ITA)
94, 95 Advertisements for *Bass* shoes. Fig. 94 mainly in blue and green shades; Fig. 95 in shades of brown. (USA)
96 Full-page ad for *Bass* children's shoes. Full-colour photograph. (USA)
97, 98 From a campaign with full-page advertisements for Kerkerbachbahn AG, home builders, attempting here to pull in investments for a hotel project. Black-and-white photographs, red text. (GER)

91–93 Hier wird den Konsumenten die Zigarettenmarke *Milde Sorte* durch eine Werbekampagne für Sportkleidung dieser Marke in Erinnerung gerufen. Vollständige Anzeigen und eine der Farbaufnahmen. (ITA)
94, 95 «Gehen Sie in *Bass* oder barfuss.» Anzeigen für *Bass*-Schuhe. Abb. 94 vorwiegend in Blau- und Grüntönen, Abb. 95 in Brauntönen. (USA)
96 Ganzseitiges Inserat für Kinderschuhe von *Bass*. Farbaufnahme. (USA)
97, 98 Aus einer Kampagne mit ganzseitigen Anzeigen für das Wohnungsbauunternehmen Kerkerbachbahn AG, das hier um Investitionen in ein Hotel wirbt, in dem Reiter und Pferd gut untergebracht sein sollen. Aufnahmen in Schwarzweiss, Text in Rot. (GER)

91–93 On évoque ici la marque de cigarette *Milde Sorte* dans le cadre d'une campagne en faveur des vêtements de sport de la même marque. Annonces complètes plus l'une des photos couleur. (ITA)
94, 95 «Promenez-vous en *Bass* ou pieds nus.» Annonces pour les chaussures *Bass*. Fig. 94 tons bleus et verts surtout, 95 divers bruns. (USA)
96 Annonce pleine page pour les chaussures *Bass* pour enfants. (USA)
97, 98 Campagne d'annonces pleine page pour le promoteur immobilier Kerkerbachbahn AG, invitant à investir dans un hôtel qui offre le même confort au cavalier et à son cheval. Photos noir et blanc, texte rouge. (GER)

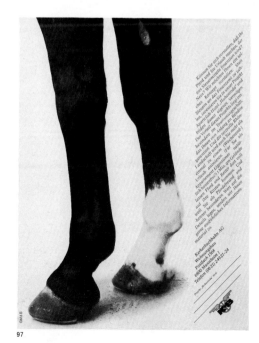

97

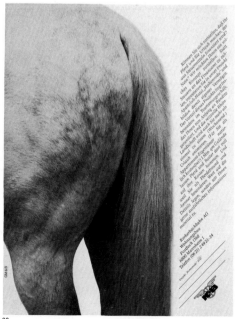

98

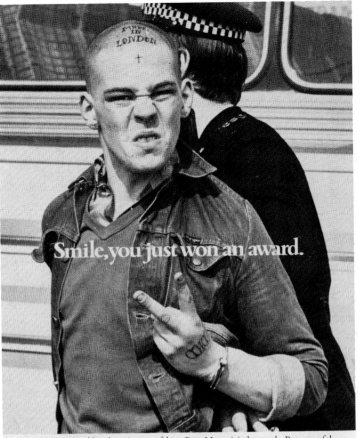

Smile, you just won an award.

Laughing Boy (above) was just one of the shots that clinched a British Press Award for Daily Express photographer John Downing.

He was named Photographer of the Year.

At the same time, the Daily Express team that covered the Iranian Embassy siege, Robert McGowan, Peter Hardy, Ian Black and Peter Mason, jointly won the Reporter of the Year Award. Which is proof that for news and pictures the Daily Express is hard to beat.

And it's not just the British Press Awards jury who think so.

There are another 6,271,000* judges who agree. Every day.

Did your sports department have a winning season last year?

Dennison
Retail
Systems

TRG

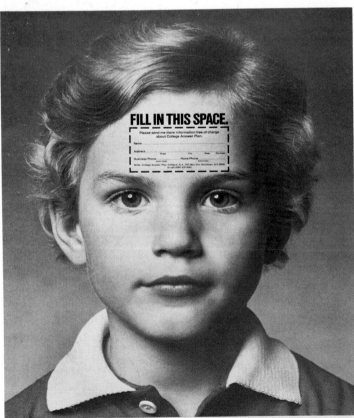

FILL IN THIS SPACE.

Please send me more information free of charge about College Answer Plan.

Name
Address
Business Phone   Home Phone

Write: College Answer Plan, Citibank, N.A., P.O. Box 640, Tarrytown, N.Y. 10591
or call (800) 431-1042

We'll send you the best way to prepare for your child's education.

Easier said than done, right? But giving your child a college education is the most important gift you'll ever give him. And the most expensive too. But thanks to Citibank now there's a way you can prepare for it—The College Answer Plan. It's a unique and comprehensive program that makes the most of your money and your child's future.

First, we start you on a high yield savings program.* And as soon as your account starts to build and earn even higher interest rates, then it really starts to add up. Especially when all your interest can be tax free to you. So the sooner you start saving, the more interest you'll start earning. And by the time your child is ready to go to college, your investment will be too.

What's more, The College Answer Plan can help you and your child pick just the right school. And with our nationwide search, we can locate scholarships to save you even more money. So stop wondering how you'll be able to provide for your child's education. And call us at (800) 431-1042 for information. Or send in this coupon. It may be one of the few things you'll have to cut out to secure your child's future.

◆ COLLEGE ANSWER PLAN. **CITIBANK**

THE CITI NEVER SLEEPS.®

Is ladies underwear starting to fall off on the East Coast?

Dennison
Retail
Systems

TRG

99 Black-and-white advertisement for the *Daily Express* pointing to the awards this newspaper's journalists have won—here particularly in the field of photography. (GBR)
100, 102–104 Full-page advertisements and photograph taken from a trade journal campaign for *Dennison Retail Systems TRG*. Analyses and marketing forecasts are the main themes here in regard to the retail business in which this company specialises. In full colour. (USA)
101 Newspaper ad in black and white for the Citibank offering educational savings programmes. (USA)

99 Schwarzweisses Inserat für den *Daily Express*, das auf die Auszeichnungen hinweist, welche diese Zeitung erhalten hat – hier besonders für Photographie. (GBR)
100, 102–104 Ganzseitige Anzeigen und Aufnahme aus einer Fachzeitschriften-Kampagne für *Dennison*, ein Beratungsunternehmen, das sich auf den Einzelhandel spezialisiert hat. Hier wird auf Analysen und Marktprognosen hingewiesen. Alle Aufnahmen sind mehrfarbig. (USA)
101 Zeitungsinserat in Schwarzweiss für eine Bank, die hier Ausbildungs-Sparprogramme anbietet. (USA)

99 Annonce noir et blanc pour le *Daily Express*, qui fait état des distinctions remportées par ce journal, ici surtout par ses photographes. (GBR)
100, 102–104 Annonces pleine page et photo utilisées dans une campagne que *Dennison*, conseils spécialisés dans le commerce de détail, a lancée dans des revues professionnelles. On attire ici l'attention sur les analyses et pronostics sur l'évolution des marchés réalisés par cette firme. Toutes les photos sont polychromes. (USA)
101 Annonce noir et blanc pour une banque offrant un plan d'épargne en faveur de la formation. (USA)

103

104

PHOTOGRAPHER / PHOTOGRAPH:

99 John Downing
100, 102–104 Peter Rice
101 Michael Pateman

DESIGNER / GESTALTER / MAQUETTISTE:

100, 102–104 Uldis Purins
101 Gary Goldsmith

ART DIRECTOR / DIRECTEUR ARTISTIQUE:

99 Gerhard Stamp
100, 102–104 Uldis Purins
101 Gary Goldsmith

AGENCY / AGENTUR / AGENCE – STUDIO:

99 Boase Massimi Pollitt Univas Partnership Ltd.
100, 102–104 Gregory Fossella Associates
101 Doyle Dane Bernbach

Advertisements
Anzeigen
Annonces

105

SWITCHED ON

ITN HOUSE

106

105, 106 Photograph and complete advertisement for *ITN House*—facilities for video studios. (GBR)
107 For a book entitled *Typography Today*, published by the *Seibundo Shinkosha* company. (JPN)
108 Tradejournal advertisement for *Continental Insurance*. In black and white. (USA)
109 Dogs biting postmen. Double-spread magazine advertisement for the German Post Office, taken from an image campaign series. (GER)
110 Advertisement taken from a campaign printed in trade magazines. (GBR)
111 Newspaper advertisement for The Marquette National Bank's pay-by-phone account. (USA)

105, 106 Aufnahme und vollständiges Inserat für *ITN House*, Ausstatter von Video-Studios. (GBR)
107 Für ein Buch des Verlags *Seibundo Shinkosha*, mit dem Titel «Typographie heute». (JPN)
108 Fachzeitschriften-Inserat für die *Continental*-Versicherungsgesellschaft. Schwarzweiss. (USA)
109 Doppelseitiges Zeitschrifteninserat aus einer Image-Kampagne für das deutsche Bundesministerium für das Post- und Fernmeldewesen. (GER)
110 Inserat als Hinweis auf die Leistungen der «Vereinigten britischen Mälzer». (GBR)
111 Zeitungsinserat einer Bank, die einen Überweisungsdienst per Telephon anbietet. (USA)

105, 106 Photo et annonce complète pour *ITN House*, qui installe des studios vidéo. (GBR)
107 Pour un livre des Editions *Seibundo Shinkosha*, «La typographie aujourd'hui». (JPN)
108 Annonce de revue professionnelle pour une compagnie d'assurances. Noir-blanc. (USA)
109 Annonce de magazine double page, dans une campagne d'image globale de marque du ministère fédéral allemand des PTT: «Voilà le facteur!» (GER)
110 Annonce mettant en vedette les performances des «Malteries britanniques réunies». (GBR)
111 Annonce de journal d'une banque offrant un service de virements par téléphone. (USA)

Advertisements

Anzeigen

Annonces

PHOTOGRAPHER / PHOTOGRAPH:

105, 106 Bob Marchant
107 Yasuhiro Asai
108 Carl Fischer
109 Peter Droste
110 Richard Prescott
111 Dave Olsen

DESIGNER / GESTALTER / MAQUETTISTE:

105, 106 Susan Bingham
107 Helmut Schmid
108 Matthew Haligman
109 Detlef Krüger/Manfred Kamp
110 Peter Rose

Die Post ist da.

109

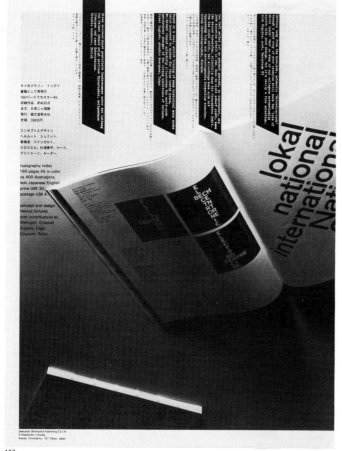

107

Some of our key roles are played by the people you're most unlikely to meet.

110

It's easy to tell who's been to the Continental Booth.

It's RIMS conference time again. Where you can hear dozens of lectures.
Talk to countless spokesmen. And pore through stacks and stacks of pamphlets.
Why not take a shortcut and head straight for the Continental booth.
It'll prove to be a truly uplifting experience.

Continental Insurance
The resources to respond

108

The phone is mightier than the pen.

Marquette Pay-by-Phone
Those who pay by the pen, should think again.

111

ART DIRECTOR / DIRECTEUR ARTISTIQUE:

105, 106 Susan Bingham
107 Helmut Schmid
108 Matthew Haligman
109 Jürgen Heymen
110 Peter Rose
111 Tom Nelson

AGENCY / AGENTUR / AGENCE – STUDIO:

105, 106 Button Design Contracts
107 Helmut Schmid
108 Doyle Dane Bernbach
109 GGK
110 GBA
111 Red Barron Inc.

Glücklich unter die Haube zu kommen, ist gar nicht so einfach...

...aber einen Film davon zu machen mit Bauer. **BAUER** von **BOSCH**

112

112 Advertisement for *Bauer* cameras. The wind was generated by a helicopter. (SWI)
113 Trade magazine advertisement of *Ingersoll-Rand*, pointing out that Japan's superiority is a result of insufficient investments on the part of the competition in the United States. (USA)
114 Full-colour advertisement for *Fiat*'s new "Panda" economy car. (ITA)
115, 116 From a *Stow/Davis* advertising campaign. The photographs are in full colour. (USA)
117, 118 From a trade journal campaign of the *Hüttenes-Albertus* chemical company, here for a raw-material combination for artificial resin and the PTC product group's synthetic moulding sands. (GER)

112 Anzeige für *Bauer*-Filmkameras. Der Wind wurde mit einem Helikopter erzeugt. (SWI)
113 «Mythos gegen Realität.» Fachzeitschriften-Inserat eines Maschinenherstellers, der hier die Überlegenheit der Japaner auf mangelnde Investitionen ihrer Konkurrenten zurückführt. (USA)
114 Mehrfarbiges Inserat für den neuen Kleinwagen «Panda» von *Fiat*. (ITA)
115, 116 Aus einer Kampagne für Büromöbel von *Stow/Davis*. Mehrfarbige Aufnahmen. (USA)
117, 118 Aus einer Fachblatt-Kampagne der Chemiewerke *Hüttenes-Albertus*, hier für eine Rohstoffkombination für Kunstharze und für die PTC-Produktgruppe für synthetische Formsande. (GER)

112 Annonce pour les caméras *Bauer*. L'effet de vent vient d'un rotor d'hélicoptère. (SWI)
113 Annonce de revue professionnelle où un atelier de construction mécanique récuse le mythe de la supériorité japonaise. En fait, les concurrents des Japonais investissent trop peu. (USA)
114 Annonce polychrome pour la nouvelle petite «Panda» de *Fiat*. (ITA)
115, 116 Campagne pour les meubles de bureau *Stow/Davis*. Photos polychromes. (USA)
117, 118 Campagne de la société de produits chimiques *Hüttenes-Albertus* dans des revues spécialisées: un adjuvant pour les résines synthétiques, un autre pour les sables de moulage. (GER)

Myth vs. reality.

By reputation some foreign workers appear productive beyond comprehension.
In reality, the image is illusory.
Productivity gains of workers are as much a result of the intelligent capital investments of their employers as anything else.
American industries simply have not kept pace. According to a comprehensive analysis by the New York Stock Exchange, if this country's rate of investment had equalled Japan's during 1973-1979, the economic growth rate of both countries would have been the same.
In short, a worker is only as good as his tools.
At Ingersoll-Rand our concern is productivity. We provide the products the U.S. needs to refurbish its industries ... everything from hand and power tools that speed assembly lines to air compressors that enable 40 percent productivity gains in textile plants through air weaving.
We know when given the right tools, American workers are equal to or better than any others in the world.
Hands down.

INGERSOLL-RAND.

Panda: quella che fa tutte le cose in grande.

Panda sei grande! *FIAT*

113   114

62

More decisions are made in Stow|Davis offices than anywhere else.

115

TROTZ WASSER... ...KEIN FALL!

117

As you struggle to the top, it helps to have a comfortable place to rest.

116

DIE HAUT... ...DAZWISCHEN

118

119–122 Double-spread trade magazine advertisements for cabinets manufactured by the *Long-Bell* company. Here the advantages of the various models are listed, which the retailer or customer can assemble himself (Figs. 119, 121, 122), as well as their careful production (Fig. 120). (USA)
123 Example from a three-page image advertising campaign for IBM computers. The copy is about (cheese) marketing. (GER)
124 Trade journal advertisement from a campaign for the *Amoco* chemical company, dealing here with various products that are derived from oil such as industrial insulation, fabrics, clothes etc. (USA)

119–122 Doppelseitige Fachzeitschriften-Anzeigen und eine Aufnahme für Schränke der Marke *Long-Bell*. Hier wird auf die Vorteile der Modelle hingewiesen, die der Händler oder der Kunde selbst zusammensetzen kann (Abb. 119, 121, 122), sowie auf die sorgfältige Verarbeitung (Abb. 120). (USA)
123 Beispiel aus einer Image-Kampagne mit dreiseitigen Inseraten für IBM-Computer. Hier geht es um (Käse)-Marketing. (GER)
124 «Wie man Energie aus Chemikalien gewinnt.» Fachzeitschriften-Inserat aus einer Kampagne für die Chemiewerke *Amoco*. Hier geht es um Produkte, die aus Öl gewonnen werden. (USA)

119–122 Annonces double page de revues professionnelles et une photo pour les armoires *Long-Bell*. On en vante les avantages: à monter soi-même (fig. 119, 121, 122), finition parfaite (fig. 120). (USA)
123 Exemple des annonces sur trois pages d'une campagne de prestige pour les ordinateurs IBM: «Ce que renferme l'ordinateur.» Il s'agit ici de la commercialisation du fromage. (GER)
124 «Conserver de l'énergie grâce à la chimie.» Annonce de revue professionnelle figurant dans une campagne de la société de produits chimiques *Amoco*: les produits dérivés du pétrole, textiles, vêtements, isolants domestiques et industriels, etc. (USA)

Advertisements
Anzeigen
Annonces

119

120

121

122

64

Was im Computer drin ist:

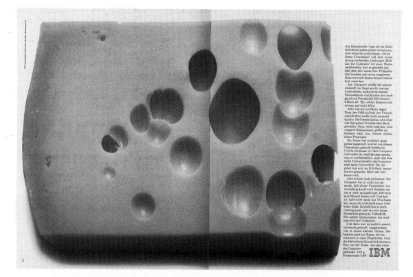

123

PHOTOGRAPHER / PHOTOGRAPH:

DESIGNER / GESTALTER / MAQUETTISTE:

ART DIRECTOR / DIRECTEUR ARTISTIQUE:

AGENCY / AGENTUR / AGENCE – STUDIO:

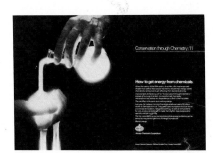

124

125

126, 127 Examples from a magazine advertising campaign for *Lancia*, here for the Coupé 200 I. E. and the *Lancia* Delta. In Fig. 127 the founder of *Lancia*, Vincenzo Lancia, can be seen on the left in the photograph. Both photographs in full colour. (GER)
128, 129 Full-page advertisements in black and white taken from a trade magazine campaign for *Zanussi*, here for dishwashing machines and hot-plates for large kitchens. (GER)
130 Photograph taken from a full-page trade magazine advertisement for *Sikkens* coloured lacquers for motorcars. (SPA)

126, 127 Beispiele aus einer Zeitschriften-Kampagne für *Lancia*, hier für das Coupé 200 I. E. und den *Lancia* Delta. In Abb. 127 ist der Vater des *Lancia*, Vincenzo Lancia, auf dem Photo links zu sehen. Von den wenigen reizvausten *Lancia* Bis eine. Beide Aufnahmen in Farbe. (GER)
128, 129 Ganzseitige Inserate in Schwarzweiss aus einer Fachzeitschriften-Kampagne für *Zanussi*, hier für Geschirrspülmaschinen und Herde für Grossküchen. (GER)
130 Aufnahme aus einem ganzseitigen Fachzeitschriften-Inserat für *Sikkens*-Autofarben. (SPA)

126, 127 Exemples d'annonces pour une campagne *Lancia* dans les magazines, ici pour le coupé 200 I. E. et la *Lancia* Delta. Sur la photo à gauche de la fig. 127, on voit le créateur des *Lancia*, Vincenzo Lancia. Les deux photos sont en polychromie. (GER)
128, 129 Annonces pleine page d'une campagne dans les revues professionnelles pour *Zanussi*; ici pour des lave-vaisselle et cuisinières pour cuisines industrielles. En noir et blanc. (GER)
130 Photo illustrant une annonce pleine page pour les vernis d'automobiles *Sikkens*, dans les revues professionnelles. (SPA)

126

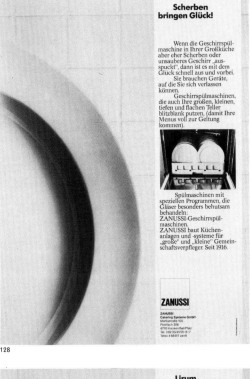

128

127

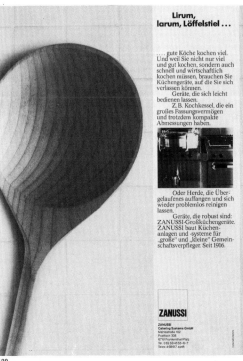

129

130

PHOTOGRAPHER / PHOTOGRAPH / PHOTOGRAPHE:

126, 127 Ben Oyne
128, 129 Detlef Schmalow
130 Miguel Martinez

DESIGNER / GESTALTER / MAQUETTISTE:

128, 129 Axel Gottschall
130 Luis Azagra/Javier Parcerisas

ART DIRECTOR / DIRECTEUR ARTISTIQUE:

126, 127 Uli Weber
128, 129 Axel Gottschall
130 Fernando Ellakuria

AGENCY / AGENTUR / AGENCE – STUDIO:

126, 127 Leonhardt & Kern
128, 129 Gottschall, Martens & Blume
130 Slogan S.A.

Advertisements
Anzeigen
Annonces

YOU CAN'T BE
TOO WELL ARMED TODAY

Since 1979, although the carpet industry
has been shrinking, Horizon's sales have
increased at a rate of 47% per year,
compounded annually. Retailers nationwide
have found that majoring with Horizon means
faster turnover, increased sales,
and higher profits.
The Horizon formula works because it
focuses on the needs of our customers.
Behold...

Horizon Carpets/Calhoun, Georgia

131

PHOTOGRAPHER / PHOTOGRAPH / PHOTOGRAPHE:

131 Arthur Tilley
132 Graham Kirk
133 Peter Smith
134–137 Chico Bialas

DESIGNER / GESTALTER / MAQUETTISTE:

131 Tom Wood
132 Peter Maisey
133 David Waters/Paul Rutterford
134–137 Günter Classen/Beate Lorber

ART DIRECTOR / DIRECTEUR ARTISTIQUE:

131 Tom Wood
132, 133 Peter Maisey
134–137 Axel Hinnen

AGENCY / AGENTUR / AGENCE – STUDIO:

131 Creative Services
132, 133 First City Advertising
134–137 GGK

LOOKS GOOD, TASTES GOOD, SMELLS AWFUL.

The appetising aroma of freshly
fried fish is fine, when it accompanies the
fish.

But the smell is awful when it
doesn't.

It's the same with any kind of
cooking, the smell often lingers long after
the food has been eaten.

Cooking smells fill your kitchen,
your hair, your clothes and, if not checked,
your entire house.

It's nice for your guests to savour

the aroma of good cooking when they
arrive.

But a little unsavoury when they
depart to the same smell.

If all of this is too awful to
contemplate, you need a Power-lectric
cooker hood.

With one of these, a simple press
of a button will help eliminate all cooking
smells, fumes, steam and grease (and
reduce the need for frequent

redecoration in your kitchen too).

Drawn into the hood by powerful
fans and filtered through charcoal and
grease retainers or expelled from your
kitchen permanently, via wall ducts;
depending on the hood you choose.

Power-lectric are by far the largest
and most experienced manufacturers of
cooker hoods in the country, producing
more units than all other UK
manufacturers put together.

And every one we make is

carefully designed to blend in with any
kind of kitchen decor.

Unobtrusively.

Go along to your local Electricity
Board shop, leading department store or
any good electrical retailer soon and see
the comprehensive range of Power-lectric
cooker hoods.

power lectric

Like a breath of fresh air.

132

The best looking roof under the sun

It takes a downpour to fully
appreciate Eternit asbestos cement
slates. Just like natural slate, their full
beauty is revealed when they get wet.

They still make very handsome
roofs when they're dry, of course.
The slates are tough, but as slim as
natural slate, and offer far greater
design possibilities than thick concrete
tiles. There are three aesthetically
pleasing colours – blue-black, brown,
and rose-red. And they can cost less
than some concrete tiles.

Every slate is guaranteed and
supported by the Eternit back-up
service, which offers architecturally
qualified design advice and technical
advice, something no other
manufacturer provides.

If you're looking for a beautiful
roof that does more than keep the rain
out, specify Eternit slates.

Eternit®
For the best-looking roof
in the business Eternit it

Eternit Building Products Ltd.
Meldreth, Nr Royston, Hertfordshire, SG8 5RL
Tel: 0763 60421

133

Sehen, 3. Teil: Wenn Heinz Ketelhut damals bei PHOTO PORST nicht die PORST sound 500 XL macro gekauft hätte, dann hätte er wahrscheinlich nie im Leben zu Gabriele Dorothea Renate Claassen-Lorber gesagt: „Los, springen Sie mal", und sie wäre nie auf die Idee gekommen, mit zugehaltener Nase, angezogenen Knien, wildem Schrei und zum Vergnügen der Hotelgäste in den Swimmingpool zu plumpsen. Nicht nur einmal, sondern siebenmal hintereinander, weil Herr Ketelhut gar nicht genug davon auf seinen Film kriegen konnte. Und seine Freunde in Düsseldorf hätten nie diesen Film gesehen mit der originalgetreuen Wiedergabe von Gabriele Dorothea Renate Claassen-Lorbers unglaublichem Schrei.

134

Sehen, 25. Teil: Sie frühstückten auf der Terrasse des Hotels in Ibiza. Ulla hatte das geblümte Kleid an. Joachim Hoh filmte sie mit seiner PORST MS 60 und blendete ab. Eine Stunde später am Strand richtete er die Kamera wieder auf Ulla, blendete auf und filmte sie auf dem Felsen im Meer. Nach dem Urlaub bekam er von PHOTO PORST den Film zurück und führte Ulla die Vorteile der automatischen Auf- und Abblendautomatik vor. Sie traute ihren Augen kaum: Da saß sie im geblümten Kleid und schwupp, war das Kleid weg, und sie hatte sich in eine Meerjungfrau verwandelt.

135

Advertisements
Anzeigen
Annonces

131 Double-spread trade magazine advertisement for *Horizon* carpets. (USA)
132 Double-spread advertisement for cooker hoods manufactured by the *Power Lectric* company. In full colour. (GBR)
133 Double-spread advertisement for *Eternit* asbestos cement slates. (USA)
134–137 Double-spread magazine advertisements from a big campaign for photographic equipment from *Photo Porst*. Each one shows a photograph being taken with a *Porst* camera and gives a humorous commentary on the event. (GER)

131 Doppelseitiges Fachzeitschriften-Inserat für *Horizon*-Teppiche: «Man kann nicht gut genug ausgerüstet sein.» (USA)
132 «Sieht gut aus, schmeckt gut, riecht furchtbar.» Doppelseitiges Inserat für Küchen-Dampfabzugshauben von *Power Lectric*. In Farbe. (GBR)
133 «Das schönste Dach unter der Sonne.» Doppelseitiges Inserat für *Eternit*-Dachplatten. (USA)
134–137 Doppelseitige Zeitschriften-Inserate aus einer Image-Kampagne für *Photo Porst*. Die Photos sind von humorvollen Kommentaren zu den jeweiligen Ereignissen begleitet. (GER)

131 Annonce double page de revue professionnelle pour les tapis *Horizon*: «On ne saurait être assez bien équipé.» (USA)
132 «Ça a l'air appétissant, ça a bon goût, mais ça pue.» Annonce double page pour les hottes de cuisine *Power Lectric*. En couleur. (GBR)
133 «Le plus beau toit sous le soleil.» Annonce double page pour les plaques d'*Eternit*. (USA)
134–137 Annonces de magazines double page, pour une campagne d'image globale de marque de *Photo Porst*. Chaque photo est accompagnée d'un commentaire plein d'humour. (GER)

Sehen, 1. Teil: Als der Künstler Aristide Maillol, der 1861 in Paris geboren wurde und 1944 dort starb, in seinem Atelier vor Scheiche zurücklest, um sich die gerade Vollendete anzuschauen, die er „Die Strom" nannte, weil sie so was hingegossen dalag, dachte er sicher nicht daran, daß Axel Hennen am 2.3.1980 vier Schritte zurücklest, um mit seiner PORST comparostille OC 14 von Maillols Strom ein Königsbild zu machen, das es nur bei PHOTO PORST gibt und das er immer, wenn er Lust hat, aus seiner PORST-Bibliothek holen und sich darüber freuen kann, daß er nun doch einen kleinen Maillol hat.

137

136

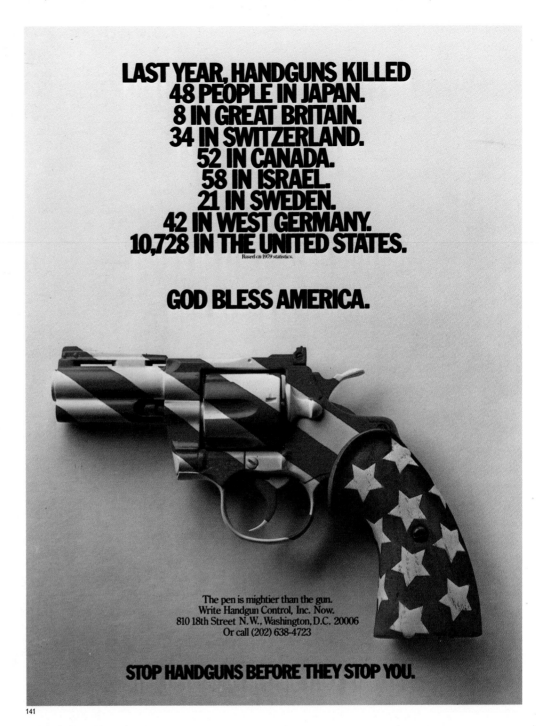

PHOTOGRAPHER / PHOTOGRAPH / PHOTOGRAPHE:

138–140 K. P. Ohlenforst
141 Dennis Manarchy
142 Peter Michael
143 Dennis Chalkin
144, 145 Don Dempsey

DESIGNER / GESTALTER / MAQUETTISTE:

138–140 Klaus Möller
142 Paulo de Andrade
144, 145 Armando Milani

Advertisements
Anzeigen
Annonces

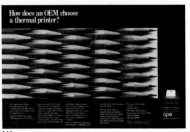

138–140 Examples from a series of full-page, full-colour advertisements for *Tupperware* receptacles. (GER)
141 Advertisement of an organization against the unrestricted use
firearms in America. (USA)
142 Trade journal advertisement for *Brasinca*, supplier for the
automobile industry. Various colours on silvery grey. (BRA)
143 Advertisement for the *Maxell* company, producers of magnetic-
cassettes. (USA)
144, 145 Complete advertisement and photograph for *Olivetti* printers. Pencils in warm shades of yellow. (USA)

138–140 Beispiele aus einer Serie von ganzseitigen, farbigen Inseraten für *Tupperware*-Frischbehälter. (GER)
141 Inserat einer Organisation gegen den uneingeschränkten Be-
sitz von Waffen, ein aktuelles Thema in den USA. (USA)
142 Fachzeitschriften-Inserat für *Brasinca*, Zulieferant für die Auto-
industrie. Verschiedene Farben auf Silbriggrau. (BRA)
143 «Wir machen sehr magnetische Bänder.» Anzeige für Tonband-
Kassetten von *Maxell*. (USA)
144, 145 Vollständiges Inserat und Aufnahme für *Olivetti*-Drucker.
Bleistifte in warmen Gelbtönen. (USA)

138–140 Exemples d'annonces pleine page en couleurs pour les
récipients *Tupperware* pour garder les aliments au frais. (GER)
141 Annonce d'une organisation qui tente de mobiliser la population américaine contre le port d'armes sans restriction. (USA)
142 Annonce de revue professionnelle pour *Brasinca*, fournisseur
de l'industrie automobile. Divers tons sur gris argent. (BRA)
143 «Nous fabriquons des bandes très magnétiques.» Annonce
pour les cassettes à bandes magnétiques de *Maxell*. (USA)
144, 145 Annonce complète et photo l'illustrant. Publicité pour les
imprimantes *Olivetti*. Crayons aux tons jaunes chauds. (USA)

142

ART DIRECTOR / DIRECTEUR ARTISTIQUE:

138–140 Klaus Möller
141 Rick Boyko
142 Alfredo Aquino
143 Cathie Campbell
144, 145 Tom Weisz

AGENCY / AGENTUR / AGENCE – STUDIO:

138–140 MPW Univas
142 CBBA Propaganda S. A.
143 Scali, McCabe, Sloves
144, 145 Weisz, Greco Ltd.

143

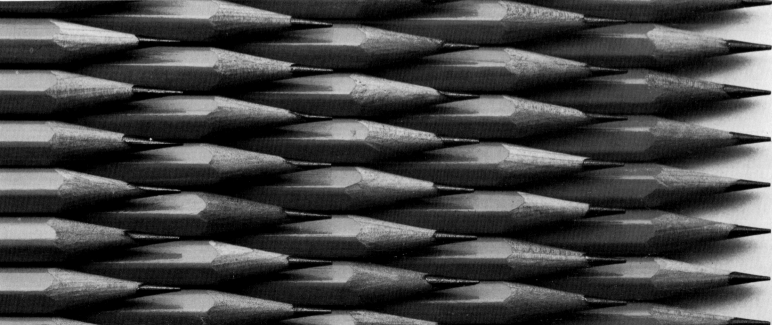

145

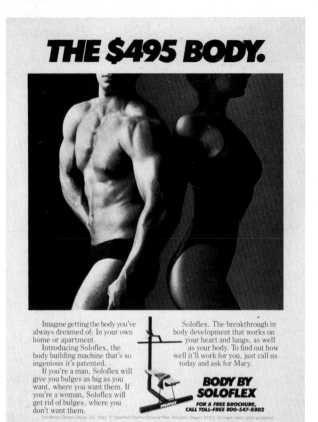

THE $495 BODY.

Imagine getting the body you've always dreamed of. In your own home or apartment.

Introducing Soloflex, the body building machine that's so ingenious it's patented.

If you're a man, Soloflex will give you bulges as big as you want, where you want them. If you're a woman, Soloflex will get rid of bulges, where you don't want them.

Soloflex. The breakthrough in body development that works on your heart and lungs, as well as your body. To find out how well it'll work for you, just call us today and ask for Mary.

BODY BY SOLOFLEX

FOR A FREE BROCHURE, CALL TOLL-FREE 800-547-8802

The Wilson Design Group, Inc. Dept. 17, Hawthorn Farms Industrial Park, Hillsboro, Oregon 97123. All major credit cards accepted.

146

WARNING: THE USE OF THIS PRODUCT MAY BE HAZARDOUS TO YOUR SHIRT COLLECTION.

There's nothing funny about the way Soloflex can develop your body. In your own home or apartment.

Soloflex is the body building machine that's so ingenious it's patented. Anything you can do on health club equipment you can do on Soloflex.

You decide how far you want to go. Soloflex will pump up your muscles as big as you want them, where you want them.

You can outmuscle your old shirts, or look sensational in your new shirts.

And Soloflex won't cost you the shirt off your back. It's only $495. To find out how much it can do for you, call us today and ask for Lisa.

BODY BY SOLOFLEX

FOR A FREE BROCHURE, CALL TOLL-FREE 800-547-8802

The Wilson Design Group, Inc. Dept. 17, Hawthorn Farms Industrial Park, Hillsboro, Oregon 97123. All major credit cards accepted.

147

PETER LINDBERGH AUF KODAK EKTACHROME 400 FILM

KODAK REALISATIONEN

AUCH BEI WENIG LICHT KONTRASTREICHE FARBEN. SCHÄRFE DA, WO SIE SEIN SOLL.

148

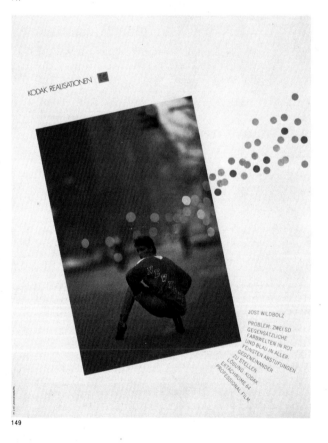

KODAK REALISATIONEN

JOST WILDBOLZ

PROBLEM: ZWEI SO GEGENSÄTZLICHE FARBWELTEN IN ROT UND BLAU IN ALLER FEINSTEN ABSTUFUNGEN GEGENEINANDER ZU STELLEN. LÖSUNG: KODAK EKTACHROME 64 PROFESSIONAL FILM

149

146, 147 Advertisements for *Soloflex* home trainers. In black and white. (USA)
148–150 From a series of advertisements in which well-known photographers comment on *Kodak* diapositive films. Fig.148: Peter Lindbergh on the *Kodak* Ektachrome 400. Dealing here with colour contrasts—red and grey-brown—and sharp focussing with little available light; Figs.149, 150: Jost Wildbolz and Uwe Omner for *Kodak* Ektachrome 64: comparison of red and blue in the finest of gradations, and reliability of the planned colour effect. (GER)

146, 147 Inserate für *Soloflex*-Heimtrainierer. In Schwarzweiss. (USA)
148–150 Aus einer Serie von Inseraten, in denen bekannte Photographen *Kodak*-Diafilme kommentieren. Abb.148: Peter Lindbergh mit *Kodak* Ektachrome 400. Es ging um Farbkontraste – hier Rot und Grau-Braun – und Schärfe bei wenig Licht. Abb.149, 150: Jost Wildbolz und Uwe Omner für *Kodak* Ektachrome 64. Die Aufgaben: Gegeneinanderstellung von Rot und Blau in allerfeinsten Abstufungen und Zuverlässigkeit der geplanten Farbwirkung. (GER)

146, 147 Pour les engins de musculation *Soloflex*. Noir-blanc. (USA)
148–150 Exemples d'annonces où des photographes réputés commentent des films diapos *Kodak*. Fig.148: Peter Lindbergh avec le *Kodak* Ektachrome 400. Il s'agissait de couleurs contrastantes – ici le rouge et le brun gris – et de la netteté obtenue sous une faible lumière. Fig.149, 150: Jost Wildbolz et Uwe Omner avec le *Kodak* Ektachrome 64. Il s'agissait ici de mettre en contraste le rouge et le bleu dans les nuances les plus fines à obtenir, en respectant parfaitement l'effet chromatique recherché. (GER)

UWE OMMER.
WIRD DIE FARBE
BEWUSST
EINGESETZT,
UM EINE BESTIMMTE
WIRKUNG
ZU ERZIELEN,
SO MUSS DER FILM
ZUVERLÄSSIG,
D. H. BERECHENBAR SEIN.
KODAK EKTACHROME 64
PROFESSIONAL FILM.

UNTAS | HAMBURG PF 9/81

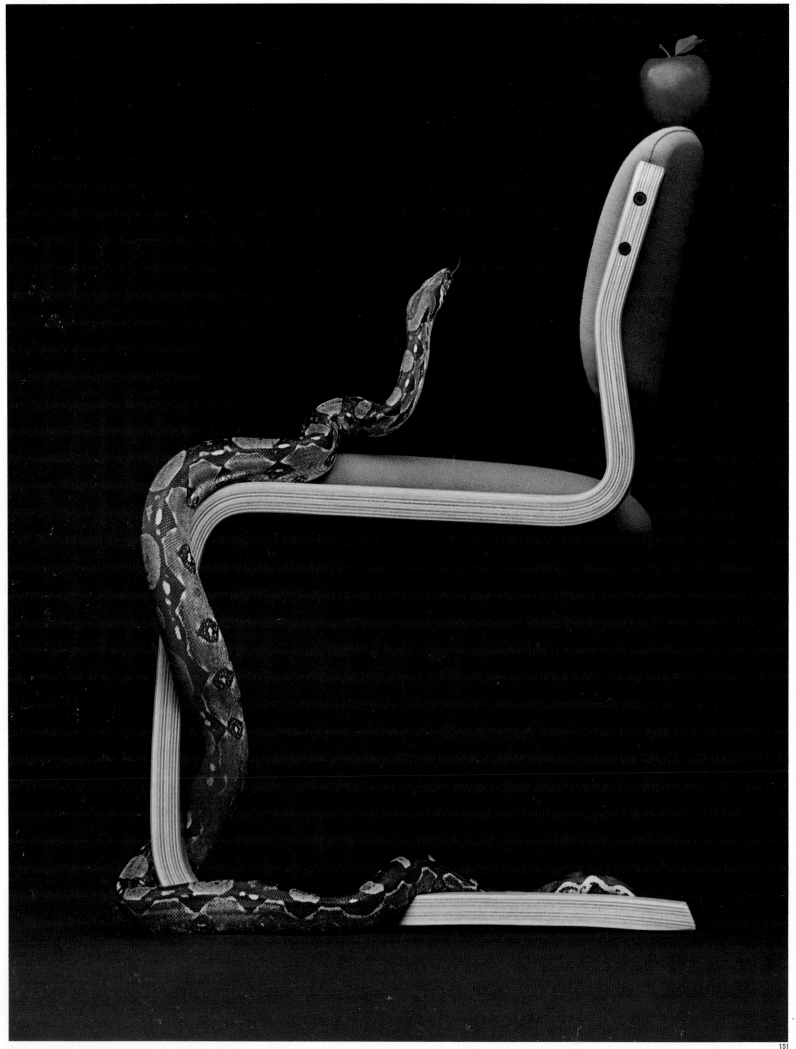

151a

PHOTOGRAPHER / PHOTOGRAPH:

151, 151a Hickson Bender
152 Rick Etkin
153 Michael Furman
154 Hermann-Josef Giesen
155 Dietmar Henneka

DESIGNER / GESTALTER / MAQUETTISTE:

152 Rick Etkin
153 Partners Design
154, 155 Dirk Barelmann

ART DIRECTOR / DIRECTEUR ARTISTIQUE:

151, 151a Bob Bender/Doug Fisher
152 Rick Etkin
153 Partners Design
154, 155 Bernd Kreutz

AGENCY / AGENTUR / AGENCE – STUDIO:

151, 151a Lord, Sullivan & Yoder
152 Water Street Photokinetics
154, 155 Troost Campbell-Ewald

151, 151a Photograph and complete ad for *Harter* office furniture. (USA)
152 Self-promotional advertisement for a photo studio. (CAN)
153 Full-page full-colour advertisement for *Thonet* chairs. (USA)
154 From a campaign of the association of German opticians, showing a phoropter instrument. (GER)
155 Example from an advertising campaign for *Geha* pens which are equipped with ink checking windows. (GER)

151, 151a Aufnahme und vollständiges Inserat für *Harter*-Büromöbel. (USA)
152 «Täglich frisch.» Eigenwerbungsinserat für ein Photostudio. (CAN)
153 Ganzseitiges, mehrfarbiges Inserat für *Thonet*-Stühle. (USA)
154 Aus einer Kampagne der Leistungsgesellschaft deutscher Augenoptiker. Gezeigt wird ein Phoropter zur Bestimmung von Brillengläsern. (GER)
155 Beispiel aus einer Kampagne für *Geha*-Schreibgeräte, hier mit Hinweis auf die Tintenkontrollfenster. (GER)

151, 151a Photo et annonce complète pour les meubles de bureau *Harter*. (USA)
152 Annonce d'un studio photo: «créations fraîches tous les jours.» (CAN)
153 Annonce pleine page polychrome pour les sièges *Thonet*. (USA)
154 Annonce utilisée dans une campagne pour la société d'optique allemande: appareil Phoropter pour déterminer les dioptries. (GER)
155 Exemple d'annonce pour une campagne *Geha* destinée à faire connaître son matériel d'écriture. On décrit ici l'avantage que représente dans les stylos *Geha* le regard permettant de contrôler le niveau d'encre. (GER)

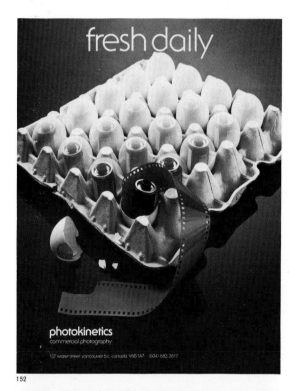

152

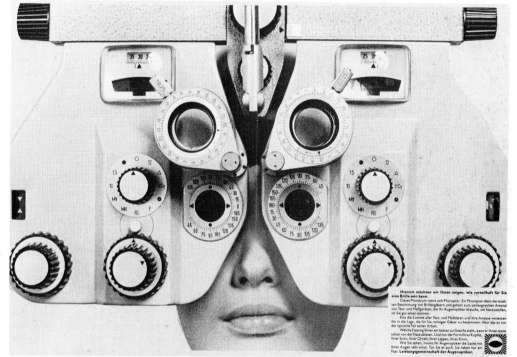

154

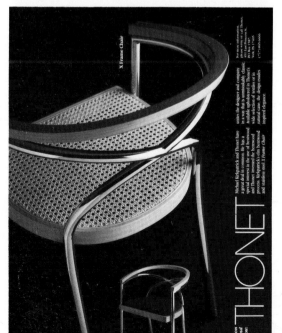

153

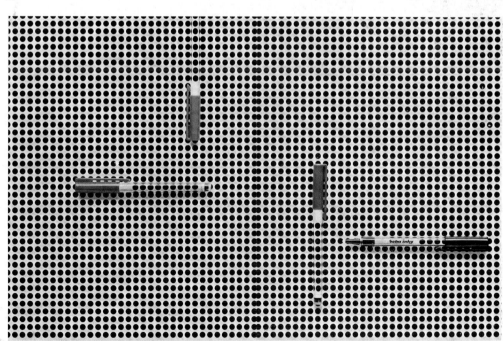

155

Die 32 Kontrollfenster sind die wichtigsten der vielen Punkte, die für diesen Tintenschreiber sprechen.

156

Advertisements
Anzeigen
Annonces

156–159 Photographs and complete advertisements taken from a campaign for *Rolf Benz* furniture. For this series, the photographer worked with white props and strong light-shadow effects. The sofas shown here are in white and the models are wearing white clothes. (GER)
160 Full-page advertisement for *Vuokko* furniture and installation textiles. Material in black and white as well as red and white stripes. (FIN)
161 Full-page advertisement from a campaign for *deSede* furniture. Photograph in shammy-like shades. (SWI)

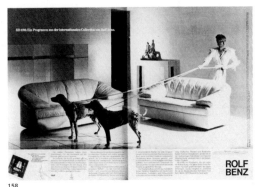

158

PHOTOGRAPHER / PHOTOGRAPH:

156–159 Conny J. Winter
160 Adam Korpak
161 Christian Vogt

DESIGNER / GESTALTER / MAQUETTISTE:

156–159 Wolfgang Weiss
160 Studio Nurmesniemi
161 Tschudi & Hauri

ART DIRECTOR / DIRECTEUR ARTISTIQUE:

156–159 Wolfgang Weiss
160 Antti Nurmesniemi

AGENCY / AGENTUR / AGENCE – STUDIO:

156–159 CC-Marketing
160 Studio Nurmesniemi
161 Tschudi & Hauri

Vuokko

Printed interior fabrics designed by Vuokko Eskolin-Nurmesniemi and furniture experiments designed by Antti Nurmesniemi.

Bedruckte Einrichtungsstoffe von Vuokko Eskolin-Nurmesniemi und Möbelexperimente von Antti Nurmesniemi.

Tissus de décoration imprimés, créés par Vuokko Eskolin-Nurmesniemi, et meubles expérimentaux par Antti Nurmesniemi.

160

deSede fotografiert von Christian Vogt

161

156–159 Aufnahmen und vollständige Inserate aus einer Werbekampagne für Möbel von *Rolf Benz.* Für diese Serie arbeitete der Photograph mit weissen Raumaufbauten und starken Licht-Schatten-Effekten. Die hier vorgestellten Sofas sind weiss, die Modelle tragen weisse Kleidung. (GER)
160 Ganzseitiges Inserat für *Vuokko*-Möbel und Einrichtungstextilien. Die Stoffe sind schwarz und weiss sowie rot und weiss gestreift. (FIN)
161 Ganzseitiges Inserat aus einer Werbekampagne für *deSede*-Möbel. Aufnahme in chamois-ähnlichem Ton. (SWI)

156–159 Photos et annonces complètes dans une campagne réalisée pour les ameublements *Rolf Benz.* Pour cette série, le photographe s'est servi de décors blancs et de contrastes clair-obscurs très marqués. Les divans présentés ici sont blancs, les modèles également habillés de blanc. (GER)
160 Annonce pleine page pour les meubles et tissus d'ameublement *Vuokko.* Les étoffes sont à rayures noires et blanches et rouges et blanches. (FIN)
161 Annonce pleine page pour une campagne en faveur des ameublements *deSede.* Photo dans une teinte évoquant le chamois. (SWI)

159

162–164 "There is a need. Why not make better business out of it?" Three examples from a commercial campaign whose aim was to introduce *feh* paper handkerchiefs, toilet and kitchen rolls to German retailers. The subject—value-for-money quality and an attractive profit margin for the retail trade, was to be presented as dramatically as possible. In black and white. (GER)
165 Double-spread trade magazine advertisement using three-dimensional caricatures of Labour Party leaders and spoof political copy for *Lego* toys, aimed at leaving no doubt in the consumer's mind as to which company leads in this field. (GBR)

162–164 Drei Beispiele aus einer Handelskampagne, deren Ziel es war, die Marke *feh* für Papiertaschentücher, Toiletten- und Küchenrollen beim deutschen Lebensmittelhandel einzuführen. Das Thema, preiswerte Markenqualität und eine attraktive Spanne für den Handel, sollte möglichst dramatisch dargestellt werden. Alle Aufnahmen in Schwarzweiss. (GER)
165 «Auf dem Spielzeugmarkt gibt es keinen Zweifel darüber, wer an der Spitze ist.» Das doppelseitige Fachzeitschriften-Inserat für *Lego*-Spielzeug zeigt Karikaturen von drei Führern der britischen Labour-Partei. (GBR)

162–164 Campagne pour les mouchoirs en papier, rouleaux de papier WC et de papier de cuisine *feh* à l'intention des détaillants de l'alimentation: «Le besoin existe (fig. 162)... Assez de taches! (fig. 163)... Ne le laissez pas s'égoutter (fig. 164)... Faites-en une bonne affaire!» Mise en vedette de la bonne relation prix–marge. Photos en noir et blanc. (GER)
165 «Sur le marché des jouets, notre leadership est indiscutable.» Cette annonce de revue professionnelle double page en faveur des jouets de construction *Lego* met en scène trois leaders du parti Labour (portraits réalisés à l'aide d'éléments de construction *Lego*). (GBR)

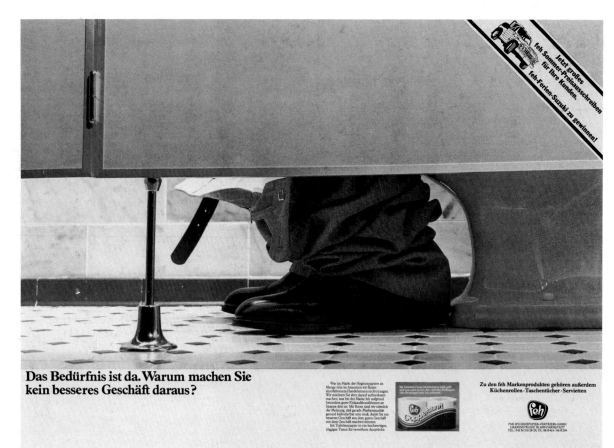

Das Bedürfnis ist da. Warum machen Sie kein besseres Geschäft daraus?

162

Genug gekleckert. Machen Sie ein besseres Geschäft!

163

PHOTOGRAPHER / PHOTOGRAPH:

162–164 Reinhard Hennig
165 John Lawrence-Jones

DESIGNER / GESTALTER:

162–164 Reinhard Kunz

ART DIRECTOR:

162–164 Heinz Böldl
165 Malcolm Gaskin

AGENCY / AGENTUR / AGENCE:

162–164 Doyle Dane Bernbach
165 TBWA Ltd.

**Nicht einfach laufen lassen!
Machen Sie ein besseres Geschäft.**

164

In the toy market, there's no question who's the leader.

Let the opposition look left and right for a new direction.
We're standing by the policies that have kept us leaders through a year of recession.

More investment in the railways. Increased support for the space programme. More to improve and encourage development of our towns.

All backed by new ideas, new initiative.

And to make interest rates soar, a higher level of spending in the public sector than ever before.

Lastly, to get the country back to work, let us remind you that we are committed to a National Building Competition.

This is the way ahead. This is the road to a higher standard of living.

And, you know, this can only be achieved by U-turning.

You turning LEGO® bricks into prosperity.

The world's most popular toy.
©1981 LEGO GROUP ®LEGO is a registered trademark.

166

167

166–169 Examples from a campaign for ITT products, using the slogan "What one wears this spring". All photographs are in full colour. (GER)
170, 171 From a series of full-page advertisements in trade magazines for the *Container Corporation of America*. Fig. 170 with coffee-brown containers on a sand-coloured ground; Fig. 171 in full colour, lettering and cardboard box in white on a dark ground. (USA)

166–169 Beispiele aus einer Kampagne für ITT-Geräte, unter dem Motto «Was man dieses Frühjahr trägt». Alle Aufnahmen sind mehrfarbig. (GER)
170, 171 Aus einer Reihe von ganzseitigen Anzeigen in Fachzeitschriften für die *Container Corporation of America*. Abb. 170 mit kaffeebraunen Behältern auf sandfarbenem Grund, Abb. 171 mehrfarbig, Schrift und Karton weiss auf dunklem Grund. (USA)

166–169 Exemples des annonces réalisées pour la campagne en faveur des appareils ITT lancée sous le slogan «Ce qu'on porte ce printemps». Toutes les photos en polychromie. (GER)
170, 171 Eléments d'une série d'annonces pleine page pour la *Container Corporation of America*, publiées dans des revues spécialisées. Fig. 170: récipients couleur café sur fond sable; fig. 171: en polychromie, texte et carton blanc sur fond sombre. (USA)

Advertisements
Anzeigen
Annonces

168

Frühlingserwachen. Der CRC 4000.
Clock-Radio und Rechner in einem. Seite 3

Ein echt starkes Stück.
Der Touring 120. Seite 4

Überspielen Sie's lächelnd. Neu.
der RC 6600. Doppelcassette. Seite 6

Dieser Frühling wird farbig.
Der Ideal Color 3122. Seite 7

Angeln Sie sich einen Millionär.
Alles über den SL 500. Seite 8

Was man
dieses Frühjahr trägt

Technik der Welt **ITT**

169

170

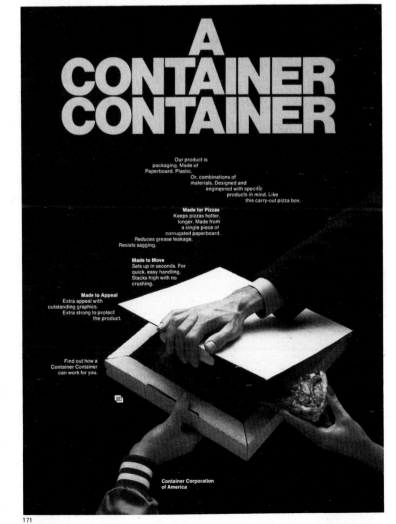

171

PHOTOGRAPHER / PHOTOGRAPH / PHOTOGRAPHE:

166–169 Wolfgang Klein
170 Jim Matusik
171 Robert Keeling

DESIGNER / GESTALTER / MAQUETTISTE:

170, 171 Kathy Forsythe

ART DIRECTOR / DIRECTEUR ARTISTIQUE:

166–169 Reinhardt Anthes
170, 171 Kathy Forsythe

AGENCY / AGENTUR / AGENCE – STUDIO:

166–169 Heumann, Ogilvy & Mather
170, 171 CCA Communications Dept.

PHOTOGRAPHER / PHOTOGRAPH / PHOTOGRAPHE:

172, 173 Daniel Aron
174, 175 Andrew Unangst
176 Hunter Freeman

172, 173 Examples from an image campaign for *Bayer*. Fig. 172: "Life would be too mechanical without comfort", dealing here with *Bayer dralon* fabrics used for coverings in a *Peugeot 604*; Fig. 173: "Life would be less tasteful without good things." The material for the *Moulinex* kitchen apparatus was manufactured by *Bayer*. (FRA)
174–176 Photograph and complete advertisement for IBM. Fig. 174 and 175 deal with IBM office machines; Fig. 176 deals with IBM's participation with machines and personnel in career-training centres. (USA)

172, 173 Aus einer Image-Kampagne für *Bayer*. Abb. 172: «Ohne Komfort wäre das Leben zu mechanisch.» Es geht um Bezüge aus *Bayer-Velour-Dralon*, hier am Beispiel eines *Peugeot 604* gezeigt. Abb. 173: «Ohne gute Sachen hätte das Leben weniger Geschmack.» Das Material für die Küchenmaschine stammt von *Bayer*. (FRA)
174–176 Aufnahme und vollständige Inserate für IBM. In Abb. 174 und 175 geht es um IBM-Büromaschinen, in Abb. 176 um IBMs Beteiligung an Berufsausbildungszentren mit Geräten und Personal. (USA)

172, 173 Annonces figurant dans une campagne d'image globale de marque réalisée pour *Bayer*. La fig. 172 se rapporte aux tissus d'ameublement *Bayer* en velours *dralon*. La fig. 173 montre des équipements de cuisine faits de matériaux *Bayer*. (FRA)
174–176 Photo et annonces complètes pour IBM. Les fig. 174 et 175 concernent des machines de bureau IBM, la fig. 176 traite de la participation d'IBM aux centres de formation professionnelle qui s'équipent d'appareils de cette firme et ont recours à du personnel d'instruction IBM. (USA)

172

173

Advertisements
Anzeigen
Annonces

174

Office heroes in the War of 9 to 5.

It's happening all over the country.

People in offices struggle heroically against the increasing complexity of increasing amounts of work.

At IBM, we know that pencils, memo pads and even telephones are no longer enough to win all the battles in the War of 9 to 5.

IBM office systems can help.

We have a wide range of computers, word processors, electronic typewriters, printers and copiers that help unite your business and your people and help information flow more smoothly.

Of course, that doesn't guarantee that people who work in offices will win every battle they get into.

But, with IBM office systems, at least they'll be in a fair fight.

With more than 40 years of experience, no one is more committed to the office than we are—where it is now and where it will be.

Where will you be? **IBM**

175

Jobs.

If you have the right skills, you might get one.

But for many people, getting those skills can seem like an impossible task.

Since 1968, in partnership with other companies and local community groups, IBM has supported a national job training program for the disadvantaged.

IBM provides equipment, supplies, and in some cases, people, to job training centers from New York to Los Angeles.

The results: more than 150,000 graduates have been trained for careers in office administration, computer operations, and computer programming.

This year, 11 new centers are scheduled to open.

They'll help even more people get the skills they need. And that helps open a lot of doors that used to be closed. **IBM**

176

DESIGNER / GESTALTER / MAQUETTISTE:

174–176 Seymon Ostilly

ART DIRECTOR:

172 Isabelle Hintsy
173 Yves Goube
174–176 Seymon Ostilly

AGENCY / AGENTUR / AGENCE:

172, 173 Chevassus/Vadon
174–176 Lord, Geller, Federico, Einstein

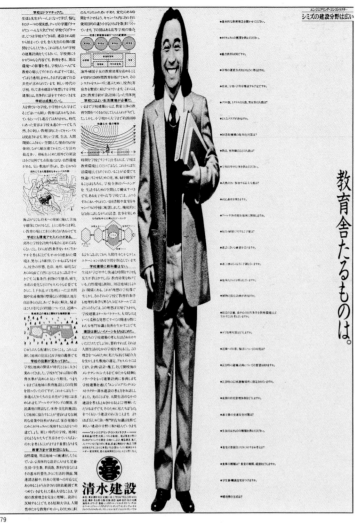

179

180

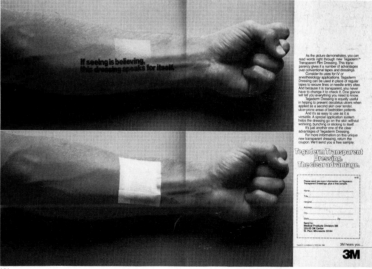

181

PHOTOGRAPHER / PHOTOGRAPH / PHOTOGRAPHE:

177, 178 Marc David Cohen
179 Shintaro Shiratori
180 Michel Dubois
181 Kent Severson

DESIGNER / GESTALTER / MAQUETTISTE:

177, 178 Mark McDowell
179 Hiromu Sato
180 Philippe Mercier
181 William Zabowski

ART DIRECTOR / DIRECTEUR ARTISTIQUE:

177, 178 Peter Belliveau
179 Masahiro Sobue
180 Philippe Mercier
181 William Zabowski

AGENCY / AGENTUR / AGENCE – STUDIO:

177, 178 Lavey/Wolff/Swift
180 LBP
181 Martin/Williams Advertising

177, 178 Photograph and complete trade magazine advertisement for *Mycelex*, a broad-spectrum antifungal treatment from *Miles Pharmaceuticals*. (USA)
179 Newspaper advertisement for the building firm *Shimizu Construction Co.* (JPN)
180 Research for *Makinon* lenses is the subject of this double-spread advertisement. Black lens on a sand-coloured ground, sky turning from pink into brown. (FRA)
181 Advertisement for *Tegaderm Transparent Dressing* made by the 3M company. (USA)

177, 178 Aufnahme und vollständiges Fachzeitschriften-Inserat für *Mycelex*, ein Breitspektrum-Mittel gegen Pilzinfektionen von *Miles Pharmaceuticals*. (USA)
179 Zeitungsinserat für das Bauunternehmen *Shimizu Construction Co.* (JPN)
180 Forschung für *Makinon*-Objektive ist das Thema dieser doppelseitigen Anzeige. Schwarzes Objektiv auf sandfarbenem Grund, Himmel von Rosa in Braun übergehend. (FRA)
181 Hier soll der Vorteil transparenter Pflaster von 3M verdeutlicht werden. (USA)

177, 178 Photo et annonce de revue professionnelle où elle figure. Publicité pour le *Mycelex*, un antifongique à large spectre d'activité préparé par *Miles Pharmaceuticals*. (USA)
179 Annonce de journal pour l'entreprise de construction *Shimizu Construction Co.* (JPN)
180 Le sujet de cette annonce double page, c'est la recherche dont sont issus les objectifs *Makinon*. Objectif noir sur fond sable, ciel variant de rose à brun. (FRA)
181 Publicité visant à mettre en évidence l'avantage d'un pansement transparent de 3M. (USA)

178

Advertisements
Anzeigen
Annonces

2

Booklets

Folders

Catalogues

Programmes

Broschüren

Faltprospekte

Kataloge

Programme

Brochures

Dépliants

Catalogues

Programmes

Brügmann Meisterprofil
Red Pine

182

Brügmann Meisterprofil

Red Pine

Dieses neue Profilholz aus dem Hause Brügmann eignet sich für jeden Einsatz – für den gesamten Wohnungs- und Objektbau sowie für jeden Alt- und Neubau. Dem jeweiligen Raumcharakter entsprechend gibt es das Brügmann Meisterprofil in unterschiedlichen Holzarten aus den wichtigsten Einschlaggebieten der Welt: vom rustikal und astig Lebhaften bis zum dezent Eleganten. Das Brügmann Meisterprofil ist durch und durch massiv und oberflächenveredelt, zeigt eine lebhafte Struktur und ist dicker und breiter als je zuvor. Aufgrund dieser markanten Eigenschaften ist es sehr montagefreundlich, wärme- und schalldämmend und dadurch energiesparend. Das Meisterprofil bringt ein gutes, behagliches Klima in jeden Raum und ist fertig montiert außerordentlich preisgünstig.

Brügmann Meisterprofil eignet sich für Wand- und Deckenbekleidungen im gesamten Innenausbau besonders gut. Nicht nur für das private Zuhause, sondern auch für den Ladenbau, für Restaurants, für den Sportstättenbau – kurz, für den gesamten Objekt-bau. Die gewählte starke Dimensionierung bringt alle guten Eigenschaften des Holzes voll zur Wirkung, seine Holzfestigkeit, seine Formbeständigkeit und seine Schönheit. Ein Profilholz für den Meister, der seine Kunden solide und gut beraten will.
Brügmann Meisterprofil aus Red Pine in der Abmessung 18x144 mm wird in modernen Hobelwerken in der Bundesrepublik Deutschland unter ständiger Qualitätskontrolle hergestellt und kommt ausschließlich folienverpackt in den Handel.
Über Arbeitszeitersparnis durch schnelle Montage, über den nicht unbedeutenden Beitrag zur Heizkostenersparnis, über den verbesserten Schallschutz sowie über Raumklima und Wohlbehagen gibt der technische Prospekt ausführlich Auskunft.

W. Brügmann & Sohn GmbH
Elisabethstraße 5 · Postfach 728
4600 Dortmund 1
Telefon 0231/527731-35 · Telex 08 22 302

183

Brügmann Meisterprofil
Nordische Kiefer

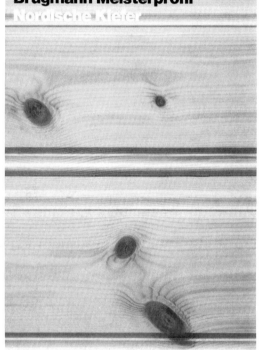

184

Brügmann Meisterprofil

Nordische Kiefer

Dieses neue Profilholz aus dem Hause Brügmann eignet sich für jeden Einsatz – für den gesamten Wohnungs- und Objektbau sowie für jeden Alt- und Neubau. Dem jeweiligen Raumcharakter entsprechend gibt es das Brügmann Meisterprofil in unterschiedlichen Holzarten aus den wichtigsten Einschlaggebieten der Welt: vom rustikal und astig Lebhaften bis zum dezent Eleganten. Das Brügmann Meisterprofil ist durch und durch massiv und oberflächenveredelt, zeigt eine lebhafte Struktur und ist dicker und breiter als je zuvor. Aufgrund dieser markanten Eigenschaften ist es sehr montagefreundlich, wärme- und schalldämmend und dadurch energiesparend. Das Meisterprofil bringt ein gutes, behagliches Klima in jeden Raum und ist fertig montiert außerordentlich preisgünstig.

Brügmann Meisterprofil eignet sich für Wand- und Deckenbekleidungen im gesamten Innenausbau besonders gut. Nicht nur für das private Zuhause, sondern auch für den Ladenbau, für Restaurants, für den Sportstättenbau – kurz, für den gesamten Objekt-bau. Die gewählte starke Dimensionierung bringt alle guten Eigenschaften des Holzes voll zur Wirkung, seine Holzfestigkeit, seine Formbeständigkeit und seine Schönheit. Ein Profilholz für den Meister, der seine Kunden solide und gut beraten will.
Brügmann Meisterprofil aus Nordischer Kiefer in den Abmessungen 18x146 mm, 18x196 mm wird in modernen Hobelwerken in der Bundesrepublik Deutschland unter ständiger Qualitätskontrolle hergestellt und kommt ausschließlich folienverpackt in den Handel.
Über Arbeitszeitersparnis durch schnelle Montage, über den nicht unbedeutenden Beitrag zur Heizkostenersparnis, über den verbesserten Schallschutz sowie über Raumklima und Wohlbehagen gibt der technische Prospekt ausführlich Auskunft.

W. Brügmann & Sohn GmbH
Elisabethstraße 5 · Postfach 728
4600 Dortmund 1
Telefon 0231/527731-35 · Telex 08 22 302

185

PHOTOGRAPHER / PHOTOGRAPH / PHOTOGRAPHE:

182–185 Siegfried Himmer
186 Lazlo Stern
187 Poul Ib Henriksen
188 Robert Pütz

DESIGNER / GESTALTER / MAQUETTISTE:

182–185 Siegfried Himmer
186 Rene Vidmer
187 Poul Ib Henriksen

186

Booklets / Prospekte / Brochures

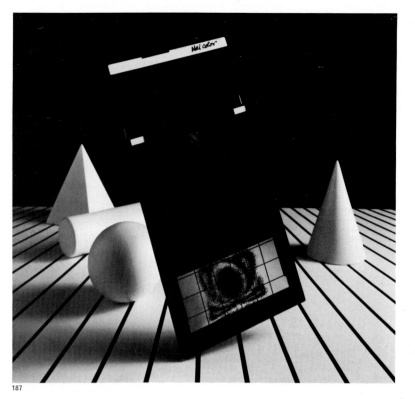

187

182–185 Examples from a sales kit for sectional wood manufactured by W. Brügmann & Son Ltd., in Dortmund. Here the recto and inside spreads for the "Red Pine" and "Nordic Pine" with photographs taken from the range of application. (GER)
186 Double spread from a catalogue with spiral binding for the paper quality *Kromokote* made by *Champion Papers*. The advantages of this paper are listed from A to Z. The compositor's case is in light brown with shades of gold and silver. (Reproduced with permission of Champion International Corporation.) (USA)
187 A photograph was used on the cover of this photo laboratory's price-list. Mainly in white and black, photograph in the cassette in red, yellow and light blue. (DEN)
188 Photograph for a prospectus with the slogan "My bath is my island". The prospectus deals with bathroom installations made by the *Ideal-Standard* company. The photo studio in question also used this photograph for a self-promotional prospectus. (GER)

182–185 Beispiele aus einer Verkaufsmappe für Profilholz von W. Brügmann & Sohn GmbH, Dortmund. Hier die Vorder- und Innenseiten für die Qualitäten «Red Pine» und «Nordische Kiefer» mit Aufnahmen aus dem Anwendungsbereich. (GER)
186 Doppelseite aus einem Katalog mit Spiralbindung für die Papierqualität *Kromokote* von *Champion Papers*. Hier werden die Vorteile des Papiers von A–Z dargelegt. Setzkasten in Hellbraun mit Gold- und Silbertönen. (Mit freundlicher Genehmigung der Champion International Corporation.) (USA)
187 Für diesen Umschlag der Preisliste eines Photolabors wurde ein Photo verwendet. Vorwiegend in Weiss und Schwarz, Aufnahme in der Kassette rot, gelb und hellblau. (DEN)
188 Aufnahme für einen Prospekt mit dem Slogan «Mein Bad ist meine Insel». Es geht hier um Badezimmereinrichtungen von *Ideal-Standard*. Das Photostudio verwendete diese Aufnahme ebenfalls für einen Eigenwerbungs-Prospekt. (GER)

182–185 Exemples tirés d'une documentation de vente pour les profilés en bois de W. Brügmann & Fils Sàrl, Dortmund: première page de couverture et pages intérieures relatives aux qualités «Red Pine» et «Pin nordique» avec des photos qui en illustrent l'application. (GER)
186 Double page d'un catalogue à reliure spirale pour la qualité de papier *Kromokote* de *Champion Papers*. On indique ici de A à Z les avantages inhérents au papier. Casse brun clair, avec des teintes or et argent. (Avec autorisation de Champion International Corporation.) (USA)
187 Une photo illustre cette couverture de prix courant pour un laboratoire photo. Les tons blancs et noirs y sont prédominants. La photo figurant dans la cassette est exécutée en rouge, jaune et bleu clair. (DEN)
188 Photo pour un prospectus placé sous la devise «Ma salle de bains est mon île». Il s'agit ici d'équipements *Ideal-Standard* pour salles de bains. L'atelier photo a également utilisé ce cliché pour un prospectus destiné à son autopromotion. (GER)

ART DIRECTOR / DIRECTEUR ARTISTIQUE:

182–185 Siegfried Himmer
186 Rene Vidmer
187 Poul Ib Henriksen
188 Robert Pütz

AGENCY / AGENTUR / AGENCE – STUDIO:

182–185 Pro Publica
188 Robert Pütz GmbH & Co.

188

189

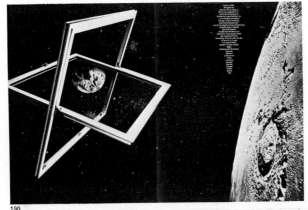

190

PHOTOGRAPHER / PHOTOGRAPH / PHOTOGRAPHE:

189 E. König
190 Egbert Burmester/NASA
191, 192 Mechthild Wilhelmi/Tony Wacker/Egbert Burmester
193–195 Don A. Sparks

DESIGNER / GESTALTER / MAQUETTISTE:

189–192 Dorothea Steinhof/Manfred Siegler
193–195 James Hellmuth

191

**Booklets
Prospekte
Brochures**

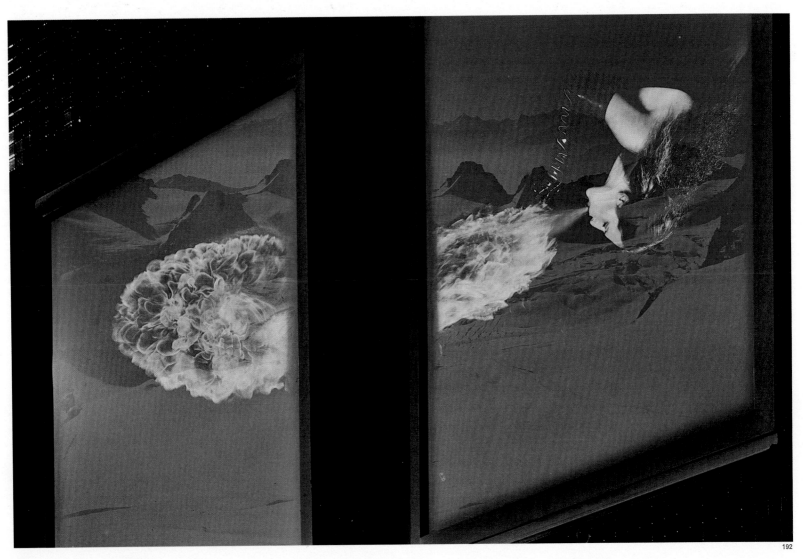

PHOTOGRAPHER / PHOTOGRAPH / PHOTOGRAPHE:

189 E. König
190 Egbert Burmester/NASA
191, 192 Mechthild Wilhelmi/Tony Wacker/Egbert Burmester
193–195 Don A. Sparks

DESIGNER / GESTALTER / MAQUETTISTE:

189–192 Dorothea Steinhof/Manfred Siegler
193–195 James Hellmuth

192

193

194

Office Chair with flair

195

ART DIRECTOR / DIRECTEUR ARTISTIQUE:

189–192 Paul Bodo Köchel
193–195 James Hellmuth

AGENCY / AGENTUR / AGENCE – STUDIO:

189–192 COMmunication Agency Köchel GmbH
193–195 James Hellmuth Design

189–192 From a large-format image brochure for *Kömmerling* plastic windows, sent to building contractors and architects. Instead of a detailed text, the optics here are meant to communicate the subjects, each one of which takes up at least one double spread. Figs.189, 190: "Window to the world", cover with luminous yellow windows in Manhattan's skyscrapers, and the first double spread; Figs.191, 192: Complete, unfolded four-page spread and both inside spreads dealing with the subject of insulation. The picture was obtained with superimposed transparencies. (GER)
193–195 From a catalogue for *Rudd International*, makers of furniture. Shown here are various chair models. In full colour. (USA)

189–192 Aus einer grossformatigen Image-Broschüre für *Kömmerling*-Kunststoff-Fenster, die an Bauherren und Architekten gerichtet ist. Die Optik sollte anstelle eines umfangreichen Textes die Themen kommunizieren, die auf jeweils mindestens einer Doppelseite dargestellt wurden. Abb.189, 190: «Das Fenster zur Welt», Umschlag mit gelberleuchteten Fenstern in Manhattans Wolkenkratzern und die erste Doppelseite; Abb.191, 192: Vollständige, aufgeklappte Seite und die beiden Innenseiten zum Thema Isolation. Es handelt sich um eine Sandwich-Aufnahme. (GER)
193–195 Aus einem Katalog für *Rudd International*, Hersteller von Möbeln. Hier stapelbare Konferenzstühle, eine Stuhlreihe und ein Drehstuhl. In Farbe. (USA)

189–192 Eléments d'une brochure de prestige au grand format réalisée pour les fenêtres plastiques *Kömmerling* et destinée aux maîtres d'œuvre et aux architectes. Les divers sujets sont interprétés visuellement sur au moins une page double. Fig. 189, 190: «La fenêtre ouverte sur le monde», couverture montrant les fenêtres illuminées (jaunes) des gratte-ciel de Manhattan, et première double page; fig.191, 192: page intérieure complètement dépliée et les deux pages intérieures traitant de l'isolation. Photo en sandwich. (GER)
193–195 Catalogue pour les ameublements *Rudd International:* chaises empilables pour salles de conférences, gamme de chaises, chaise pivotante. En couleurs. (USA)

196

197

Booklets / Prospekte / Brochures

198

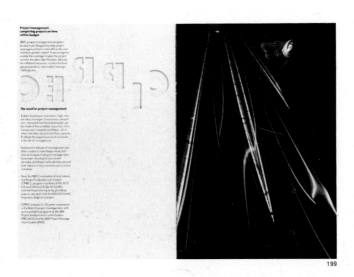

199

PHOTOGRAPHER / PHOTOGRAPH / PHOTOGRAPHE:

196–200 Bill Farrell

DESIGNER / GESTALTER / MAQUETTISTE:

196–200 Richard Rogers

AGENCY / AGENTUR / AGENCE – STUDIO:

196–200 Richard Rogers

196–200 Taken from an IBM brochure dealing with efficient project management with the aid of control- and analyses-computer programmes developed by IBM. The full-page photographs in Figs.196, 197 and 200 show a sphere—for example, ship and airplane construction—for which these planning methods were developed; Figs.198, 199: The cover with cut-out letters designating the programme, and the first double spread. (USA)

196–200 Aus einer Broschüre der IBM, in der es um effizientes Projekt-Management mit Hilfe der von IBM entwickelten Kontroll- und Analysen-Computerprogramme geht. Die ganzseitigen Aufnahmen in Abb.196, 197 und 200 zeigen einige der Bereiche, z. B. den Schiffs- und Flugzeugbau, für welche diese Planungsmethoden entwickelt wurden. Abb.198, 199: Der Umschlag mit ausgestanzten Buchstaben, die die Bezeichnung des Programms ergeben, und die erste Doppelseite. Alle Aufnahmen in Farbe. (USA)

196–200 Brochure IBM traitant de la gestion efficace de projets à l'aide de programmes d'analyse et de contrôle développés pour les ordinateurs IBM. Illustration des domaines couverts par ces méthodes de planification: construction navale et aéronautique, etc. (fig.196, 197, 200). Fig.198, 199: la couverture aux lettres découpées qui composent le titre du programme; et la première double page de l'opuscule. (USA)

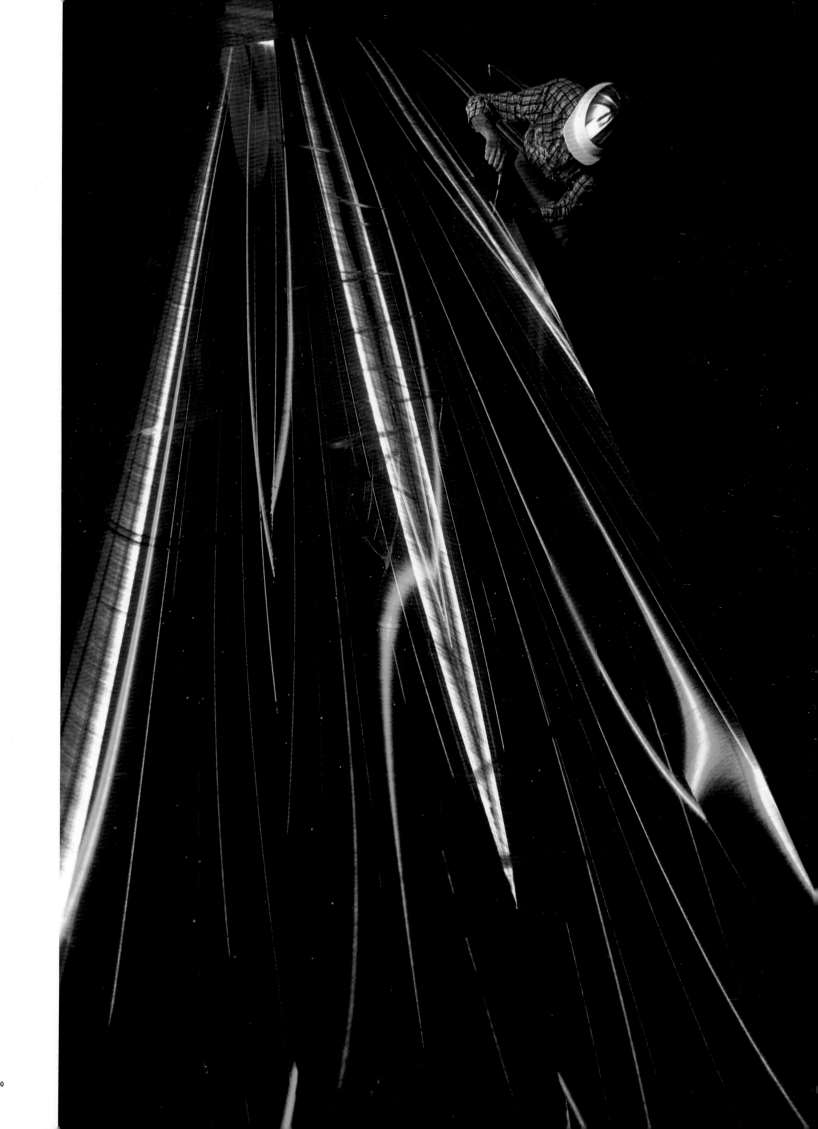

201

203

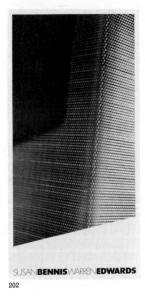

SUSAN**BENNIS**WARREN**EDWARDS**

202

PHOTOGRAPHER:

201, 202 John Pilgreen
203 Roland Schneider
204, 206 Charles Moretz
205 Bard Martin
207 François Robert

DESIGNER / GESTALTER:

201, 202 Stan Eisenman
203 Hubert Hasler
204, 206 John Graham
205 Al Karsten
207 Ron Coates

Booklets
Prospekte
Brochures

ART DIRECTOR / DIRECTEUR ARTISTIQUE:

201, 202 Stan Eisenman/Dennis Dollens
203 Hubert Hasler
205 Andrew Kner
207 Ron Coates

AGENCY / AGENTUR / AGENCE – STUDIO:

201, 202 Eisenman & Enock Inc.
203 H. Hasler
204, 206 Graham-Solano
207 Boller-Coates-Robert

201, 202 Detail of the photograph and complete cover of a prospectus for *Susan Bennis/Warren Edwards*, shoe designers. (USA)
203 Cover of a prospectus for Technorama, a museum in Winterthur, Switzerland, devoted to science and technology. (SWI)
204, 206 Two of six photographs commissioned by the New York Port Authority, used as wall decorations in a well-known restaurant at the World Trade Center. (USA)
205 Cover of a *New York Times* advertising insert. (USA)
207 Black-and-white photo from a furniture catalogue. (USA)

201, 202 Detail der Aufnahme und Umschlag eines Prospekts der Schuh-Designer *Susan Bennis/Warren Edwards*. (USA)
203 Umschlag eines Prospekts für das Technorama, ein Museum in Winterthur, das der Wissenschaft und Technik gewidmet ist. (SWI)
204, 206 Aufnahmen, die von der New Yorker Hafenbehörde in Auftrag gegeben und als Wanddekoration im «Fenster zur Welt», Restaurant im World Trade Center, verwendet wurden. (USA)
205 Umschlag einer Werbebeilage der *New York Times*. (USA)
207 Schwarzweisser Umschlag eines Möbelstoff-Katalogs. (USA)

201, 202 Détail de la photo et couverture complète d'un prospectus des stylistes en chaussures *Susan Bennis/Warren Edwards*. (USA)
203 Couverture d'un prospectus du Technorama, Musée de la science et de l'industrie à Winterthour. (SWI)
204, 206 Deux des six photos commanditées par l'Autorité portuaire de New York et utilisées comme décoration murale de «La Fenêtre ouverte sur le monde», le restaurant du World Trade Center. (USA)
205 D'un supplément publicitaire du *New York Times*. (USA)
207 Couverture d'un catalogue (tissus d'ameublement). (USA)

204

GIFT'S!

205

206

BEN ROSE DEEP END

A New Collection of Woolen Upholstery Fabrics

207

95

Alle Artikel
REINE BAUMWOLLE

Art. 252066 mit kleinem Karo,
Knopfleiste und Samtband. Gr. 36–44.
Weiß/Erika 136. Weiß/Banane 195.

208

209

**Booklets
Prospekte
Brochures**

PHOTOGRAPHER / PHOTOGRAPH / PHOTOGRAPHE:

208 H. P. Mühlemann
209 Essat Cicic
210 Lois Greenfield
211, 212 Michel Tcherevkoff

DESIGNER / GESTALTER / MAQUETTISTE:

208 Kreativ-Team Ulrich & Fehlmann
209 Gregor Balk
210 Frank Young

ART DIRECTOR / DIRECTEUR ARTISTIQUE:

208 Hans Ulrich
209 Karl-Heinz Schwaiger
210 Frank Young
211, 212 Terry Huntington

AGENCY / AGENTUR / AGENCE – STUDIO:

208 Kreativ-Team Ulrich & Fehlmann
209 Sportive Werbeproduktion
210 Ovesey & Co., Inc.
211, 212 Clairol, Inc.

211

For a full description of the fabulous Capezio legwear, see next page.

208 Recto of a small leporello prospectus for women's nightdresses in western-style made by the *Scherle* company. (GER)
209 Verso of a prospectus for *elho Sportswear*. The anoraks' greyish-green shades are repeated in the background. (GER)
210 Double spread from a catalogue for *Capezio*. (USA)
211, 212 Photographs from a catalogue for *Klorane* hair-care products. Fig. 211 refers to the assertion that natural products make up at least five per-cent of the ingredients; Fig. 212 shows four special-care shampoos. Liquids and product colours are in shades of chamois, red and two kinds of yellow. (USA)

208 Vorderseite eines kleinen Leporello-Prospekts für Damen-nachtwäsche im Herrenhemden-Westernstil von *Scherle*; hier ein rot-weiss-kariertes Modell. (GER)
209 Rückseite eines Faltprospekts für *elho Sportswear*. Das Grau-grün der Anoraks wiederholt sich im Hintergrund. (GER)
210 Doppelseite aus einem Katalog für *Capezio*-Ballett-, Theater- und Sportkleidung; hier die «Beinkleider». (USA)
211, 212 Aufnahmen aus einem Katalog für *Klorane*-Haarpflegepro-dukte. Abb. 211 bezieht sich auf die Behauptung, dass Naturpro-dukte mindestens 5% der Bestandteile ausmachen; Abb. 212 zeigt vier Spezialpflege-Shampoos. Flüssigkeiten und Produktfarben: Chamois, Rot und zwei Gelbtöne. (USA)

208 Recto d'un petit prospectus en accordéon pour la lingerie fine de nuit de *Scherle* dans le style des chemises messieurs du Far-Ouest; ici, un modèle à carreaux rouges et blancs. (GER)
209 Verso d'un dépliant pour les vêtements sport *Sportswear elho*. Anoraks et arrière-plan gris vert. (GER)
210 Double page d'un catalogue pour les costumes de ballet et de théâtre et les tenues de sport *Capezio*. (USA)
211, 212 Photos illustrent un catalogue des produits capillaires *Klorane*. La fig. 211 explicite l'affirmation que ces produits con-tiennent au moins 5% de composants naturels; la fig. 212 présente quatre variétés de shampooings spéciaux. Liquides et couleurs des produits: chamois, rouge, deux jaunes. (USA)

Booklets
Prospekte
Brochures

213

214

PHOTOGRAPHER / PHOTOGRAPH:

213, 214 Ronnie Poon
215–217 Denis Jobron

DESIGNER / GESTALTER / MAQUETTISTE:

215–217 Henri Chauvin

ART DIRECTOR / DIRECTEUR ARTISTIQUE:

213, 214 Dennis Walker/Brian Farrow
215–217 Henri Chauvin

AGENCY / AGENTUR / AGENCE – STUDIO:

213, 214 Macy's California Advertising
215–217 Dolci France SA

213, 214 Complete cover and photograph from a catalogue for *Macy's* department store, issued on the occasion of a special Independence Day sale. (USA)
215–217 Photograph on the verso, one double spread and recto of the cover of a catalogue for *Xavier Danaud* shoe fashions for the 1982 autumn/winter collection. Fig. 216: black on a white ground, the shoes in red; Fig. 217 in brilliant pink, orange and red with white and black. (FRA)

213, 214 Vollständiger Umschlag und Aufnahme für einen Katalog des Kaufhauses *Macys*, herausgegeben aus Anlass eines Sonderverkaufs zum Unabhängigkeitstag der Vereinigten Staaten. (USA)
215–217 Aufnahme der Rückseite, eine Doppelseite und Vorderseite des Umschlags eines Katalogs für Schuhe von *Xavier Danaud* im Herbst/Winter 1982. Abb. 216: Schwarz vor weissem Grund, Schuhe in Rot; Abb. 217 in leuchtendem Pink, Orange und Rot mit Weiss und Schwarz. (FRA)

213, 214 Couverture complète et photo illustrant un catalogue du grand magasin *Macys* publié à l'occasion d'une vente spéciale organisée pour la Journée de l'indépendance américaine, le 4 juillet. (USA)
215–217 Photo de la 4e page de couverture, double page et première page de couverture d'un catalogue du chausseur *Xavier Danaud* pour sa collection d'automne et d'hiver 1982. Fig. 216: noir sur fond blanc, les chaussures rouges; fig. 217 rose, orange et rouge vif, avec du noir et du blanc. (FRA)

215

216

XAVIER DANAUD

217

218

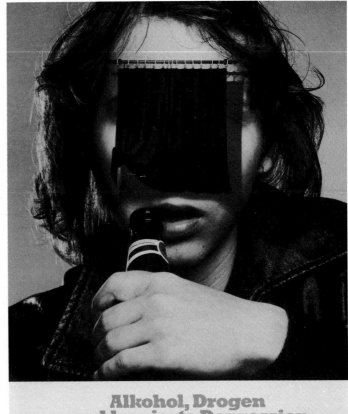

Alkohol, Drogen und larvierte Depression.

220

award winning homeware · décor®

219

221

PHOTOGRAPHER / PHOTOGRAPH / PHOTOGRAPHE:

218, 219 Edy Gaber
220 Felix Heiber/Peter Häfliger
221, 222 Casimir Bart
223 Yasuhiro Asai/Tadanobu Fukuda

DESIGNER / GESTALTER / MAQUETTISTE:

218, 219 Andy Schmid
220 Christian Lang
221, 222 Peter Cordy
223 Helmut Schmid

ART DIRECTOR / DIRECTEUR ARTISTIQUE:

218, 219 Andy Schmid
220 Christian Lang
221, 222 Peter Cordy/Casimir Bart
223 Shigeshi Omori

AGENCY / AGENTUR / AGENCE – STUDIO:

220 Werbung Ciby-Geigy
221, 222 Artagon Photographics

222

223

218, 219 Double spread and cover of a catalogue for plastic kitchenware, -tools, storage containers etc. of the *décor* range by *Brian Davis*—a design that won an award in Australia. Fig. 218 is also in bright colours. (AUS)
220 Photograph taken from a folder for the anti-depressive medicament *Ludiomil* made by *Ciba-Geigy*. Dealt with here is a form of depression concealed by drug addiction or alcoholism, as well as depressive reactions to withdrawal cures. (SWI)
221, 222 Photograph in actual size and complete cover of a small prospectus for *Creative Source*, an annual for applied graphics and photography in Canada. (CAN)
223 Recto of a large-format menu for the "Sun Valley" family restaurant in Japan. (JPN)

218, 219 Doppelseite und Umschlag eines Katalogs für Küchen-Kunststoffgeschirr und -behälter der Marke *décor* von *Brian Davis*, ein Design, das in Australien ausgezeichnet wurde. Abb. 218 ebenfalls mit leuchtenden Farben. (AUS)
220 Aufnahme aus einem Faltprospekt für das Antidepressivum *Ludiomil* von *Ciba-Geigy*. Es geht hier um eine Form der Depression, die sich häufig hinter Drogen- oder Alkoholsucht verbirgt, sowie um depressive Reaktionen bei Entzugskuren. (SWI)
221, 222 Aufnahme in Originalgrösse und vollständiger Umschlag für einen kleinen Prospekt über ein Jahrbuch angewandter Graphik und Photographie in Kanada, *Creative Source*. (CAN)
223 Vorderseite einer grossformatigen Menü-Karte für das Familien-Restaurant «Sun Valley». (JPN)

218, 219 Double page et couverture d'un catalogue de vaisselle et récipients de plastique de la marque *décor* de *Brian Davis*. Design primé en Australie. La fig. 218 est elle aussi exécutée en couleurs vives. (AUS)
220 Photo illustrant un dépliant pour l'antidépresseur *Ludiomil* de *Ciba-Geigy*. Il s'agit ici d'une forme de dépression masquée par la toxicomanie et l'alcoolisme, ainsi que des réactions dépressives qu'entraînent les cures de désintoxication. (SWI)
221, 222 Photo au format original et couverture complète d'un petit prospectus pour un annuel canadien d'art graphique appliqué et de photographie, *Creative Source*. (CAN)
223 Recto d'un menu au grand format pour le restaurant des familles «Sun Valley». (JPN)

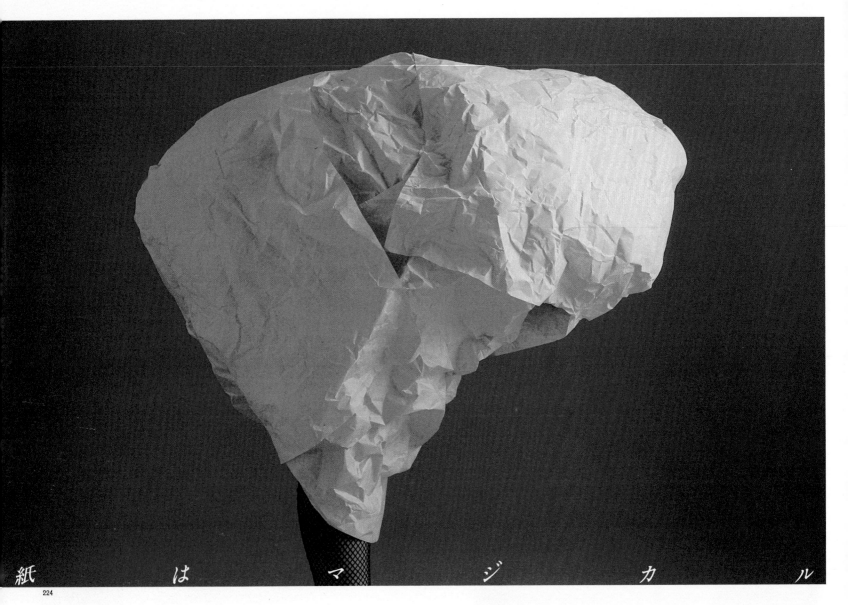

紙 は マ ジ カ ル

224

224 Photograph from a prospectus for *Sanyo* electric apparatuses, here for a vacuum-cleaner with an automatic removal of the dust-bag. (JPN)
225 Cover for a brochure about music in Burma, from a series about Asian music. (JPN)
226 Recto of a leporello invitation card for the opening of a showroom. (USA)
227 Invitation to an exhibition of photography at the Maeght gallery in Barcelona. (SPA)
228 Self-promotion of Tom Colombi, taken from the *Art Directors Index to Photographers*, published by *RotoVision*, Geneva. (SWI)

224 «Zauber-Papier.» «Wundersame Papierkassette ... die ausgeworfen wird, nachdem sie angeschwollen ist. Es ist ihr Schicksal.» Aufnahme aus einem Prospekt für elektrische Geräte von *Sanyo*, hier für Staubsauger mit automatischer Entfernung des Staubbeutels. (JPN)
225 Umschlag für eine Broschüre über Musik in Burma, aus einer Reihe über asiatische Musik. (JPN)
226 Vorderseite einer Leporello-Einladungskarte zur Einweihung eines Showrooms. (USA)
227 Einladung zu einer Photographie-Ausstellung in der Galerie Maeght in Barcelona. (SPA)
228 Eigenwerbung von Tom Colombi. (Aus *Art Directors' Index to Photographers, RotoVision*.) (SWI)

224 «Papier magique.» «Merveilleuse cassette en papier... éjectée lorsqu'elle enfle. C'est là son destin.» Photo illustrant un prospectus d'appareils électriques pour *Sanyo*, ici pour un aspirateur avec éjection automatique du sac à poussière. (JPN)
225 Couverture d'une brochure consacrée à la musique birmane. Série sur la musique d'Asie. (JPN)
226 Recto d'une carte d'invitation en accordéon pour l'inauguration d'un hall d'exposition. (USA)
227 Invitation à une exposition photo organisée à la Galerie Maeght de Barcelone. (SPA)
228 Autopromotion de Tom Colombi. (Parue dans *Art Directors' Index to Photographers*.) (SWI)

ILLUSTRATED STORY OF MUSIC
ASIAN MUSIC
アジアの音楽 —— ビルマの音楽を訪ねて.

BURMA

225

226

227

ART DIRECTOR / DIRECTEUR ARTISTIQUE:

224 Jo Negoro
225 Naomi Tanaka
226 David Perkins
228 Tom Colombi

AGENCY / AGENTUR / AGENCE – STUDIO:

224 Kent
225 Dentsu/Gull Design
226 David Perkins & Associates

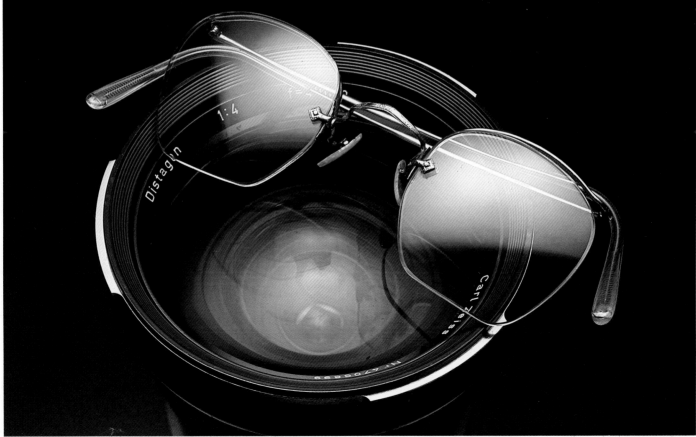

228

Booklets / Prospekte / Brochures

229, 230 Examples from a series of black-and-white photographs for *Xerox* on the subject of in house safety measures. (USA)
231 Double spread from a catalogue for *Innsbruck* ski fashions for the 1983 season. (GER)
232, 233 Detail of the photograph and complete cover of a brochure for *Yamaha*-Vision, a new model that is here presented in detail. (USA)

229, 230 «Sicherheit ist der Schlüssel.» Beispiele aus einer Serie von Schwarzweiss-Aufnahmen für *Xerox* zum Thema Sicherheit innerhalb des Betriebs. (USA)
231 Doppelseite aus einem Katalog für Innsbruck-Skimode für die Saison 1983. (GER)
232, 233 Detail der Aufnahme und vollständiger Umschlag einer Broschüre für *Yamaha*-Vision, ein neues Modell, das den Konsumenten darin vorgestellt wird. (USA)

229, 230 «La sécurité, c'est la clef.» Exemples de photos noir et blanc composant une série *Xerox* sur le thème de la sécurité dans l'entreprise. (USA)
231 Page double d'un catalogue pour les modes de ski *Innsbruck* durant la saison de 1983. (GER)
232, 233 Détail de la photo et couverture complète d'une brochure réalisée pour *Yamaha*-Vision, et présentant un nouveau modèle de moto. (USA)

232

233

PHOTOGRAPHER / PHOTOGRAPH / PHOTOGRAPHE:

229, 230 Michael Furman
231 Essat Cicic
232, 233 Mark Coppos

DESIGNER / GESTALTER / MAQUETTISTE:

229, 230 Ford, Byrne & Associates
231 Helmut Mätzler
232, 233 Amy Miyano

ART DIRECTOR / DIRECTEUR ARTISTIQUE:

231 Karl-Heinz Schwaiger
232, 233 Brent Thomas

AGENCY / AGENTUR / AGENCE – STUDIO:

229, 230 Ford, Byrne & Associates
231 Sportive Werbeproduktion
232, 233 Chiat Day Inc.

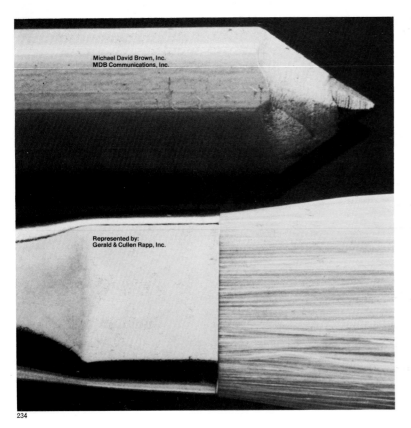

234

235

PHOTOGRAPHER / PHOTOGRAPH:

234 Thomas W. Radcliffe
235 Naotaroh Misoni
236–237a Terry Heffernan
238 Dirk Bakker
239 Nikolay Žurek

DESIGNER / GESTALTER / MAQUETTISTE:

234 Kathleen Wilmes Herring/
     Marilyn Worseldine
235 Seiyoh Nishikawa
236–237a Mark Anderson
238 Charles Byrne/Charleen Catt
239 Douglas Tinney

ART DIRECTOR / DIRECTEUR ARTISTIQUE:

235 Seiyoh Nishikawa
238 Charles Byrne
239 Nikolay Žurek

237a

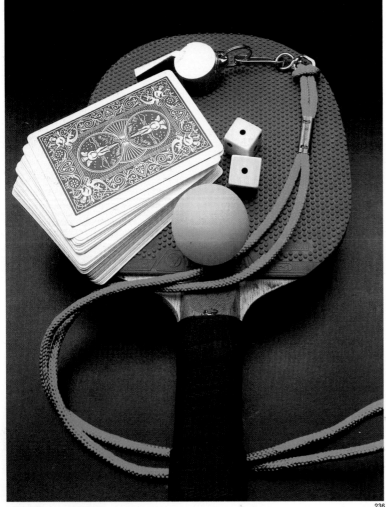

236

237

234 Detail of the cover illustration of the self-promotional brochure for a design studio. (USA)
235 From a catalogue of a manufacturer of Japanese lacquered wooden boxes and crockery. (JPN)
236–237a Photographs and complete double spread from a handbook for *Apple* computers, dealing with computers in schools and computer games. (USA)
238 Complete cover of a catalogue about glass artistry on the occasion of a touring exhibition. (USA)
239 Photograph taken from an *Ampex Corporation* brochure, presenting this company's most important clients; here the German Federal Post Office. (USA)

234 Detail der Umschlagillustration einer Eigenwerbungs-Broschüre für ein Design-Studio. (USA)
235 Doppelseite aus einem Katalog für lackierte japanische Holzkästchen und Geschirr. (JPN)
236–237a Aufnahmen und vollständige Doppelseite aus einem Handbuch für *Apple*-Computer. Themen: Computer in der Schule und Computer-Spiele. (USA)
238 Vollständiger Umschlag eines Katalogs über Glaskunst anlässlich einer Wanderausstellung. (USA)
239 Aufnahme aus einer Broschüre der *Ampex Corporation*, die darin ihre wichtigsten Kunden aufführt; hier die Deutsche Bundespost. (USA)

234 Détail de la couverture de la brochure autopromotionnelle d'un studio de design. (USA)
235 Double page du catalogue d'un fabricant de coffrets de bois laqué et de vaisselle japonais. (JPN)
236–237a Photos et double page complète d'un manuel d'ordinateur *Apple*. Les thèmes traités: l'ordinateur à l'école; les jeux d'ordinateur. (USA)
238 Couverture complète du catalogue d'une exposition itinérante sur l'art du verre. (USA)
239 Photo tirée d'une brochure de l'*Ampex Corporation* où sont énumérés les principaux clients de cette société, ici les P.T.T. allemands. (USA)

AGENCY / AGENTUR / AGENCE – STUDIO:

234 Michael David Brown, Inc.
236–237a Mark Anderson
     Graphic Design
238 Colophon

238

Booklets / Prospekte / Brochures

239

PHOTOGRAPHER / PHOTOGRAPH / PHOTOGRAPHE:

240, 241 Christian von Alvensleben
242, 243 Gian Carlo Durante

DESIGNER / GESTALTER / MAQUETTISTE:

240 Hannes Rausch
242, 243 Angelo Zenzalari

ART DIRECTOR / DIRECTEUR ARTISTIQUE:

240, 241 Christian von Alvensleben
242, 243 Angelo Zenzalari

AGENCY / AGENTUR / AGENCE – STUDIO:

240 Schretter & Rausch
242, 243 CEP

241

240, 241 Full-page photographs from a large-format self-promotional newspaper printed on re-cycled paper, for the photographer Christian von Alvensleben, annoucing the change of location of his studio and home to a small village in the country. Fig. 240: Photograph for *Mateus* rosé wine; Fig. 241: As with much of his work, this knitwear dress by *Claudia Skoda* was worn by an amateur model. (GER)
242, 243 Cover illustrations for catalogues of the *Paoline* publishing company, here for audio tapes, in brown shades and white; and for children's and young people's books, mainly green and blue. (ITA)

240, 241 Ganzseitige Aufnahmen aus einer grossformatigen Eigenwerbungs-Zeitung des Photographen Christian von Alvensleben, auf Umweltpapier gedruckt. Er gibt hier die Verlegung seines Ateliers aufs Land, nach Bargfeld-Stegen, bekannt. Abb. 240: Aufnahme für *Mateus*-Rosé; Abb. 241: Wie viele seiner Arbeiten wurde dieses Strickkleid von *Claudia Skoda* mit einem Laien-Modell photographiert. (GER)
242, 243 Umschlagillustrationen für Kataloge des Verlegers *Paoline*, hier für Audio-Kassetten, in Brauntönen und Weiss, und für Kinder- und Jugendbücher, vorwiegend grün und blau. (ITA)

240, 241 Photos pleine page pour le journal autopromotionnel au grand format du photographe Christian von Alvensleben tiré sur papier recyclé, annonçant ici son déménagement à la campagne, à Bargfeld-Stegen. Fig. 240: Photo pour rosé *Mateus*; fig. 241: l'artiste a photographié cette robe tricot *Claudia Skoda* comme à son habitude sur un modèle non professionnel. (GER)
242, 243 Illustrations de couvertures pour des catalogues de l'éditeur *Paoline*: pour des cassettes audio (divers bruns, blanc), pour des livres d'enfants et de jeunes (vert, bleu). (ITA)

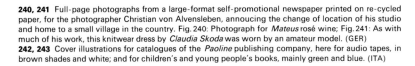

242

243

245

PHOTOGRAPHER / PHOTOGRAPH / PHOTOGRAPHE:

244 Otto Kasper
245 Siegbert Kercher
246 Uwe Behrendt

DESIGNER / GESTALTER / MAQUETTISTE:

244 Joseph Poelzelbauer
246 Uwe Behrendt

ART DIRECTOR / DIRECTEUR ARTISTIQUE:

244 Otto Kasper
245 Henning Moschinski
246 Uwe Behrendt

AGENCY / AGENTUR / AGENCE – STUDIO:

245 Moschinski & Partner

244 Self-promotion of the photographer Otto Kasper from Singen. (GER)
245 Example from a series of self-promotional photographs with fruit and vegetables on white lamella, by S. Kercher, who also took the photograph for the cover of this edition of *Photographis*. (GER)
246 Unfolded prospectus for the autumn-winter collection 1981/82 of the *Wrangler* company. Blue jeans and brightly coloured chequered shirts. (GER)

244 Eigenwerbung des Photographen Otto Kasper aus Singen. (GER)
245 Beispiel aus einer Reihe von Eigenwerbungsaufnahmen mit Früchten und Gemüsen auf weissen Lamellen von S. Kercher, der auch die für den Umschlag dieser Ausgabe von *Photographis* verwendete Aufnahme machte. (GER)
246 Auseinandergefalteter Prospekt für die Herbst-Winter-Kollektion 1981/82 von *Wrangler*. Blaue Jeans, Flanell-Hemden buntkariert. (GER)

244 Autopromotion du photographe Otto Kasper de Singen. (GER)
245 Exemple d'une série de photos autopromotionnelles de fruits et de légumes sur des lamelles blanches par S. Kercher, qui a aussi réalisé l'illustration utilisée pour la couverture de la présente édition de *Photographis*. (GER)
246 Prospectus déplié pour la collection d'automne et d'hiver 1981/82 de *Wrangler*. Jeans bleus, chemises flanelle à carreaux de diverses couleurs. (GER)

246

247

Booklets / Prospekte / Brochures

247–250 Photographs and an unfolded spread from a self-promotional brochure of Stephenson Inc., printers and lithographers. Excerpts are shown here from a book entitled *Washington the Capital* which was printed by this company and published by Thomasson-Grand Inc. Fig. 247 shows an impressionistic picture of the city; Figs. 248, 249 a three-part spread and photograph of the verso in actual size; Fig. 250 a bird's-eye view of a military cemetery. (USA)

247–250 Aufnahmen und eine aufgeklappte Seite aus einer Eigenwerbungsbroschüre der Druckerei Stephenson Inc. Es handelt sich um Auszüge aus einem von Stephenson gedruckten Buch mit dem Titel *Washington the Capital*, herausgegeben von Thomasson-Grant Inc. Abb. 247 zeigt ein Stimmungsbild der Stadt; Abb. 248, 249 eine dreiteilige Seite und Detailaufnahme in Originalgrösse; Abb. 250 einen Soldatenfriedhof aus der Vogelperspektive. (USA)

247–250 Photos et l'une des pages tripartites dépliée, tirées d'une brochure autopromotionnelle de l'imprimerie et atelier litho Stephenson Inc. Il s'agit d'extraits de l'ouvrage *Washington the Capital* (Washington la capitale) sorti des presses de Stephenson pour le compte des Ed. Thomasson-Grant Inc. Fig. 247: impression générale, fig. 248, 249 page tripartite et détail de la photo au verso au format original; fig. 250: cimetière militaire vu du ciel. (USA)

248

249

250

PHOTOGRAPHER / PHOTOGRAPH / PHOTOGRAPHE:
247–250 Robert Llewellyn

DESIGNER / GESTALTER / MAQUETTISTE:
247–250 Leo Mullen

ART DIRECTOR / DIRECTEUR ARTISTIQUE:
247–250 Leo Mullen

AGENCY / AGENTUR / AGENCE – STUDIO:
247–250 Invisions, Ltd.

251

Booklets / Prospekte / Brochures

251–255 From a handbook by Mia Detrick published by *Chronicle Books*, San Francisco, on the subject of «Sushi», a special kind of Japanese culinary art in which the presentation of the dishes is of paramount importance. Fig. 251: Etiquette; Fig. 252: The cover illustration; Fig. 253: Rice; Fig. 254: Raw fish; Fig. 255: Arrangement of coloured rice for special occasions. (USA)
256, 257 Photograph and complete double spread from an information brochure issued by the California Institute of the Arts. (USA)

251–255 Aus einem von *Chronicle Books* herausgegebenen Handbuch von Mia Detrick über «Sushi», eine spezielle Form der japanischen Kochkunst, bei der es in erster Linie um die Präsentation geht. Die Themen sind folgende: Abb. 251: Etikette; Abb. 252: Umschlagillustration; Abb. 253: Reis; Abb. 254: roher Fisch; Abb. 255: Arrangement aus gefärbtem Reis für spezielle Anlässe. (USA)
256, 257 Aufnahme und vollständige Doppelseite aus einer Informationsbroschüre des California Institute of the Arts, Hochschule für visuelle und darstellende Künste und Konservatorium. (USA)

251–255 Illustrations tirées d'un manuel de «sushi», cuisine décorative japonaise, publié aux Ed. *Chronicle Books*. Les sujets traités: fig. 251: étiquette; fig. 252: illustration de couverture; fig. 253: riz; fig. 254: poisson cru; fig. 255: arrangement de riz coloré pour les occasions spéciales. (USA)
256, 257 Photo et double page complète d'une brochure informative du California Institute of the Arts, qui regroupe une université des arts plastiques et visuels et un conservatoire. (USA)

252

253

254

255

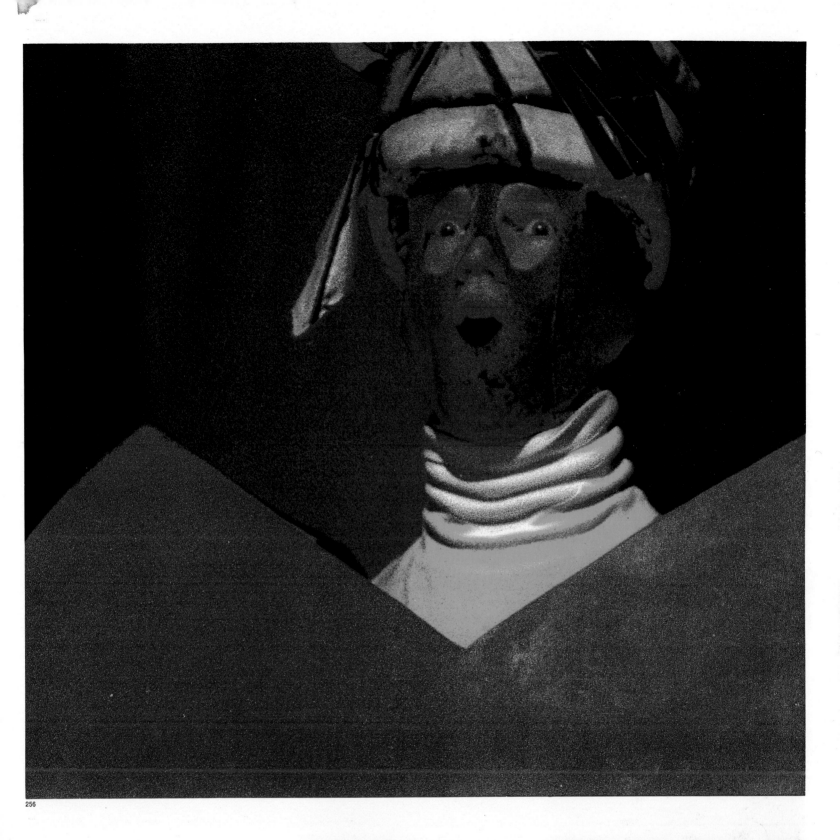

256

PHOTOGRAPHER / PHOTOGRAPH:

251–255 Kathryn Kleinman
256, 257 Dennis Gilbert

DESIGNER / GESTALTER / MAQUETTISTE:

251–255 Michael Patrick Cronan
256, 257 Julie Riefler

ART DIRECTOR / DIRECTEUR ARTISTIQUE:

251–255 Michael Patrick Cronan
256, 257 Keith Bright

AGENCY / AGENTUR / AGENCE – STUDIO:

251–255 Michael Patrick Cronan
256, 257 Bright & Associates

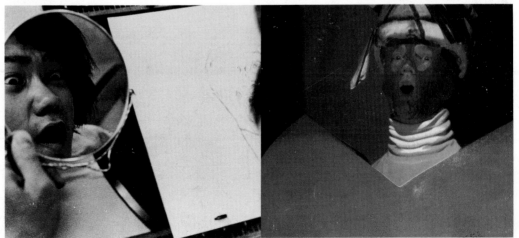

257

258

Booklets / Prospekte / Brochures

258–264 Detail of a photograph, metal cover and five double spreads from a catalogue for *Martex* home textiles made by *West Point Pepperell*. Each design is introduced with a detailed photograph of the material (see Figs. 260 and 264), which is followed by a photograph of an interior (see Figs. 261–263). The main theme is that of contrasting elements interacting to reveal unexpected harmonies. The catalogue begins with an appropriate quotation. (Stylist/Interior Designer: Bill Walter.) (USA)
265–267 Cover and introductory spreads for the chapter «Lighting rails» and «Hanging Lamps» for a *Brillant Leuchten* catalogue. Fig. 265: soft shades of green, yellowish light; Fig. 266: grey and rusty-red, yellowish light; Fig. 267: warm shades of grey with pale blue and yellow light. (GER)

258–264 Detail einer Aufnahme, Metallumschlag und fünf Doppelseiten aus einem Katalog für *Martex*-Heimtextilien von *West Point Pepperell*. Jedes Dessin wird erst mit einer Detailaufnahme des Stoffes eingeführt (s. Abb. 260 und 264), der jeweils eine Aufnahme mit Umgebung folgt (s. Abb. 261–263). Es geht hier um das Wechselspiel kontrastierender Elemente und die daraus entstehenden, unvermuteten Harmonien. Der Katalog wird mit einem entsprechenden Zitat eingeleitet. (Raumausstattung: Bill Walter.) (USA)
265–267 Umschlag und einleitende Seiten der Kapitel «Stromschienen» und «Pendelleuchten» für einen *Brillant-Leuchten*-Katalog. Abb. 265: Sanfte Grüntöne, goldgelbes Licht; Abb. 266: Grau und Rostrot, goldgelbes Licht; Abb. 267: Warme Grautöne mit blassem Blau und gelbem Licht. (GER)

258–264 «Des éléments contrastants s'associent et s'opposent, révélant des harmonies insoupçonnées»: c'est ainsi que s'ouvre le catalogue des textiles d'intérieur *Martex* de *West Point Pepperell* dont nous montrons une photo en détail, la couverture métallique et cinq doubles pages. Chaque dessin est introduit par une photo détaillée du tissu (260, 264) suivie d'une photo en situation (261–263). (Ensemblier: Bill Walter.) (USA)
265–267 Couverture et pages initiales des chapitres «Luminaires alimentés par barres collectrices» et «Plafonniers ajustables» d'un catalogue de vente réalisé pour *Brillant-Leuchten*. Fig. 265: divers tons verts adoucis, lumière jaune or; fig. 266: gris et rouille, lumière jaune or; fig. 267: divers tons gris chauds avec du bleu pâle et de la lumière jaune. (GER)

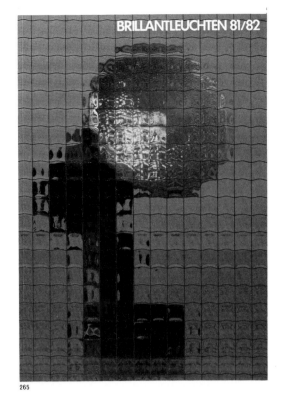

265

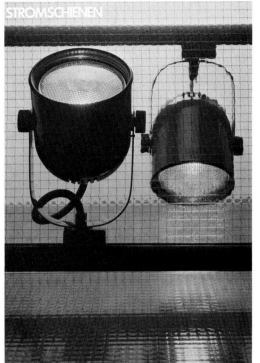

266

267

PHOTOGRAPHER / PHOTOGRAPH / PHOTOGRAPHE:

258, 261, 262, 264 Elizabeth Heyert
260, 263 Joe Standart
265 Fritz Haase
266, 267 Nikolay Žurek

DESIGNER / GESTALTER / MAQUETTISTE:

258–264 James Sebastian/Michael Lauretano
265–267 Fritz Haase

ART DIRECTOR / DIRECTEUR ARTISTIQUE:

258–264 James Sebastian

AGENCY / AGENTUR / AGENCE – STUDIO:

258–264 Designframe Inc.
265–267 Fritz Haase

259

260

261

263

262

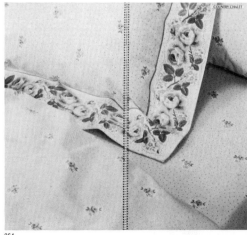

264

3

Magazine Covers

Editorial Photography

Book Covers

Trade Magazines

Corporate Publications

Annual Reports

Zeitschriften-Umschläge

Redaktionelle Photographie

Buchumschläge

Fachzeitschriften

Firmenpublikationen

Jahresberichte

Couvertures de périodiques

Photographie rédactionnelle

Couvertures de livres

Revues professionnelles

Publications d'entreprise

Rapports annuels

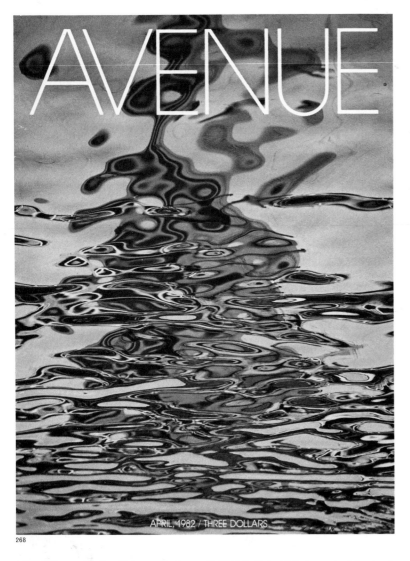

268

269

268, 269 Covers of the New York magazine *Avenue*. Fig. 268 is the first published example of "Panotage", consisting of two or more images shot and printed so as to appear as one. (USA)
270–272 Covers with full-colour photographs for *Quest*, a Canadian magazine. The issues in question contain articles about the dangers of pornography (Fig. 270), the heavyweight boxer Trevor Berbick (Fig. 271) and about sport activities for general fitness (Fig. 272). (CAN)
273, 274 Covers of *Chicago* magazine. The issues in question contain an article on summer activities and pleasures and a readers' poll of Chicago's best and worst restaurants. (USA)
275, 276 Covers of *Epicurean* magazine, a periodical devoted to eating and drinking. The illustration in Fig. 275 refers to Christmas recipes made from cherries. (AUS)

268, 269 Umschläge von Ausgaben des New Yorker Magazins *Avenue*. Abb. 268 zeigt ein zum ersten Mal veröffentlichtes Beispiel von «Panotage», ein Verfahren, bei dem zwei oder mehrere Photos so aufgenommen und gedruckt werden, dass sie ein Bild ergeben. (USA)
270–272 Umschläge für drei Ausgaben von *Quest* mit Artikeln über die Gefahren der Pornographie (Abb. 270), über einen Boxer (Abb. 271) und über Ausgleichssport (Abb. 272). (CAN)
273 Für eine Ausgabe der Zeitschrift *Chicago*, mit einem Beitrag über Sommerfreuden. (USA)
274 Ein weiterer Umschlag für *Chicago*, hier in bezug auf einen Restaurant-Test. (USA)
275, 276 Umschläge von *Epicurean*, eine Zeitschrift über Essen und Trinken. Die Illustration in Abb. 275 bezieht sich auf Kirschrezepte für Weihnachten. (AUS)

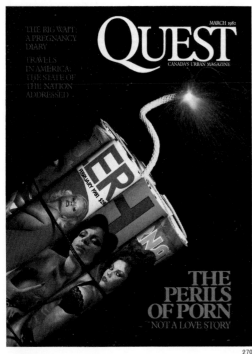
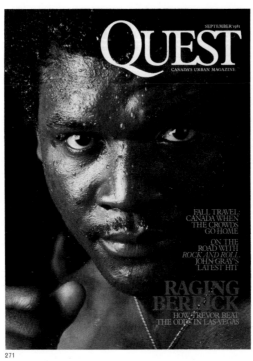

270   271

272

PHOTOGRAPHER:

268 Benno Schmidt
269 George Obremski
270, 272 Sloane Square
271 Michel Pilon
273 Dennis Manarchy
274 Tim Schultz
275 John Street
276 Peter Hendrie

DESIGNER / GESTALTER:

268 Bill Hayward
270–272 Stephen Costello
273, 274 Charles A. Thomas
275, 276 Ken Cato

ART DIRECTOR:

268 Ray Harper
269 Mary K. Baumann
270–272 Stephen Costello
273 Robert J. Post
274 Charles A. Thomas
275, 276 Ken Cato

AGENCY / AGENTUR / AGENCE:

273, 274 Chicago Magazine
275, 276 Cato Hibberd Design

PUBLISHER / VERLEGER:

268, 269 Avenue
270–272 Comac Communi-
        cations
273, 274 WFMT, Inc.
275, 276 Lawrence Publishing

273

275

274

276

268, 269 Couvertures du magazine newyorkais *Avenue*. La fig. 268 représente le premier exemple imprimé de la technique dite de «panotage» où deux ou plusieurs photos sont prises et imprimées de manière à n'en faire qu'une. (USA)
270–272 Couvertures illustrées de photos couleur pour le magazine canadien *Quest*. Elles se rapportent à des articles sur les dangers de la porno (fig. 270), le boxeur Trevor Berbick (fig. 271) et le sport équilibrant les effets stressants du travail (fig. 272). (CAN)
273 Pour un numéro du magazine *Chicago* relatant les «joies de l'été». (USA)
274 Une autre couverture de *Chicago*: résultats d'une enquête où les lecteurs étaient appelés à classer les meilleures tables de la ville et les pires. (USA)
275, 276 Couvertures d'*Epicurean*, le magazine du boire et manger. L'illustration de la fig. 275 a trait à un carnet de recettes aux cerises pour Noël. (AUS)

Magazine Covers
Zeitschriftenumschläge
Couvertures de périodiques

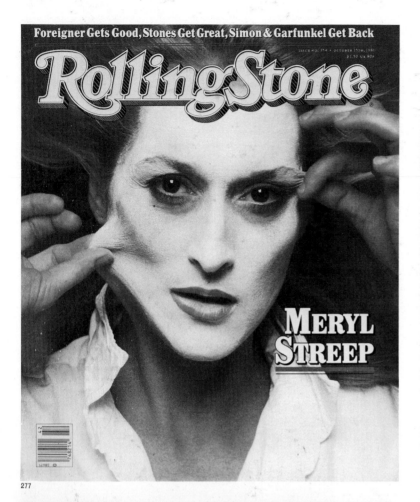

Foreigner Gets Good, Stones Get Great, Simon & Garfunkel Get Back

RollingStone

MERYL STREEP

277

The Boston Globe Magazine

November 15, 1981

A
SENSE
OF
TOUCH
By Christina Robb

278

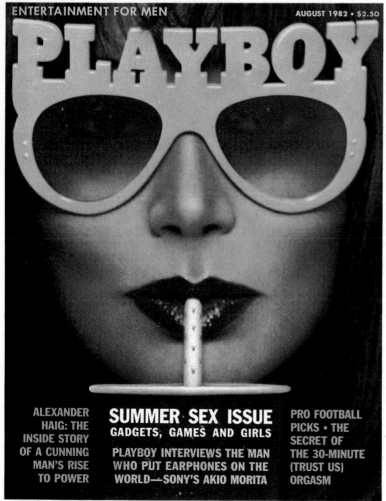

ENTERTAINMENT FOR MEN

AUGUST 1982 • $2.50

PLAYBOY

ALEXANDER HAIG: THE INSIDE STORY OF A CUNNING MAN'S RISE TO POWER

SUMMER SEX ISSUE GADGETS, GAMES AND GIRLS

PLAYBOY INTERVIEWS THE MAN WHO PUT EARPHONES ON THE WORLD—SONY'S AKIO MORITA

PRO FOOTBALL PICKS • THE SECRET OF THE 30-MINUTE (TRUST US) ORGASM

279

THE SUNDAY TIMES *magazine*

FASHION & ART: THE OTHER RUSSIAN REVOLUTION

280

277 Cover of the magazine *Rolling Stone* with a portrait of Meryl Streep. The issue in question contains an article about this actress. (USA)
278 Cover of an issue of the *Boston Globe Magazine*, with a feature about new ways to emotional and physical health by touching. (USA)
279 Cover of an issue of *Playboy*. (USA)
280 Cover of the *Sunday Times Magazine* using a model of Alexandra Exter's geometric dress designed in 1922. (GBR)
281, 282 Photograph by Karin Székessy and complete cover of an issue of *Nikon News* featuring a report on this photographer. (SWI)

277 Umschlag des *Rolling Stone* mit einem Porträt von Meryl Streep. Die Ausgabe enthält einen Bericht über diese Schauspielerin. (USA)
278 Umschlag für eine Ausgabe des *Boston Globe Magazine* mit einem Beitrag über physische und psychische Therapien durch Berührung. (USA)
279 Umschlag einer Sommer-Sex-Ausgabe des *Playboy*-Magazins. (USA)
280 «Mode und Kunst: Die andere russische Revolution.» Umschlag des *Sunday Times Magazine*. (GBR)
281, 282 Aufnahme von Karin Székessy und vollständiger Umschlag einer Ausgabe der *Nikon-News* mit einem Bericht über diese Photographin. (SWI)

277 Couverture de *Rolling Stone*, avec un portrait de Meryl Streep. Le numéro contient un article de fond sur cette actrice. (USA)
278 Couverture d'un numéro du *Boston Globe Magazine* (article sur les thérapies de contact: «le toucher qui guérit»). (USA)
279 D'un numéro du magazine *Playboy* consacré au «sexe en été». (USA)
280 «La mode et l'art: l'autre révolution russe.» Couverture du *Sunday Times Magazine*. (GBR)
281, 282 Photo de Karin Székessy et couverture complète d'un numéro de *Nikon News* où figure un rapport sur cette photographe. (SWI)

PHOTOGRAPHER / PHOTOGRAPH:

277 Annie Leibovitz
278 John Goodman
279 Tom Staebler
280 Ross Feltus
281, 282 Karin Székessy

DESIGNER / GESTALTER:

278 Ronn Campisi
279 Len Willis

ART DIRECTOR / DIRECTEUR ARTISTIQUE:

277 Mary Shanahan
278 Ronn Campisi
279 Tom Staebler
280 Michael Rand/Gilvrie Misstear
281, 282 Hans-Peter Schmid

AGENCY / AGENTUR / AGENCE – STUDIO:

281, 282 Züllig & Kiefer

PUBLISHER / VERLEGER / EDITEUR:

277 Straigt Arrow Publishers Inc.
278 The Boston Globe
279 Playboy Enterprises, Inc.
280 Times Newspapers Ltd.
281, 282 Nikon AG

281

282

283

Editorial Photography

PHOTOGRAPHER / PHOTOGRAPH / PHOTOGRAPHE:

283 Peter Strongwater
284 Jaap Teding van Berkhout
285, 287 Robert Golden
286 Jim Matusik
288 Albert Watson

DESIGNER / GESTALTER / MAQUETTISTE:

284 Jan-Willem Henssen
286 Christopher Garland

284

285

283 Double spread of an interview with the actress Ali MacGraw which appeared in the American edition of *Interview*. In black and white. (USA)
284 Photograph for a feature that appeared in the magazine *Avant Garde*. (NLD)
285, 287 Full-colour double spreads from an article about bread which is baked without yeast. From the magazine *Good Housekeeping*. (GBR)
286 Cover of *Art Direction*. In red shades. (USA)
288 Colour spread with tips for making up with *Orlane's* cosmetics, from *Vogue*. (GBR)

283 Doppelseite aus einem Interview mit der Schauspielerin Ali MacGraw, erschienen in der amerikanischen Ausgabe von *Interview*. In Schwarzweiss. (USA)
284 Aufnahme für einen Beitrag in der Zeitschrift *Avant Garde*. (NLD)
285, 287 Farbige Doppelseiten aus einem Artikel über Brote, die ohne Hefe gebacken werden, erschienen in der Zeitschrift *Good Housekeeping*. (GBR)
286 Umschlag der Zeitschrift *Art Direction*. (USA)
288 Farbige Doppelseite mit Tips für Make-up mit *Orlane*-Kosmetikprodukten. Aus *Vogue*. (GBR)

283 Double page d'une interview avec l'actrice Ali Mac-Graw publiée dans l'édition américaine d'*Interview*. Illustration noir et blanc. (USA)
284 Pour un article du magazine *Avant-Garde*. (NLD)
285, 287 Doubles pages couleur d'un article sur les pains confectionnés sans levain, paru dans le magazine *Good Housekeeping*. (GBR)
286 Couverture du magazine *Art Direction*. (USA)
288 Double page couleur de *Vogue* avec des conseils de maquillage aux produits *Orlane*. (GBR)

ART DIRECTOR / DIRECTEUR ARTISTIQUE:

283 Marc Balet
284 Jaap Teding van Berkhout
285, 287 Mike Lackersteen
286 Christopher Garland
288 Susan Mann

AGENCY / AGENTUR / AGENCE – STUDIO:

286 Xeno

PUBLISHER / VERLEGER / EDITEUR:

283 Interview Enterprises, Inc.
284 Avant-Garde Magazine
285, 287 National Magazine Co. Ltd.
286 Advertising Trade Publications, Inc.
288 Condé Nast Publications, Ltd.

ART DIRECTION

January 1982

The Magazine of Visual Communication

286

287

288

289

290

291

292

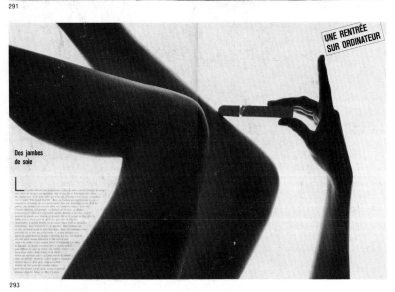

Des jambes
de soie

293

paris

SAINT LAUR

294

289, 290 Two double spreads from the American edition of *Vogue*, in which Isabella Rossellini, Ingrid Bergman's daughter, shows new weather-proof make-up: here for cold weather, manufactured by *Revlon* (Fig. 289) and for *Max Factor* make-up for rainy weather (Fig. 290). (USA)
291 Double spread with a full-colour photograph taken from *Vogue* magazine, showing decorative cosmetics for the spring manufactured by the *Elizabeth Arden* company. (GBR)
292 Double spread from the fashion section of the English edition of *Vogue* magazine, in which stores such as Harrods, Liberty's and Selfridges present their new fashions. (GBR)
293 "Legs like silk" is the slogan from an article in *Vogue* about hair removal. (FRA)
294 Full-colour *Vogue* double spread for silk creations by *Yves Saint Laurent*. (USA)
295 From a *Vogue* editorial containing suggestions for the autumn and winter fashions as well as their accessories. The photograph is in black and white. (FRA)
296, 297 Full-page photographs from *Vogue* magazine showing spontaneous, youthful fashions created by *Angelo Tarlazzi*. The male models are wearing New York Jets football outfits. (FRA)

289, 290 Zwei Doppelseiten der amerikanischen Ausgabe von *Vogue*, in welcher Isabella Rossellini, Ingrid Bergmans Tochter, die neuen wetterfesten Make-ups zeigt; hier für kaltes Wetter von *Revlon* (Abb. 289) und für regnerisches Wetter von *Max Factor* (Abb. 290). (USA)
291 Doppelseite mit Farbaufnahme in der Zeitschrift *Vogue* mit dekorativer Kosmetik von *Elisabeth Arden* für den Frühling. (GBR)
292 Doppelseite aus dem Modesektor der englischen Ausgabe der Zeitschrift *Vogue*, in der verschiedene Modehäuser wie Harrods, Liberty's und Selfridges ihre neue Mode vorstellen. (GBR)
293 «Beine wie Seide» lautet der Slogan zu einem Artikel über Haarentfernung in *Vogue*. (FRA)
294 Farbige Doppelseite aus *Vogue* für Seiden-Kreationen von *Yves Saint Laurent*. (USA)
295 Aus einem redaktionellen Beitrag in *Vogue*, mit Vorschlägen für die Herbst- und Wintermode und die Accessoires. Aufnahme in Schwarzweiss. (FRA)
296, 297 Ganzseitige Aufnahmen aus der Modezeitschrift *Vogue*, die spontane, junge Mode von *Angelo Tarlazzi* zeigt. Die männlichen Modelle im «Football»-Tenue der New York Jets. (FRA)

Editorial Photography

PHOTOGRAPHER / PHOTOGRAPH / PHOTOGRAPHE:

289, 290, 294, 296, 297 Bill King
291, 292 John Bishop/Mayer-Norten Group
293 Daniel Jouanneau
295 Albert Watson

ART DIRECTOR / DIRECTEUR ARTISTIQUE:

289, 290, 294 Alexander Liberman
291, 292 Susan Mann
293, 295–297 Jocelyn Kargère

PUBLISHER / VERLEGER / EDITEUR:

289, 290, 294 Condé Nast Publications, Inc.
291, 292 Condé Nast Publications, Ltd.
293, 295–297 Condé Nast SA

289, 290 Deux pages doubles de l'édition américaine de *Vogue* où Isabella Rossellini, la fille d'Ingrid Bergman, présente les nouveaux produits de maquillage insensibles aux intempéries: ici, pour braver le froid, des fards *Revlon* (fig. 289), et, pour braver la pluie, des fards *Max Factor* (fig. 290). (USA)
291 Double page avec une photo couleur illustrant les produits cosmétiques décoratifs d'*Elisabeth Arden* pour le printemps, dans le magazine *Vogue*. (GBR)
292 Double page de la section Mode de l'édition anglaise du magazine *Vogue*: divers magasins de modes tels que Harrods, Liberty's et Selfridges y présentent leurs nouveaux modèles. (GBR)
293 Double page avec un article dans *Vogue* sur l'épilation des jambes. En couleur. (FRA)
294 Double page couleur de *Vogue* pour les créations soie d'*Yves Saint Laurent*. (USA)
295 Contribution rédactionnelle au magazine *Vogue*, avec des propositions pour la mode d'automne et d'hiver et les accessoires idoines. Photo noir et blanc. (FRA)
296, 297 Photos pleine page publiées dans le magazine *Vogue* et présentant la jeune mode spontanée d'*Angelo Tarlazzi*. Les modèles masculins en tenue «foot» des New York Jets. (FRA)

La nouvelle mode arrive qu'il faut savoir reconnaître, apprivoiser, adopter, sans fausses notes. Ce qui paraît l'accessoire fait souvent partie intégrante de l'essentiel. Écoutez les créateurs. Bien porter leur mode, c'est la porter complète, du chapeau au talon. Rykiel : "Avec le blanc de cet hiver, jupe est courte, les jambes doivent être gainées dans le même ton pour allonger la silhouette. Les chapeaux, même le soir, sont toujours indiqués. Quand la jupe est ample, la taille doit être marquée." Kenzo : "Le blanc des manteaux est la note de calme nécessaire dans le jardin fleuri des robes imprimées. La gaieté par-dessous, la sobriété par-dessus". Gaultier : "Impératif des noirs pour allonger la silhouette". Lagerfeld : "Retour du gant géant, qui "chausse" la manche comme la botte "gantait la jambe". Mugler : "Mélangez les pastels et la fourrure. Portez des bottines à talons hauts et des corselets de crocodile. Sac, gants et chaussures devront être assortis dans les mêmes tons."

LE POINT DE VUE DE VOGUE

Le béret de marin à cabochon et voilette de S. Rykiel. Bague diamants de Tiffany. Maquillage P. Gobel.

295

296

Ombre et lumière chez Angelo Tarlazzi, le favon des détaillants d'après un récent sondage. Pourquoi ? Sans doute parce qu'il opte pour une ligne plus intuitive qu'intellectuelle. Ici, il joue des brillants et des mats, et de nouvelles proportions pour les épaules et les pantalons. Mais là-dedans, aucun rembourrage de footballeur américain. Tout est dans la coupe. Le mélange de matière, à droite, ample veste en lainage à col châle, sur une blouse à décolleté bénitier en satin et un pantalon court et fuselé en cuir. Angelo Tarlazzi. Chaussures Angelo Tarlazzi pour Guido Pasquali. Page de droite, la veste blazer en lainage à chevrons, sur une blouse en lamé décolletée en V, blousante sur un pantalon court en jersey de laine. Angelo Tarlazzi. Chaussures Angelo Tarlazzi pour Guido Pasquali. Maquillages Tyen pour Christian Dior. Coiffures Simon Marsden New York. Pour eux, uniforme de football des N.Y. Jets.

BILL KING

297

298

299

PHOTOGRAPHER / PHOTOGRAPH:

298, 299 Michel Tcherevkoff
300, 301 Gillean Proctor
302, 303 Joel Baldwin
304 Klaus Lucka
305 Harald Sund
306 Victor Skrebneski

DESIGNER / GESTALTER / MAQUETTISTE:

298, 299 Bridget DeSocio
302, 303 Tory Ettlinger
304, 306 Melissa Tardiff

ART DIRECTOR / DIRECTEUR ARTISTIQUE:

298, 299, 302–304, 306 Melissa Tardiff
300, 301 Ursula Kaiser
305 David Moore

AGENCY / AGENTUR / AGENCE – STUDIO:

300, 301 Homemaker's Magazine
305 U.S. Information Agency

PUBLISHER / VERLEGER / EDITEUR:

298, 299, 302–304, 306 The Hearst Corp.
300, 301 Comac Communications
305 International Communication Agency

298, 299 From the magazine *Town & Country*, for an article about American caviar which, after one hundred years, has once again become a top-class delicacy. (USA)
300, 301 Taken from a series in *Homemaker's Magazine* with advice for professional-looking make-up techniques and for the simplification of beauty care for today's busy woman. (CAN)
302–304 Double spreads taken from *Town & Country* magazine featuring fashion and jewellery. (USA)
305 Cover of *America Illustrated* magazine, this edition being destined for the Soviet Union. (USA)
306 Broadside double spread for an article about make-up which appeared in *Town & Country*. (USA)

298, 299 Aus dem Magazin *Town & Country* für einen Artikel über amerikanischen Kaviar. (USA)
300, 301 Aus einer Serie im *Homemaker's Magazine* mit Ratschlägen für die Schönheit, hier kunstgerechtes Augen-Make-up und die Vereinfachung der Schönheitspflege. (CAN)
302–304 Doppelseiten aus dem Magazin *Town & Country* über Mode- und Schmuckartikel. (USA)
305 Umschlag der Zeitschrift *America Illustrated*, die für die Sowjetunion bestimmt ist. (USA)
306 Querformatige Doppelseite für einen Artikel über Make-up in *Town & Country*. (USA)

298, 299 Illustration d'un article du magazine *Town & Country* qui contient une étude sur le caviar américain. (USA)
300, 301 Extraits d'une série d'articles du *Homemaker's Magazine* contenant des conseils de beauté, ici comment farder ses yeux et comment simplifier les soins de beauté. (CAN)
302–304 Doubles pages du magazine *Town & Country*: articles de mode et de bijouterie. (USA)
305 Couverture du magazine *America Illustrated* en version russe. (USA)
306 Double page, au format oblong, d'un article de *Town & Country* consacré au maquillage. (USA)

300

301

302

303

Editorial Photography

304

АПРЕЛЬ 1982 / № 305 • 50 коп.

Америка

«БОИНГ» СТРОИТ НОВЫЙ ЛАЙНЕР

40 RENTALS

305

306

HEFT NR. 45 HAMBURG, 4. NOVEMBER 1982 3,– DM 25.05 C 8041 C

stern
magazin

Krieg der Zuhälter
Organisiertes Verbrechen auf St. Pauli

307

HEFT NR. 40 HAMBURG, 30. SEPTEMBER 1982 3,– DM 25.05 C 8041 C

stern
magazin

Tauziehen um die Macht in Bonn

Das Signal von Hessen: Rot-grüne Mehrheit bald auch in Bonn?

Siegt F. J. Strauß gegen...
bitte umblättern

308

Formel Wahnsinn

Die Angst des Rennfahrers vor dem Rennen. Der Italiener Andrea de Cesaris verdreht nervös die Augen. 22 Wagen hat der Millionärssohn allein im letzten Jahr zu Schrott gefahren. Mit Sport hat die Formel 1 nichts mehr zu tun. Den Drahtziehern im Rennzirkus geht es allein ums Geld

Auto ✶ Journal

310

309

307–313 Covers and double spreads from *Stern* magazine, dealing with the following subjects: organized crime in Hamburg's St. Pauli area (Fig. 307); the political power struggle in Germany (Fig. 308 in full colour, Fig. 309 in black and white); "Formula Madness", portraying the danger of automobile racing with a photograph of the interior of a Formula-1 car which shows how little room the designers leave for the driver (Figs. 310, 311); the old piers in England, here the North Pier in Blackpool on which 3000 deck-chairs are set up for sunbathers (Fig. 312); inhuman architecture, spaces and squares—an example of which is shown in this photograph of a square fronting the university of Bochum, one end of which descends into an underground garage (Fig. 313). (GER)

307–313 Umschläge und Doppelseiten aus dem Magazin *Stern* zu folgenden Themen: das organisierte Verbrechen auf St. Pauli (Abb. 307); der politische Machtkampf in Deutschland (Abb. 308, in Farbe, und Abb. 309, in Schwarzweiss); die Gefährlichkeit des Auto-Rennsports, mit einer Aufnahme aus dem Innern eines Formel-1-Wagens, die zeigt, wie wenig Raum die Konstrukteure den Piloten lassen (Abb. 310, 311); die Piers in England, hier der North Pier in Blackpool, auf dem 3000 Liegestühle für Sonnenhungrige bereitstehen (Abb. 312); unmenschliche Architektur, Räume und Plätze, die niemand mag – als Beispiel eine Aufnahme des Platzes vor der Universität Bochum, dessen Abstieg zu einer Tiefgarage führt (Abb. 313). (GER)

307–313 Couvertures et doubles pages du magazine hebdomadaire *Stern* traitant des sujets suivants: le crime organisé dans le quartier hambourgeois de St-Pauli (fig. 307); la lutte pour le pouvoir politique en Allemagne fédérale (fig. 308 en couleur, fig. 309 noir et blanc); les dangers inhérents aux courses automobiles, avec une photo de l'intérieur d'un bolide de formule 1 montrant le peu de place que les constructeurs laissent aux pilotes (fig. 310, 311); les embarcadères anglais, ici le North Pier de Blackpool, où 3000 chaises longues attendent les mordus de bains de soleil (fig. 312); l'architecture ignorant des valeurs humaines, exemple d'une place devant l'Université de Bochum gâchée par l'entrée d'un garage souterrain (fig. 313). (GER)

Editorial Photography

PHOTOGRAPHER / PHOTOGRAPH / PHOTOGRAPHE:

307 Iver Hansen
308, 309 Christian von Alvensleben
310, 311 Joseph Emonts-Pohl
312 Richard Fischer
313 Anne Koch

DESIGNER / GESTALTER / MAQUETTISTE:

307–309 Franz Epping
310, 311 Dietmar Schulze
312 Karl-Heinz John
313 Günther Meyer

ART DIRECTOR / DIRECTEUR ARTISTIQUE:

307–313 Wolfgang Behnken

PUBLISHER / VERLEGER / EDITEUR:

307–313 Gruner & Jahr AG & Co.

312

311

313

314

315

314, 315 Double spreads from a feature in *Stern* magazine presenting men's fashions in action photographs from various sports. (GER)
316 Full-colour photograph from *Quest* magazine featuring an article about an unusual humoristic programme on Radio Toronto starring Allan McFee. (CAN)
317, 318 Full-page photograph in full colour and introductory double spread for a feature in *Quest* on the phenomenal history of the Japanese *Walkman*, a trade mark which has become the common name for a personal stereo tape recorder which can be worn in the street. (CAN)
319 "Gold nuggets of zero carats." From a series of photographs in *Stern* magazine. (GER)
320, 321 Photographs of spring and summer fashions taken from the Italian magazine *Lei*. (ITA)

314, 315 Doppelseiten aus einem in der Zeitschrift *Stern* erschienenen Artikel über Männermode, mit Action-Photos aus verschiedenen Sportarten. (GER)
316 Farbaufnahme aus dem Magazin *Quest* mit einem Artikel über eine bemerkenswerte humoristische Sendung von Radio Toronto mit Allan McFee. (CAN)
317, 318 «Zen und die Kunst der Audio-Erotik.» Ganzseitige Aufnahme in Farbe und vollständige, einleitende Doppelseite für einen Artikel in *Quest* über die Geschichte der aus Japan stammenden, auf der Strasse zu tragenden Tonbandgeräte, die als *Walkman* bekannt wurden. (CAN)
319 «Goldstücke zu Null Karat.» Aus einer Serie von Aufnahmen im Magazin *Stern*. (GER)
320, 321 Aufnahmen mit Frühlings- und Sommermode aus der italienischen Zeitschrift *Lei*. (ITA)

314, 315 Doubles pages d'un article de mode masculine dans le magazine *Stern*, illustré de photos de sportifs pris en pleine action. (GER)
316 Photo couleur du magazine *Quest* rappelant une émission humoristique d'Allan McFee. (CAN)
317, 318 «Le zen et l'art de l'érotisme audio.» Photo pleine page en couleur et double page complète en tête d'un article consacré à l'histoire du magnétophone portatif à écouteurs baptisé *walkman*. Le tout est tiré du magazine *Quest*. (CAN)
319 «Pièces d'or à zéro carat.» Exemple d'une série de photos dans le magazine *Stern*. (GER)
320, 321 Photos de la mode de printemps et d'été présentées dans le magazine italien *Lei*. (ITA)

Editorial Photography

316

317

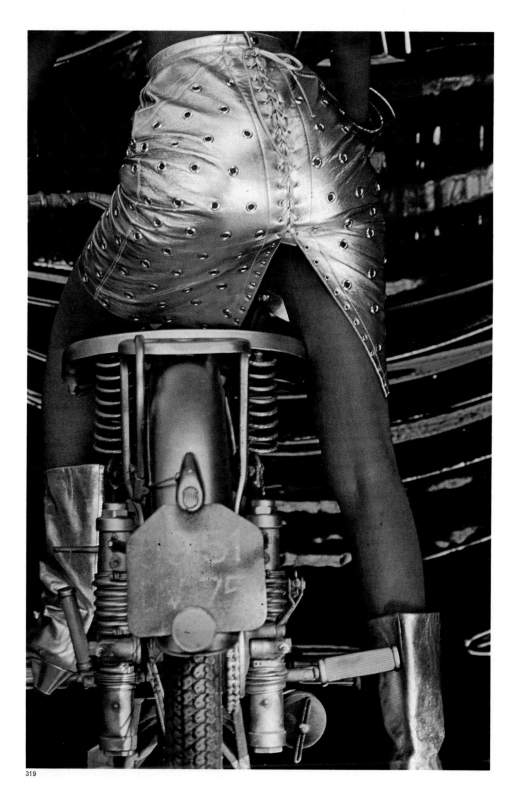

319

320

321

PHOTOGRAPHER / PHOTOGRAPH / PHOTOGRAPHE:

314, 315 Christian von Alvensleben
316 Sloane Square Studio
317, 318 Pat Lacroix
319 Peter Knapp/Mayer–Norten Group
320, 321 Verita Monselles

318

DESIGNER / GESTALTER / MAQUETTISTE:

316 Stephen Costello
317, 318 Mary Opper
320, 321 Roberto Bastianoni

ART DIRECTOR / DIRECTEUR ARTISTIQUE:

314, 315, 319 Wolfgang Behnken
316–318 Stephen Costello
320, 321 Roberto Bastianoni

AGENCY / AGENTUR / AGENCE – STUDIO:

320, 321 Fotogrammatre

PUBLISHER / VERLEGER / EDITEUR:

314, 315, 319 Gruner & Jahr AG & Co.
316–318 Comac Communications Ltd.
320, 321 Haccatre

133

322

323

322, 323 Double spreads from the *Sunday Times Magazine* with ideas for the design of living-rooms and of kitchens. Full-colour illustrations. (GBR)
324 Double-spread full-colour photograph of a church façade taken from the German edition of *Photo* magazine, for an article about the American photographer Harry Callahan. (GER)
325 Photograph from an instructional volume of photographs by Ewald Stark, entitled "Beauty as the Goal", published by *Falken Verlag*, 6272 Niedernhausen, West Germany. (GER)

322, 323 Doppelseiten aus dem *Sunday Times Magazine* mit Anregungen für die Gestaltung von Wohnräumen und Küchen. Mehrfarbige Illustrationen. (GBR)
324 Doppelseitige Farbaufnahme einer Kirchenfassade aus der deutschen Ausgabe von *Photo*, zu einem Artikel über den amerikanischen Photographen Harry Callahan. (GER)
325 Aufnahme aus einem didaktischen Photo-Bildband von Ewald Stark, mit dem Titel *Das Schöne als Ziel*, erschienen im *Falken Verlag*, D-6272 Niedernhausen. (GER)

PHOTOGRAPHER / PHOTOGRAPH / PHOTOGRAPHE:

324 Harry Callahan
325 Ewald Stark

ART DIRECTOR / DIRECTEUR ARTISTIQUE:

322, 323 Michael Rand/Lucy Sisman
324 Karl-Heinz Wendlandt
325 Ewald Stark

DESIGNER / GESTALTER / MAQUETTISTE:

322, 323 Lucy Sisman
325 Gebhardt & Lorenz

PUBLISHER / VERLEGER / EDITEUR:

322, 323 Times Newspapers Ltd.
324 New Magazines Verlagsgesellschaft mbH
325 Falken-Verlag GmbH

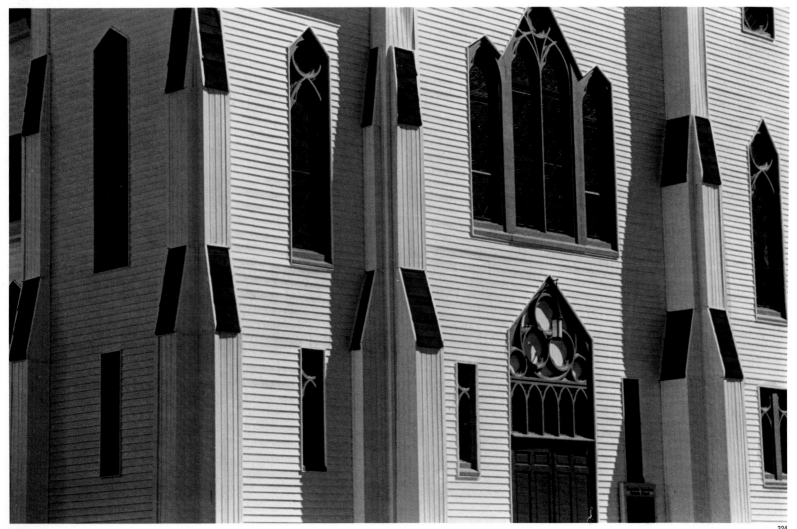

324

325

322, 323 «100 idées pour vivre et dîner.» Doubles pages du *Sunday Times Magazine* avec des options d'aménagement des livings et des cuisines. Illustrations polychromes. (GBR)
324 Photo couleur, sur page double, d'une façade d'église dans l'édition allemande de *Photo*, illustrant un article consacré au photographe américain Harry Callahan. (GER)
325 Photo tirée d'un album de photo didactique par Ewald Stark, paru aux Ed. *Falken-Verlag* (D-6272 Niedernhausen) sous le titre de *Das Schöne als Ziel* (La Beauté pour cible). (GER)

Editorial Photography

326

326, 329 Aufnahme und vollständige Doppelseite aus einem Artikel in der französischen Ausgabe von *Vogue*. Es geht hier um Accessoires und Make-up im Sommer. (FRA)
327 Doppelseite zu einem Bericht über Spiele für Kinder bei Regen, aus dem Magazin *Eltern*. (GER)
328 Doppelseitige Farbaufnahme eines Laubfrosches, der eine Fliege fängt, aus *Sunday*. (GBR)
330 Doppelseite aus einem Buch der National Geographic Society über Tierphotographie. (USA)
331 Aus einem im *American Photographer* erschienenen Artikel über den Photographen Hiro. Das durch die Vielfalt intensiver, nahe beieinanderliegender Farben entstehende Belichtungsproblem löste Hiro durch Einzelaufnahmen, die dann zusammenmontiert wurden. (USA)

326, 329 Photograph and double spread from an article in the French edition of *Vogue*. (FRA)
327 "Oh, beautiful filthy weather!" An *Eltern* magazine article about games for children which can be played in rainy weather. (GER)
328 Double-spread colour shot of a tree-frog catching a bluebottle, from *Sunday* magazine. (GBR)
330 Spread from a book published by the National Geographic Society on photographing animals. (USA)
331 From an article on the photographer Hiro in *American Photographer*. The lighting problem created by the variety of intense colours in close proximity was solved by Hiro by shooting them separately and assembling the transparencies. (USA)

OH, DU HERRLICHES SAUWETTER!

327

KERMIT TAKES A FLIER

328

329

Editorial Photography

326, 329 Photo et double page complète d'un article de l'édition française de *Vogue*: accessoires et maquillage en été. (FRA)
327 «Oh, quel merveilleux temps dégueulasse!» Double page tirée d'un rapport sur les jeux des enfants par temps de pluie publié dans le magazine *Eltern*. (GER)
328 Photo couleur (double page) d'une rainette attrapant une mouche, dans *Sunday*. (GBR)
330 Double page extraite d'un livre que la National Geographic Society consacre à la photo animalière. (USA)
331 Illustration d'un article d'*American Photographer* sur l'art du photographe Hiro, qui a résolu le trop grand voisinage de couleurs trop intenses par un montage de photos individuelles. (USA)

330

PHOTOGRAPHER / PHOTOGRAPH / PHOTOGRAPHE:

326, 329 Albert Watson
327 Norbert Schäfer
328 Kim Taylor/Bruce Coleman
330 Jonathan Blair
331 Hiro

DESIGNER / GESTALTER / MAQUETTISTE:

327 Rita Gerstenbrand
328 Colin Jenkins
330 David M. Seager

ART DIRECTOR / DIRECTEUR ARTISTIQUE:

326, 329 Jocelyn Kargère
327 Noelle Thieux
328 Clive Crook
330 David M. Seager
331 William Hopkins

PUBLISHER / VERLEGER / EDITEUR:

326, 329 Condé Nast SA
327 Gruner & Jahr AG & Co.
330 National Geographic Society
331 CBS Publications

vidual style had emerged intact.

Within a month, Avedon introduced Hiro to Alexey Brodovitch at *Harper's Bazaar*. With Avedon's backing and the set of pictures that had resulted from the New York/France collaboration, Hiro was given a chance to try out for a job as a backup for Leslie Gill, the magazine's still life master. Brodovitch gave Hiro a small shoe by Dior to photograph. In a lecture series at the New School, Brodovitch also gave the exacting dictum, which became the fundament of Hiro's career: If you look into your camera and see something you've seen before, don't click the shutter.

For weeks Hiro photographed the shoe, periodically taking the pictures to Brodovitch. The master deigned to make no other comment than a polite, "Will you try this again, please?" At last, months after the ordeal had begun, Brodovitch declared that Hiro was ready to make photographs for publication. His first assignment, a spread on a collection of shoes.

Hiro has an instinct for what Kant called "the thing in the thing." This animistic sense for the soul of matter is one of the most obvious classically Oriental traits he displays. This feeling invariably reaches further than the specific object he's photographing. Hiro creates surprise by caring equally for all the elements in his pictures, like a magnanimous director devoted as much to the excellence of his bit players as to the luminosity of his stars. When he placed a ruby necklace around a steer's hoof

Paper Shoes, 1967. The variety of intense colors in close proximity created a difficult lighting problem, which Hiro solved by shooting them separately on 8 × 10 and assembling the transparencies.

49

331

332

334

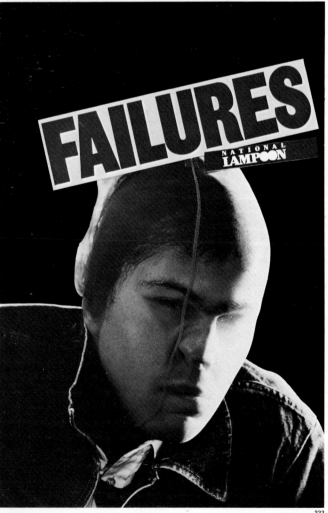

333

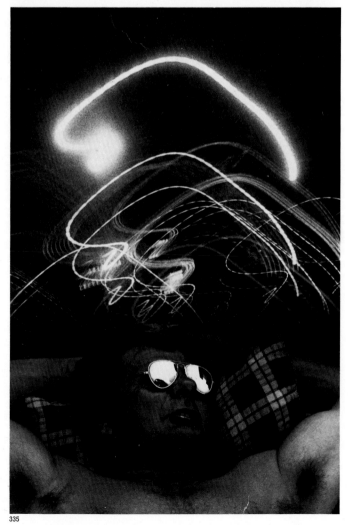

335

PHOTOGRAPHER:

332, 333 H. Brehm
334, 335 Steve Hill
336 C. Hirschfeld
337 Robert Holcepl
338, 339 Gary A. Per-
    weiler

DESIGNER:

332, 333 H. Brehm
336, 337 S. Capuano
338, 339 David Talbert

ART DIRECTOR:

332, 333 H. Brehm
334–337 Greg Paul
338, 339 David Talbert

PUBLISHER:

334–337 The Plain
    Dealer Publishing
338, 339 Cuisine
    Magazine

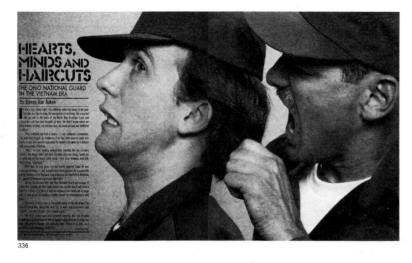

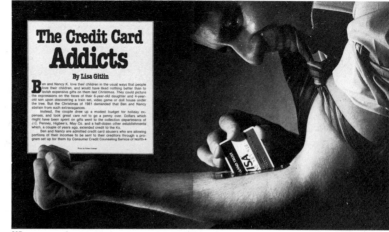

336   337

332, 333 Layouts by the photographer Heribert Brehm for a fashion feature (332) and for the "Failures" column (333), which appears regularly in *National Lampoon*. (GER)
334, 335 Black-and-white photographs for an article about dreams in *Plain Dealer Magazine*. (USA)
336, 337 Full-colour introductory spreads from articles in the *Plain Dealer Magazine*. (USA)
338, 339 Double spread and illustration taken from *Cuisine Magazine*. (USA)

332, 333 Entwürfe des Photographen Heribert Brehm für einen Modebeitrag (332) und für die Rubrik «Gescheiterte» («Failures»), die regelmässig in *National Lampoon* erscheint (333). (GER)
334, 335 Schwarzweiss-Aufnahmen aus einem Artikel über Träume im *Plain Dealer Magazine*. (USA)
336, 337 Einleitende Doppelseiten zu Artikeln im *Plain Dealer Magazine*. In Farbe. (USA)
338, 339 Doppelseite und Illustration zum Thema «Suppen», aus *Cuisine Magazine*. (USA)

332, 333 Contributions du photographe Heribert Brehm pour un article de mode (332) et la rubrique «Paumés» («Failures») publiée régulièrement dans le *National Lampoon* (333). (GER)
334, 335 Photos noir et blanc pour un article du *Plain Dealer Magazine* sur les rêves. (USA)
336, 337 Doubles pages en tête d'articles du *Plain Dealer Magazine*. En couleur. (USA)
338, 339 Double page et illustration de *Cuisine Magazine*, sur le sujet des soupes. (USA)

338

339   **139**

Von Udo Pini, Fotos John Dominis

Superbe Köche und junge Frauen soll man meiden, sagen die Franzosen, denen doch beides ständig begegnet. Denn, so spricht das Sprichwort, beiden verfällt man unweigerlich. Und beide darf man deshalb hier in einem Atemzug erwähnen, weil er auf leisen, sympathischen Zehen-Spitzen des Knoblauchs daherweht und seine Verehrer nicht mehr überzeugen muß, daß die Liebe durch die Küche, durch die Augen, durch den Magen geht. Genau diesen Weg der Verführung nähme ein solcher Teller mit einer gegarten Gemüsegemeinschaft, die ein Koch auf einem Markt in der Provence zusammenfeilschte. Er kennt die Minutenstaffel von Zuccini, Karotten, Bohnen und Beten, Fenchel, Porree, vom Blumenkohl, den Kartoffeln und den Artischocken, fischt alles gleichzeitig aus dem Wasser und stellt ein Schüsselchen von der „Butter der Provence" dazu: Aioli! Das Kunstwort aus Ail (Knoblauch) und Öl ist das Kunstwerk von einer geknofelten Sauce – den Zutaten Ei, Öl, Zitronensaft und Knoblauch nach eine Knoblauchmayonnaise, die auch einen Kochfisch oft in ganz neue Elemente befördert.

DAS GELBE VOM EI SIND KNOBLAUCH UND ÖL

Vom Gemüsebeet zur Augenweide: Ein köstlicher Teller zum Vorspeisen, zusammengekauft auf den Märkten der Provence, so verschieden wie die Garzeiten und stets gekrönt von Aioli, der unentbehrlichen Knoblauchmayonnaise. Délicieux!

16

340

Editorial Photography

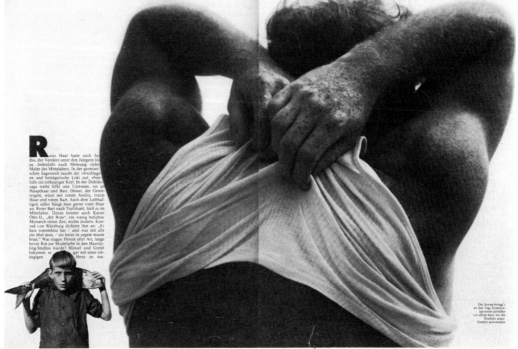

344   345

340–347 On this and the following double spread, covers and spreads from the *Frankfurter Allgemeine Magazin* are shown, the appearance of which has been decidedly marked for many years by the art director Willy Fleckhaus. The layout is of paramount importance here in addition to the photography. Figs. 340 and 341 show a double spread on the subject of garlic and the corresponding contents page; Fig. 342 shows the contents page with a reference to an article about the Lake of Constance; Fig. 343: the contents page with a restorer's tools, again as a pointer to an article on this subject; Figs. 344 and 345 show the cover and a double spread on the subject of redheads; Figs. 346 and 347: cover and double spread with a certain make of sunglasses from a feature about the discomfort experienced when peering at completely covered eyes. (GER)

340–347 Auf dieser und der folgenden Doppelseite werden Umschläge und Seiten aus dem *Frankfurter Allgemeine Magazin* gezeigt, dessen Erscheinungsbild Willy Fleckhaus als langjähriger Art Director entscheidend geprägt hat. Es geht hier nicht nur um die Photographie, sondern vor allem auch um das Layout. Abb. 340 und 341 zeigen eine Doppelseite zum Thema Knoblauch und die entsprechende Inhaltsseite; Abb. 342 die Inhaltsseite mit Anspielung auf einen Artikel über den Bodensee; Abb. 343 die Inhaltsseite mit den Geräten eines Restaurators, wiederum als Hinweis auf einen Artikel zu diesem Thema; Abb. 344 und 345 Umschlag und Doppelseite zum Thema «Rothaarige»; Abb. 346 und 347: Umschlag und Doppelseite aus einem Beitrag über das Unbehagen, das der Mensch beim Anblick eines völlig bedeckten Auges empfindet. (GER)

340–347 Les couvertures et pages du *Frankfurter Allgemeine Magazin* visibles sur cette double page, ainsi que sur la suivante, vous familiarisent avec le style de présentation original que Willy Fleckhaus, longtemps directeur artistique de ce magazine, a su donner tant à la photographie qu'au layout. Les fig. 340 et 341 montrent une double page sur le thème de l'ail et la page correspondante du sommaire; la fig. 342, la page du sommaire avec référence à un article sur le lac de Constance; la fig. 343, la page du sommaire avec les outils du restaurateur de tableaux qui renvoient à un article sur ce sujet; les fig. 344 et 345, la couverture et une page double sur le thème des rouquins; les fig. 346 et 347, la couverture et une page double d'un article sur l'œil masqué qui inquiète, dans la mode punk des écrans frontaux pare-soleil. (GER)

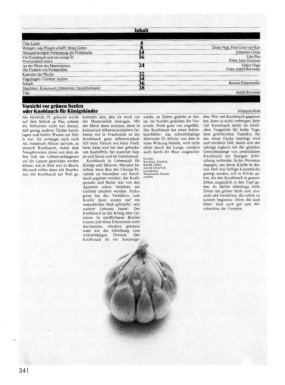

341

342

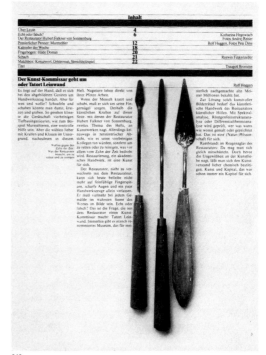

343

PHOTOGRAPHER / PHOTOGRAPH / PHOTOGRAPHE:

340, 341 John Dominis
342, 343 Andrej Reiser
344, 345 Joel Meyerowitz
346, 347 Detlef Odenhausen

ART DIRECTOR / DIRECTEUR ARTISTIQUE:

340–347 Willy Fleckhaus

PUBLISHER / VERLEGER / EDITEUR:

340–347 Frankfurter Allgemeine Zeitung GmbH

346

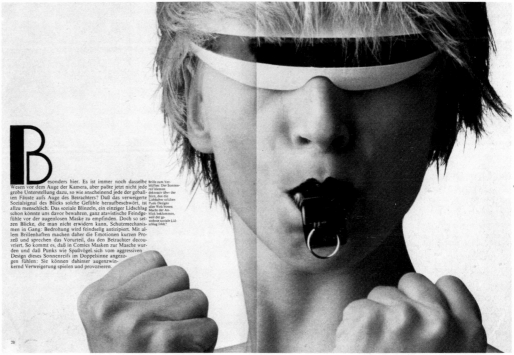

347

348–354 More examples from the *Frankfurter Allgemeine Magazin*, here contents pages for issues with articles about dogs (Fig. 348), about Berlin's "Unter den Linden" (Fig. 349), Georges Simenon (Fig. 350) and double spreads from an article about fashion and the avant garde in Russia after the 1917 Revolution (Fig. 351), for a feature on Georges Simenon (Fig. 352—see also Fig. 350), and an article about parrots (Figs. 353, 354). (GER)
355, 356 One double spread and complete page from *Photography Annual*. They present the work of Jérôme Ducrot, a French photographer who took some striking shots of female bodies pressed against glass. (USA)

348–354 Weitere Beispiele aus dem *Frankfurter Allgemeine Magazin*, hier Inhaltsseiten für Ausgaben mit Artikeln über Hunde (Abb. 348), über Berlins «Unter den Linden» (Abb. 349), Georges Simenon (Abb. 350) und Doppelseiten aus einem Artikel über Mode der Avantgarde im Russland nach der Revolution von 1917 (Abb. 351), für einen Beitrag über Georges Simenon (Abb. 352 – siehe auch Abb. 350), und aus einem Artikel über Papageien (Abb. 353 und 354). (GER)
355, 356 Doppelseite und Seite aus einem in *Photography Annual* erschienenen Porträt des französischen Photographen Jérôme Ducrot, der hier mit einer Glasplatte gearbeitet hat. (USA)

348–354 Autres exemples tirés du *Frankfurter Allgemeine Magazin*: pages du sommaire de numéros contenant des articles sur les chiens (fig. 348), l'avenue Unter den Linden à Berlin (fig. 349), l'auteur Georges Simenon (fig. 350); doubles pages d'un article sur les modes d'avant-garde prônées en Russie au lendemain de la révolution de 1917 (fig. 351), d'un reportage sur Georges Simenon (fig. 352; voir aussi la fig. 350) et d'un article consacré aux perroquets (fig. 353, 354). (GER)
355, 356 Double page et page de *Photography Annual*, montrant les effets que Jérôme Ducrot obtient avec une plaque de verre. (USA)

348

349

351

352

353

354

Ein Anschluß unter dieser Nummer

Im Lexikon sieht er zwischen Simeis, dem Schwarzmerkurort auf der Krim, dem und aus der Bibel übernommenen Vornamen befindlichen Ursprungs Simeon. Zu wundern braucht das niemanden, Georges Simenon, der Autor von mehr als achtzig Maigret-Romanen und knapp hundertdreißig sogenannten Non-Maigrets, ist als einer der raren Namen, die den Kriminalroman literarisch salonfähig gemacht haben, so berühmt, daß ihm seit langem das eigene Lexikonstichwort gebührt. Doch im Telefonbuch steht er auch, überall gelegt von einem Simenon. Und das ist schon zum Wundern.

seit sechzig Jahren schreibt er, seine Arbeit als Ausdruck der Notwendigkeit empfindet, ist so berührt, daß man es wenig Abschöttung und Verinnkspiel für normale ansähe als diese Normalität. Doch wie Wilfried Wiegand bei seinem Besuch in Lausanne erfahren hat, meint Simenon, als Schriftsteller sei er jemand, sich an die Öffentlichkeit wende und deshalb auch kein Recht habe, sich von seinem Publikum zurückziehen – und außerdem wird mein Telefon ja von Teresa bedient, und sie weiß schon, wie man mir unliebsame Anrufer vom Leib hält".

Auch er steht im Lexikon, aber in seinem Telefonbuch der Welt: Jacques Daguerre lebte zwischen 1787 und 1851. Bei seiner jahrelangen Suche nach einer Methode, Bildeindrücke auf irgendeine chemische Weise dingfest zu machen, entdeckte der Panoramamaler und Bühnenbildner die Lichtempfindlichkeit des Silberjodids und damit einen Weg, mit Hilfe der Camera obscura Bilder, wenn auch seitenverkehrt, auf Dauer festzuhalten. Einige Beispiele dieses ersten praktikablen fotografischen Verfahrens,

nach seinem Erfinder Daguerreotypie genannt, werden im folgenden gezeigt und beschrieben.

Selbst über das Motorrad, ein zweirädriges Einspurfahrzeug zur Personenbeförderung, kann im Lexikon informieren, wer im Kutschbügel gefahren", kann im Konstruktionsmerkmale der die Geschichte interessieren, angefangen bei den eisenbereiften hölzernen Zweiradgestell, das die Herren Daimler und Maybach 1885 entwickelten, bis zu den Feuerstühlen, die knapp hundert Jahre

Die Texte auch draußen im recht gekappt Georges Simenon steht im Telefonbuch

Hans-Dieter Seidel

später über die Straßen preschen. Doch was vermag die Theorie dürrer Stichwörter, wo ein Praktiker das Wort hat, dem auf zwei Rädern das Unterwegssein an sich, dem Kurventechnik und Bremsstrategie schon allein eine Lust sind? Gerold Lingnau, der Fachmann als Enthusiast, singt das rauschende, landschaftsdurchtaumelnde Lied vom "Fahren pur". Unser letztes Stichwort allerdings, das italienische Essen im allgemeinen und die "arme" Küche Neapels im besonderen, steht im Lexikon nur noch der vollkommen Abrundung (das richtige Telefonbuch hilft schon eher). Da braucht's, um eine Ahnung zu vermitteln, neben dem Blick für das Entscheidende vor allem Zunge und Geschmack, Gaumen und Nase – und es braucht nicht zuletzt die Wortgewalt eines Schriftstellers wie Gerold Späth.

PHOTOGRAPHER / PHOTOGRAPH / PHOTOGRAPHE:

350, 352 Andrej Reiser
351 Ross Feltus
353, 354 Pete Dine
355, 356 Jerome Ducrot

DESIGNER / GESTALTER / MAQUETTISTE:

348, 349 Hans-Georg Pospischil
355, 356 Brenda Suler

ART DIRECTOR / DIRECTEUR ARTISTIQUE:

348–354 Willy Fleckhaus
355, 356 Brenda Suler

PUBLISHER / VERLEGER / EDITEUR:

348–354 Frankfurter Allgemeine Zeitung GmbH
355, 356 Ziff-Davis Publishing Co.

350

356

355

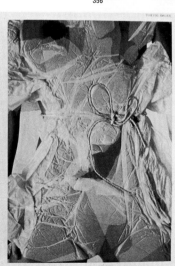

Editorial Photography

PHOTOGRAPHER:

357 Sergio Yazbek
358 Walter Bibkow
359 Ron Yablon

DESIGNER / GESTALTER:

357 Alberto Labarta
359 Edward Rosanio

ART DIRECTOR:

357 Sergio Yazbek/
    Alberto Labarta
359 Edward Rosanio

AGENCY / AGENTUR / AGENCE:

359 The Ron Yablon Agency

PUBLISHER / VERLEGER:

357 Vogue
359 Intermed Communica-
    tions, Inc.

Editorial Photography

357 Illustration from the "Eating" section in the Mexican *Vogue*. (MEX)
358 Study of a balloon taken from an article on this subject. (USA)
359 Photograph in actual size taken from *Nursing* magazine, with a feature by three chief nurses describing the difficult treatment of a pregnant minor suffering from a psychic disorder. (USA)

357 Aufnahme für den Sektor «Essen» in der mexikanischen *Vogue*. (MEX)
358 Studie eines Ballons aus einem Artikel über dieses Thema. (USA)
359 Aufnahme in Originalgrösse aus der Zeitschrift *Nursing* mit einem Beitrag von drei Oberschwestern, in dem es um die schwierige Behandlung einer schwangeren, psychisch gestörten Minderjährigen geht. (USA)

357 Illustration pour la section «Bien manger» de *Vogue*, éd. mexicaine. (MEX)
358 Etude d'un ballon illustrant un article sur ce sujet. (USA)
359 Photo au format original illustrant dans le magazine *Nursing* un rapport de trois infirmières en chef sur les difficultés du traitement d'une mineure enceinte atteinte de troubles mentaux. (USA)

357

358

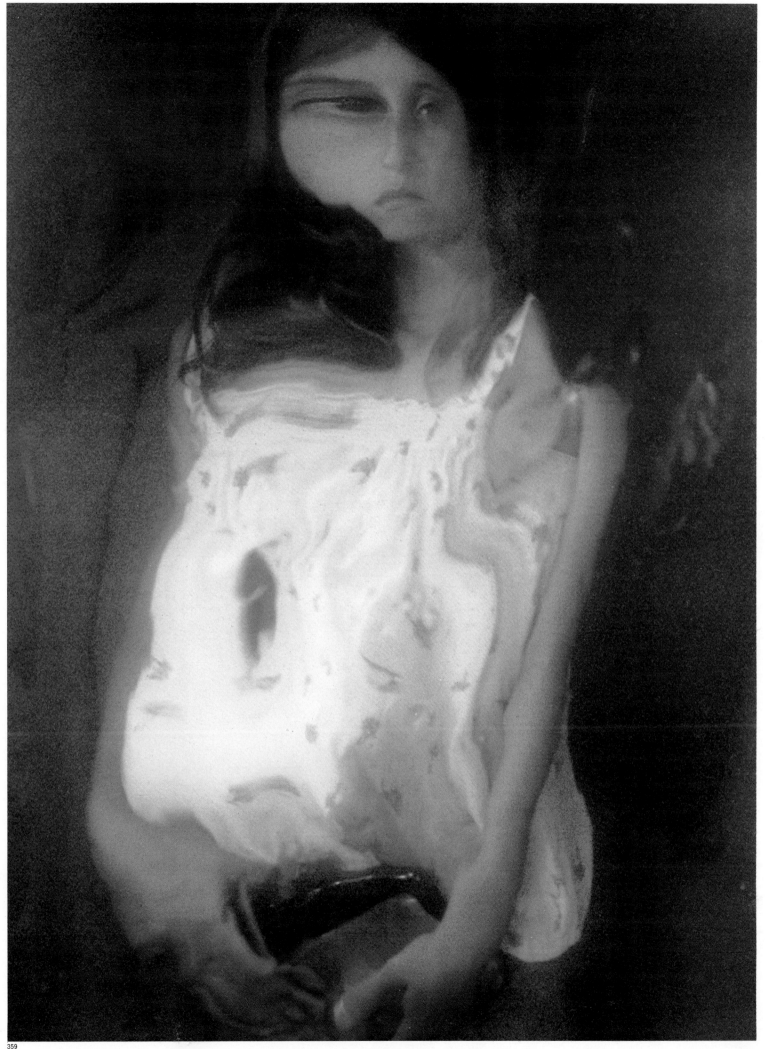

360

PHOTOGRAPHER / PHOTOGRAPH / PHOTOGRAPHE:

360 Jeff Hornbaker
361 Bill Rosenberg
362 Casimir Bart

ART DIRECTOR / DIRECTEUR ARTISTIQUE:

360, 361 John Byrne
362 Eric Devlin

PUBLISHER / VERLEGER / EDITEUR:

360, 361 Australian Penthouse
362 L'Edition JST, Inc.

360 Double-spread photograph from an article in the Australian edition of *Penthouse* magazine. (AUS)
361 Introductory double spread for a feature in the Australian edition of *Penthouse* magazine about Australia's champion freefall formation parachute team. (AUS)
362 Full-page colour photograph from *Le Mois Magazine* for an article about the use of electro-shock treatment in the field of psychiatry. (CAN)

360 Doppelseitige Aufnahme aus einem Artikel in der australischen Ausgabe des Magazins *Penthouse*. (AUS)
361 Einleitende Doppelseite für einen Beitrag in der australischen Ausgabe des Magazins *Penthouse* über das australische Meister-Team im Freifall-Fallschirmkunstspringen. (AUS)
362 Ganzseitige Farbaufnahme für einen Artikel über die Anwendung von Elektro-Schocks in der Psychiatrie, aus der Zeitschrift *Le Mois Magazine*. (CAN)

360 Photo double page illustrant un article de la version australienne du magazine *Penthouse*. (AUS)
361 Double page initiale d'un reportage sur l'équipe des as du parachutisme australien spécialistes de la voltige en chute libre, dans l'édition australienne du magazine *Penthouse*. (AUS)
362 Photo couleur pleine page pour un article sur l'utilisation de l'électrochoc en psychiatrie – «les électrochocs ou le feu par le feu» –, publié dans *Le Mois Magazine*. (CAN)

Editorial Photography

Skylarking is a serious business for Australia's champion freefall formation team.

SKYJINKS
BY RICHARD MILLS

There are six of us packed in behind the pilot of the tiny Cessna 207. Ian Lawrence interrupts his nap to grin and wink at me. Sandy Kane finds the exchange amusing and nudges Graham Jeffery. The other man in their team, George Creecy, is off on his own apparently absorbed in a small tear in the aircraft's interior lining. There is only one tense face in this plane and it belongs to me. I'm disappointed. I had expected the air to sing like a strand of number eight fencing wire, to see the psychic links between the four tighten unbearably as the time they would have to jump grew closer. The four make up '925', Australia's champion freefall team, and as we trundle through the sky in a tiny tin box, bumping and surging through the capricious atmosphere, they are so cool, there is no tension at all — except mine. Graham Jeffery scratches his nose, yawns, and stretches across to lean out the hole where the door should be. He waves a finger up and

361

Basic declarations of competition, status, age, and gender underlie all modes of dress.

MAN AS ART
BY SCOT MORRIS

S ince the charcoal, indian ocher and yellow clay, and an apron fringed with logs are a chopper in the woolt made of vegetable fibers and easy motion of good tolerance, these inhabit a way of human has lived with certain traditions, and their imaginative primes. The result is near becoming a vision new commands standards, the modern age and respect in the community.

Bodypainting, a stimulation of self is perhaps the ideal art form of the human species. Most people modify their bodies in an important aspect of social communication. Automated vocabulary, a persona, which carries messages of age, sex, and status. Decoration can reflect ones individuality while it reaffirms one's membership in the group.

The painted faces of these New Guinea military are recognized by nonverbal communication. On the second largest island in the world, where more than 700 languages are spoken, immediately becomes a

PHOTOGRAPHS BY MALCOLM KIRK

363

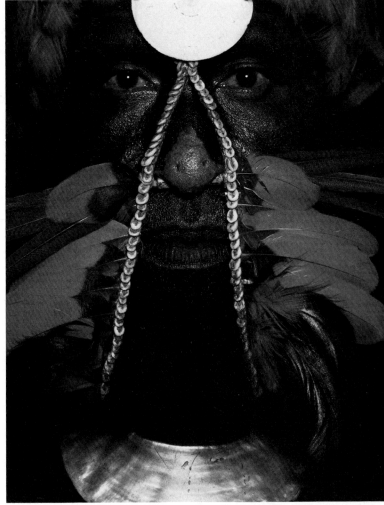

364

PHOTOGRAPHER / PHOTOGRAPH / PHOTOGRAPHE:

363–366 Malcolm Kirk
367 Gerhard Vormwald / Mayer-Norten Group
368 Heribert Brehm

ART DIRECTOR / DIRECTEUR ARTISTIQUE:

363–366 Frank Devino
367 Rainer Wörtmann
368 Manuel Ortiz

PUBLISHER / VERLEGER / EDITEUR:

363–366 Omni Publications International Ltd.
367, 368 Heinrich Bauer Verlag

365

366

367

Editorial Photography

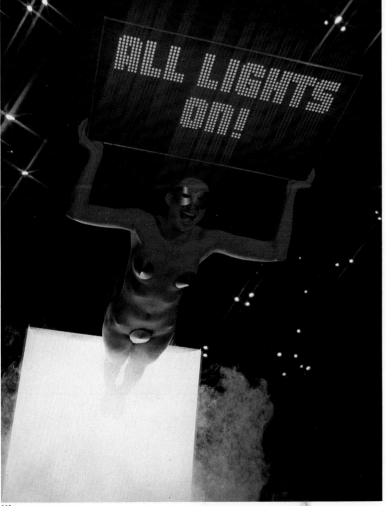

368

363–366 "Man as Art." Introductory double spread and full-page colour photographs taken from an article in *Omni* about the paintings done by natives in New Guinea. (USA)
367 "Geometry of female forms." Shot from a photographic feature in *Playboy*. (GER)
368 From a series of photographs in *Playboy* magazine featuring light graphics and girls. The photographer worked with double exposures; stars and light effects produce infinite space. (GER)

363–366 «Mensch als Kunst.» Einleitende Doppelseite und ganzseitige Farbaufnahmen aus einem Artikel in *Omni* über die Bemalungen Eingeborener Neuguineas, die sowohl den Status einer Person signalisieren, als auch die Person bei bestimmten Zeremonien völlig unkenntlich und den Mann beim Werben um die Frau schön und begehrenswert machen sollen. (USA)
367 «Geometrie der weiblichen Formen.» Aufnahme aus einem Photobeitrag im *Playboy*. (GER)
368 Aus einer Serie von Aufnahmen im *Playboy* mit Lichtgraphiken und Mädchen. Der Photograph arbeitete mit Doppelbelichtungen; Sterne und Lichteffekte lassen den Raum unendlich erscheinen. (GER)

363–366 «L'être humain en tant que forme d'art.» Double page initiale et photos couleur pleine page d'un article d'*Omni* sur les peintures corporelles des indigènes de Nouvelle-Guinée qui indiquent le statut social, sont destinées à rendre méconnaissable l'individu lors de certaines cérémonies et servent finalement à parer l'homme de ses plus belles plumes lorsqu'il courtise une femme. (USA)
367 «Géométrie des formes féminines.» Exemple d'une série de photos parues dans *Playboy*. (GER)
368 Exemples d'une série de photos dans *Playboy* où des filles sont exposées à des effets de lumière sous double exposition, l'espace étant agrandi à l'infini. (GER)

369

370

371

372

PHOTOGRAPHER / PHOTOGRAPH:

369 Ian Stone
370 Arnaud De Wildenberg
371 Dieter Zembsch
372 Dennis Manarchy
373, 374 Robert Llewellyn
375 Klaus Oberer

DESIGNER / GESTALTER / MAQUETTISTE:

369 Alex Maranzano
370 Adrian Young
371 Dieter Zembsch
372 Jeff Barnes
373, 374 John Grant
375 Pierre Mendell

ART DIRECTOR / DIRECTEUR ARTISTIQUE:

369 Marcello Minale/Brian Tattersfield
370 Rick Smolan/Andy Park
371 Dieter Zembsch
373, 374 John Grant
375 Pierre Mendell

AGENCY / AGENTUR / AGENCE – STUDIO:

369 Minale, Tattersfield & Partners
371 Dieter Zembsch
372 Alexander Communications
375 Mendell & Oberer

PUBLISHER / VERLEGER / EDITEUR:

369 Designers & Art Directors Assoc.
370 Ditla Pty Ltd
371 Schneekluth
372 Chicago Talent
373, 374 Thomasson-Grant
375 Melzer

Book Covers

373

374

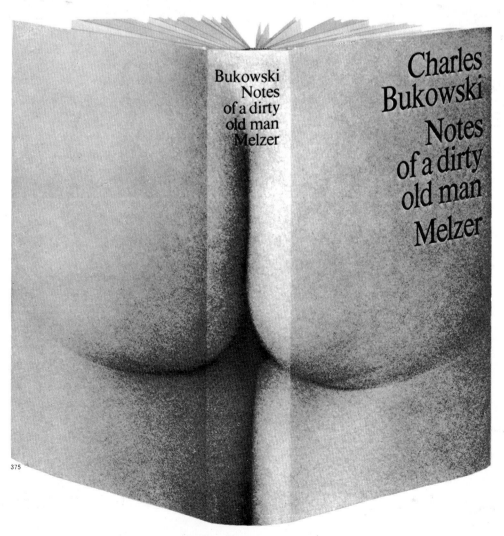

375

369 For an annual of graphic design in England. (GBR)
370 Cover in turquoise and blue for a picture-book with photographs by a hundred photographers. (AUS)
371 Dust-jacket for a volume of poetry. (GER)
372 For an annual of graphic design in Chicago. (USA)
373, 374 Cover and photograph in actual size of a book of photographs about Washington D.C. (USA)
375 Dust-jacket of a provocative book by Charles Bukowski. (GER)

369 Für ein Jahrbuch über Graphik-Design in England. (GBR)
370 Umschlag in Türkis und Blau für einen Bildband über Australien, mit Aufnahmen von hundert Photographen. (AUS)
371 Schutzumschlag für einen Gedichtband. (GER)
372 Für ein Jahrbuch über Graphik-Design in Chicago. (USA)
373, 374 Umschlag und Aufnahme in Originalgrösse für einen Photoband über Washington. (USA)
375 Schutzumschlag für ein provokatives Buch von Charles Bukowski («Notizen eines alten Lüstlings»). (GER)

369 Pour un annuel anglais de l'art graphique. (GBR)
370 Couverture turquoise et bleu d'un album photo sur l'Australie réalisé par cent photographes différents. (AUS)
371 Jaquette d'un recueil poétique. (GER)
372 Pour un annuel des réalisations graphiques à Chicago. (USA)
373, 374 Couverture et photo au format original d'un album photo consacré aux beautés de «Washington la capitale». (USA)
375 Jaquette d'un livre provocateur de Charles Bukowski («Blocnotes d'un vieux débauché»). (GER)

376

377

378

379

PHOTOGRAPHER / PHOTOGRAPH / PHOTOGRAPHE:

376–380 Yohichi Satoh
381, 382 Ruedi Hofstetter

DESIGNER / GESTALTER / MAQUETTISTE:

376–380 Kohzoh Fuse/Ai Ienaka
381, 382 Walter Neukomm

ART DIRECTOR / DIRECTEUR ARTISTIQUE:

376–380 Hiroshi Miyazaki
381, 382 Beat Keusch

AGENCY / AGENTUR / AGENCE – STUDIO:

376–380 Yohichi Satoh

PUBLISHER / VERLEGER / EDITEUR:

376–380 Snow Brand Milk Product Co.
381, 382 Kodak SA

380

381

376–380 Cover photographs and complete cover of a magazine specialising in food marketing. Fig. 376: light green and white in front of a brilliant blue ground running into black; Fig. 377: the golden yellow and red ochre colours are repeated in the background; Fig. 378: light yellow, red and green in front of a dark ground; Fig. 379: vanilla, rich brown, blue ground. In order to obtain the desired special effects, the photographer employed a combined technique with retouchings and airbrushing. (JPN)
381, 382 Complete double spread and detail of the photograph from a report on the photographer Ruedi Hofstetter that appeared in *Angewandte Fotografie*, a *Kodak* publication. (SWI)

376–380 Umschlagaufnahmen und vollständiger Umschlag einer Zeitschrift, die sich mit Lebensmittel-Marketing befasst. Abb. 376: Hellgrün und Weiss vor leuchtend blauem Grund, der in Schwarz ausläuft; Abb. 377: Die Farben des goldgelben Eierkuchens und der braunroten Kirschen wiederholen sich im Hintergrund; Abb. 378: Hellgelb, Rot und Grün vor dunklem Grund; Abb. 379: Vanille mit Schokoladenbraun vor blauem Grund. Bei allen Aufnahmen wurden die gewünschten speziellen Effekte mit Hilfe von Retuschen und Spritztechnik erreicht. (JPN)
381, 382 Vollständige Doppelseite und Detail der Aufnahme aus einem Bericht über den Photographen Ruedi Hofstetter in *Angewandte Fotografie*, eine Publikation von *Kodak*. (SWI)

376–380 Photos de couverture et couverture complète d'un magazine spécialisé dans le marketing alimentaire. Fig. 376: vert clair et blanc sur fond bleu rayonnant dégradé en noir; fig. 377: les couleurs de l'omelette jaune or et des cerises rouge brun sont reprises à l'arrière-plan; fig. 378: jaune clair, rouge, vert sur fond sombre; fig. 379: vanille, avec du brun chocolat, sur fond bleu. (JPN)
381, 382 Double page complète et détail de la photo d'une étude sur le photographe Ruedi Hofstetter parue dans *Angewandte Fotografie*, une publication *Kodak*. (SWI)

382

Trade Magazines
Fachzeitschriften
Revues professionnelles

153

383

Nr. 11 November 1980 · 7 DM

B 5155 EX

PHOTO

BILDER:

DIE MINUTE DES
JAHRES: EIN LAND
FOTOGRAFIERTE
SICH SELBST

IMPOSANTE
RÜCKENAKTE VON
FRANZ REINBOLDT

THOMAS HÖPKERS
HANDSCHRIFT

ERIC HOSKINGS
SCHÖNSTE TIERBILDER

VIDEO:

MITSUSHITAS MINI-
VIDEO-KAMERA

WIRBEL UM SONYS
VIDEO-MOVIE

JOURNAL:

DIE ARBEITEN
VON ALFRED
EISENSTAEDT

KODAK/POLAROID
EIN VERGLEICH

...UND 10 WEITERE
ARTIKEL ZUR
AKTUELLEN
PHOTO-SZENE

TECHNIK:

DIE NEUE ZENZA-
BRONICA SQ

DIE NEUE CHINON-
GENERATION

MINOLTAS
WEATHERMATIC
IN DER PRAXIS

384

385

progresso

APRILE 1982
L. 3.000

4

FOTOGRAFICO

386

Trade Magazines

PHOTOGRAPHER / PHOTOGRAPH:

383 Ruedi Hofstetter
384 Gérard Pétremand
385 Herbert Migdoll
386 Verita Monselles
387 Hans H. Siwik

DESIGNER / GESTALTER / MAQUETTISTE:

383 Walter Neukomm

ART DIRECTOR / DIRECTEUR ARTISTIQUE:

383 Beat Keusch
384 Karl-Heinz Wendlandt
385 Robin McDonald
386 Alberto Piovani
387 Michael Tafelmaier

PUBLISHER / VERLEGER / EDITEUR:

383 Kodak SA
384 New Magazines Verlagsgesellschaft
385 Horizon Publishers, Inc.
386 Progresso Fotografico
387 Verlag Grossbild-Technik GmbH

383 Cover of *Angewandte Fotografie*, a trade magazine published by *Kodak*. (SWI)
384 Full-colour cover of the German edition of *Photo* magazine. (GER)
385 A double-exposure solarized photograph of a ballet, taken from *Horizon* magazine. (USA)
386 Cover of *Progresso Fotografico*. Mainly in violet with blue, orange lettering. (ITA)
387 Photograph from an article in the trade magazine *International Photo Technik*. (GER)

383 Umschlag von *Angewandte Fotografie*, eine von *Kodak* herausgegebene Fachzeitschrift. (SWI)
384 Mehrfarbiger Umschlag der deutschen Ausgabe des Magazins *Photo*. (GER)
385 Mit Doppelbelichtung und Solarisation entstandenes Photo eines Balletts, aus *Horizon*. (USA)
386 Umschlag von *Progresso Fotografico*. Vorwiegend violett mit Blau, Schrift orange. (ITA)
387 Aufnahme aus einem Artikel in der Fachzeitschrift *International Photo Technik*. (GER)

383 Couverture d'*Angewandte Fotografie*, revue professionnelle publiée par *Kodak*. (SWI)
384 Couverture polychrome de l'édition allemande du magazine *Photo*. (GER)
385 Photo de ballet, dans *Horizon*, réalisée en double exposition et solarisation. (USA)
386 Couverture de *Progresso Fotografico*. Tons violets dominants, bleu, texte orange. (ITA)
387 Photo illustrant un article du magazine professionnel *International Photo Technik*. (GER)

387

388

AMERICAN
PHOTOGRAPHER

$2.00 MAR 1982

Nastassia Kinski photographed by Richard Avedon

389

390

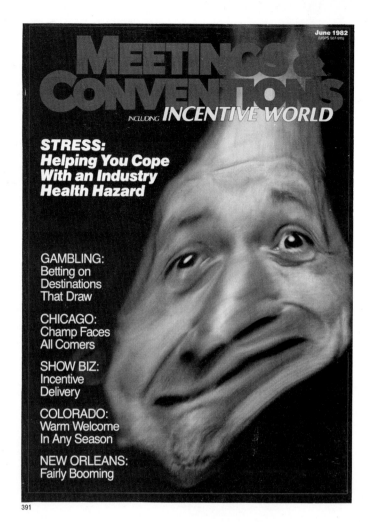

391

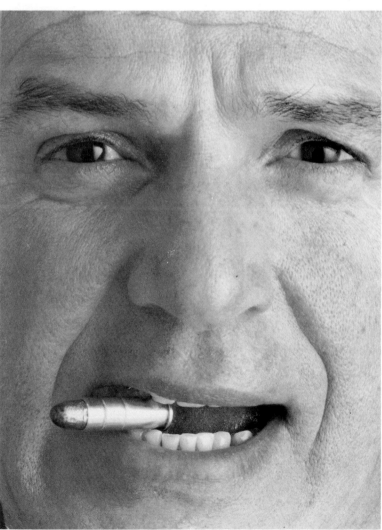

392

PHOTOGRAPHER / PHOTOGRAPH:

388 Heribert Brehm
389 Richard Avedon
390 Alexander Orloff
391 John Manno
392 Tom Chambers

DESIGNER / GESTALTER / MAQUETTISTE:

388 Heribert Brehm
389 Louis F. Cruz
391 Bruce Giacoppo
392 Jim Lienhart

ART DIRECTOR / DIRECTEUR ARTISTIQUE:

389 William Hopkins
390 John Kuchera
391 Bruce Giacoppo
392 Jim Lienhart

AGENCY / AGENTUR / AGENCE – STUDIO:

390 Hutchins/Y & R
392 Jim Lienhart Design

PUBLISHER / VERLEGER / EDITEUR:

388 Photo-Reporter
389 CBS Publications
390 Eastman Kodak Co.
391 Ziff-Davis Publishing
392 Savings & Loan News

388 Cover illustration of *Photo-Reporter*, a French trade magazine. (FRA)
389 Nastassja Kinski on the opened cover of the magazine *American Photographer*, which nominated this Richard Avedon photograph as one of the best spreads in 1981. (USA)
390 The dawn ritual at the Basle carnival. Cover illustration for *International Photography*, a *Kodak* publication. (USA)
391 Cover of the magazine *Meetings & Conventions*, on the subject of stress. (USA)
392 Cover illustration of an issue of the banking magazine *Savings & Loan News*. (USA)

388 Umschlagillustration der französischen Fachzeitschrift *Photo-Reporter*. (FRA)
389 Nastassja Kinski auf dem aufgeklappten Umschlag von *American Photographer*. Diese Aufnahme Richard Avedons wurde als eine der besten von 1981 ausgezeichnet. (USA)
390 Morgenstreich der Baseler Fastnacht. Umschlagillustration für *International Photography*, eine Publikation von *Kodak*. (USA)
391 Umschlag der Zeitschrift *Meetings & Conventions* zum Thema Stress. (USA)
392 Die Umschlagillustration dieser Ausgabe der Bankfachzeitschrift *Savings & Loan News* bezieht sich auf ein Wortspiel im englischen Text; Thema sind Kredite. (USA)

388 Illustration de couverture du magazine professionnel français *Photo-Reporter*. (FRA)
389 Nastassja Kinski sur la couverture dépliée du magazine *American Photographer*. Photo de Richard Avedon primée comme l'une des meilleures réalisées en 1981. (USA)
390 Mise en branle matinale du cortège du Carnaval de Bâle. Illustration de couverture pour *International Photography*, une publication de *Kodak*. (USA)
391 Couverture du magazine *Meetings & Conventions*. Le sujet: le stress. (USA)
392 L'illustration de couverture pour ce numéro du magazine bancaire spécialisé *Savings & Loan News* met en scène un jeu de mots anglais, sur le thème des crédits. (USA)

David Webb, *Stanley Silberstein, son of Nina Silberstein (America's first lady of jewelry), is the man who introduced the fantastic Webb designs to the international set. The jeweler is an adventurous soul and sizing up big, beautiful jewels like these is certainly an exciting and rewarding pastime. Luscious Irish beauty Clare Beresford, daughter of Lord and Lady Decies, wears a diamond and emerald necklace and earrings from the Webb collection. Make-up: Pinecone Russets by Germaine Monteil. Dress: Tracy Mills. Hair and make-up styled by Anthony Clavet.*

393

394

395

393 Taken from a feature in *Town and Country* magazine about New York's most famous jewellers. Here, a society lady (Clare Beresford) and the jeweller Stanley Silberstein inspecting a large Smaragd on the lady's diamond necklace. (USA)
394 From an article in *International Photo Technik* on an association of photo-designers. (GER)
395 Photograph in actual size from an interview with John Swannell in *Zoom* magazine. (FRA)

393 Aus einem Beitrag in der Zeitschrift *Town and Country* über New Yorks berühmteste Juweliere. Hier eine Dame der Gesellschaft (Clare Beresford) und der Juwelier Stanley Silberstein beim Inspizieren eines grossen Smaragds am Diamanten-Collier. (USA)
394 Aus einem Artikel in *International Photo Technik* über den BFF. (GER)
395 Aufnahme in Originalgrösse aus einem Interview mit John Swannell in *Zoom*. (FRA)

393 Illustration d'une étude parue dans le magazine *Town & Country* sur les grands joailliers newyorkais. On voit ici l'un de ces spécialistes, Stanley Silberstein, examiner une grosse émeraude dans la rivière de diamants d'une dame de la société (Clare Beresford). (USA)
394 Pour un article d'*International Photo Technik* sur une association de photographes. (GER)
395 Photo au format original illustrant une interview de John Swannell dans *Zoom*. (FRA)

PHOTOGRAPHER / PHOTOGRAPH:

393 Henry Wolf
394 C. J. Winter
395 John Swannel

DESIGNER / GESTALTER / MAQUETTISTE:

395 Christian Guillon

ART DIRECTOR / DIRECTEUR ARTISTIQUE:

393 Melissa Tardiff
394 Michael Tafelmaier
395 Joël Laroche

PUBLISHER / VERLEGER / EDITEUR:

393 The Hearst Corporation
394 Verlag Grossbild-Technik GmbH
395 Publicness

Editorial Photography

Trade Magazines

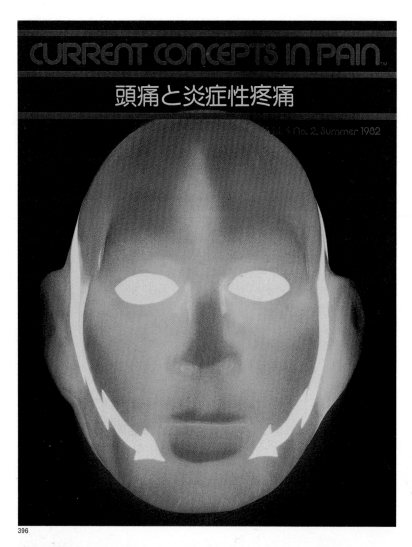

CURRENT CONCEPTS IN PAIN™

頭痛と炎症性疼痛

Vol. 4 No. 2, Summer 1982

396

ARTHRON™

Vol. 1 No. 2 Summer 1982

397

CURRENT CONCEPTS IN PAIN™

頭痛と炎症性疼痛

Vol. 3 No. 4, Winter 1981

398

Pharmascan® Geigy

Vegetarianism in Children

399

PHOTOGRAPHER / PHOTOGRAPH:

396, 398, 400 François Robert
397 John Alderson
399 Ed Gallucci

DESIGNER / GESTALTER / MAQUETTISTE:

396–398, 400 Bruno Ruegg
399 Larry Stires

ART DIRECTOR / DIRECTEUR ARTISTIQUE:

396–398, 400 Bruno Ruegg
399 Larry Stires

AGENCY / AGENTUR / AGENCE – STUDIO:

396–398, 400 Sieber & McIntyre
399 Ciba-Geigy Design

PUBLISHER / VERLEGER / ÉDITEUR:

396–398, 400 CPE Divison of
    Sieber & McIntyre
399 Ciba-Geigy Pharmaceuticals

400

396, 398 Examples from a series of medical trade publications, *Current Concepts in Pain*, dealing with the combatting of pain. Here covers are shown from issues of the Japanese edition. Fig. 398 in grey shades with a white telephone. (JPN)
397 Cover of *Arthron*, another specialised medical magazine (see Figs. 396, 398) issued by the *Professional Communication Agency*. (USA)
399 Cover for *Ciba-Geigy* pharmaceutically specialised features entitled *Pharmascan*. Dealt with here is the vegetarian feeding of children and the problems arising from it. (USA)
400 Detail of the cover illustration of *Current Concepts in Trauma Care*, a specialised medical magazine dealing with psychic illnesses and disorders. See also Figs. 396–398. (USA)

396, 398 Beispiele aus einer Reihe von medizinischen Fachpublikationen zum Thema der Schmerzbekämpfung, *Current Concepts in Pain*; hier Umschläge von Nummern der japanischen Ausgabe. Abb. 398 in Grautönen mit weissem Telephon. (JPN)
397 Umschlag von *Arthron*, einer weiteren medizinischen Fachzeitschrift (s. Abb. 396, 398), hier über Gelenkerkrankungen. (USA)
399 Umschlag für pharmazeutische Fachbeiträge in der *Pharmascan*-Reihe, herausgegeben von *Ciba-Geigy*. Hier geht es um die vegetarische Ernährung von Kindern und die damit verbundenen Probleme. (USA)
400 Detail der Umschlagillustration von *Current Concepts in Trauma Care*, eine medizinische Fachpublikation, die sich mit psychischen Erkrankungen befasst; siehe auch Abb. 396–398. (USA)

396, 398 Couvertures tirées d'une série de publications médicales de la *Professional Communication Agency* sur le sujet de la douleur, *Current concepts in Pain*, ici de l'édition en langue japonaise. Fig. 398: divers gris, téléphone blanc. (JPN)
397 Couverture d'*Arthron*, une autre revue médicale (cf. 396, 398); le sujet traité ici: les maladies articulaires. (USA)
399 Couverture d'articles pharmaceutiques de *Ciba-Geigy* réunis sous le titre de *Pharmascan*. Il s'agit ici de l'alimentation végétarienne des enfants et des problèmes qu'elle soulève. (USA)
400 Détail de l'illustration de couverture de *Current Concepts in Trauma Care*, une publication médicale spécialisée dans l'étude des traumatismes psychiques. Cf. aussi les fig. 396–398. (USA)

Trade Magazines
Fachzeitschriften
Revues professionnelles

401

402

Trade Magazines
Fachzeitschriften
Revues professionnelles

PHOTOGRAPHER / PHOTOGRAPH:

401, 403 Uwe Ommer
402 Simon Bocanegra
404 Irving Penn

DESIGNER / GESTALTER / MAQUETTISTE:

401–403 Christian Guillon
404 Louis F. Cruz

ART DIRECTOR / DIRECTEUR ARTISTIQUE:

401–403 Joël Laroche
404 William Hopkins

PUBLISHER / VERLEGER / EDITEUR:

401–403 Publicness
404 CBS Publications

401–403 Covers of the photographic trade magazine *Zoom*. Fig. 402: structures in various shades of grey and silver, red title, silver lettering; Fig. 403: whiteish oilskin, light brown skin, golden jewellery, greenish grey background, red title, white lettering. (FRA)
404 Full-page photograph from the American edition of *Vogue*. This photograph of a woman inserting her contact lenses was singled out by *American Photographer* magazine for an award as one of the best magazine spreads of 1981. (USA)

401–403 Umschläge der Photofachzeitschrift *Zoom*. Abb. 402: Aufbauten in verschiedenen Grau- und Silbertönen, Titel rot, Schrift silber; Abb. 403: weissliche Regenhaut, hellbraune Haut, Schmuck goldfarben, grüngrauer Hintergrund, Titel rot, Schrift weiss. (FRA)
404 Ganzseitige Aufnahme aus der amerikanischen Ausgabe von *Vogue*. Dieses Photo einer Frau beim Einsetzen von Kontaktlinsen wurde von dem Photomagazin *American Photographer* als eine der besten zehn Magazinseiten im Jahre 1981 ausgezeichnet. (USA)

401–403 Couvertures de la revue professionnelle de photographie *Zoom*. Fig. 402: structures exécutées en divers tons gris et argent, titre rouge, texte argent; fig. 403: pelure blanchâtre, peau brun clair, bijoux or, fond gris vert, titre rouge, texte blanc. (FRA)
404 Photo pleine page illustrant l'édition américaine de *Vogue*. Cette photo d'une femme insérant ses verres de contact a été primée par le magazine photo *American Photographer* comme l'une des dix meilleures pages de magazines en 1981. (USA)

403

パッケージは，情報メディアだ.

405

Trade Magazines
Fachzeitschriften
Revues professionnelles

PHOTOGRAPHER / PHOTOGRAPH / PHOTOGRAPHE:
405–410 Kou Chifusa/Nishi Azabu

DESIGNER / GESTALTER / MAQUETTISTE:
405–410 Jin Sato/Uji Kato

ART DIRECTOR / DIRECTEUR ARTISTIQUE:
405–410 Jin Sato

AGENCY / AGENTUR / AGENCE – STUDIO:
405–410 Art Publicity Co., Ltd.

PUBLISHER / VERLEGER / EDITEUR:
405–410 Gulliver Printing Co., Ltd.

405–410 Double spreads and covers of *Ad Paper*, a monthly publication of the Gulliver Printing Co. Ltd. that is addressed to advertising agencies and design studios. Each issue is devoted to a special theme and supplies material information, statistics and know-how, etc. Figs. 405 and 407: double spread and cover of an issue on packaging, Fig. 407 with bright blue cap. Figs. 406 and 410: cover and double spread from an issue on the subject of direct mail, with airmail envelope in the two colour shots in transparent plastic. Fig. 408: also on the subject of direct mail, green leaf, white lettering (address of Ronald Reagan), white robe. Fig. 409: colour photograph on the subject of handbills. (JPN)

405–410 Doppelseiten und Umschläge von *Ad Paper*, einer monatlich erscheinenden Publikation der Druckerei Gulliver Printing Co., Ltd., die sich an Werbeagenturen und Studios richtet. Jede Ausgabe ist einem Spezialthema gewidmet und bietet entsprechende Informationen über Material, Statistiken, Know-how etc. Abb. 405 und 407: Doppelseite und Umschlag einer Ausgabe über Verpackungen, Abb. 407 mit leuchtend blauer Kappe; Abb. 406 und 410: Umschlag und Doppelseite aus einer Nummer zum Thema Direktwerbung per Post. Der Luftpostumschlag in beiden Farbaufnahmen aus durchsichtigem Plastik; Abb. 408: zum Thema Direktwerbung. Grünes Blatt mit weisser Aufschrift (Adresse Ronald Reagans) in weissem Gewand; Abb. 409: mehrfarbige Aufnahme zum Thema Werbedrucksachen mit Flugblattcharakter. (JPN)

405–410 Doubles pages et couvertures d'*Ad Paper*, une publication mensuelle de l'imprimerie Gulliver Printing Co., Ltd. destinée aux agences et aux studios publicitaires. Chaque numéro est consacré à un thème particulier, avec une documentation sur les matériaux, les statistiques, le know-how, etc. Fig. 405 et 407: Double page et couverture d'un numéro sur les emballages, la fig. 407 avec un bonnet bleu vif; fig. 406 et 410: couverture et double page d'un numéro sur la publicité directe par voie postale; l'enveloppe avion des deux photos couleur est en plastique transparent; fig. 408: sur le thème de la publicité directe; feuille verte et inscription blanche (à l'adresse de Ronald Reagan) sur vêtement blanc, fig. 409: photo polychrome sur le thème des imprimés publicitaires. (JPN)

408

ダイレクトメール Ⅱ
1981-3-NO.18
100YEN

406

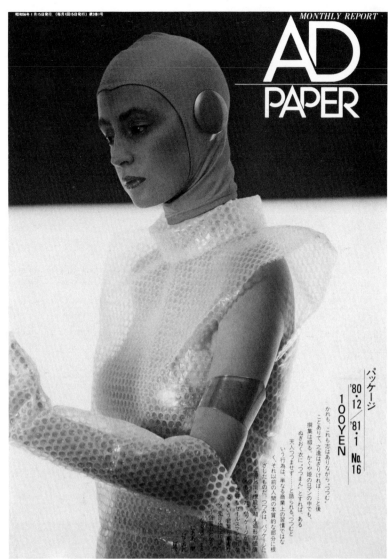

パッケージ
'80・12
'81・1
No.16
100YEN

407

顧客の行動を誘発する"仕掛け"が効果を左右する。

409

例え、1回の反響が少なかったとしても、次回には、より確実な効果を得られるのがDMだ。

410

411

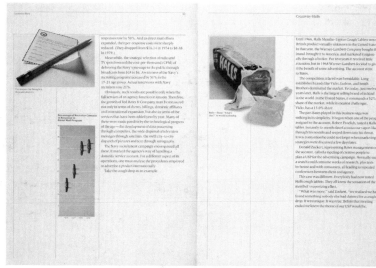

412

413

414

Corporate Publications
Firmenpublikationen
Publications d'entreprise

411, 412 Two double spreads from a company brochure for *Ted Bates*. The colour photographs refer to the various clients of this advertising agency. (USA)
413, 414 Double spreads with colour photographs from the 1981 annual report of Macmillan, Inc., publishers in the field of education. (USA)
415–419 Complete double spread and photographs in actual size from the *Compendium* company brochure, a design systems corporation that deals with every facet of design. (USA)

411, 412 Zwei Doppelseiten aus einer Firmenbroschüre der Werbeagentur Ted Bates & Company. Die Farbaufnahmen beziehen sich auf verschiedene Kunden der Agentur. (USA)
413, 414 Doppelseiten mit Farbaufnahmen aus dem Jahresbericht 1981 von Macmillan, Inc., Verlag für Schul- und Lehrbücher. (USA)
415–419 Vollständige Doppelseite und Aufnahmen in Originalgrösse aus einer Firmenbroschüre für *Compendium*, ein Unternehmen, das sich sowohl mit der Gestaltung von Gebäudekomplexen als auch mit dem Entwurf von Briefköpfen befasst. Im Begleittext geht es um das Wesen guten Designs. (USA)

411, 412 Deux doubles pages d'une brochure promotionnelle de l'agence publicitaire Ted Bates & Company. Les photos couleur se rapportent à des clients de l'agence. (USA)
413, 414 Doubles pages illustrées de photos couleur dans le rapport annuel pour 1981 de Macmillan, Inc., un éditeur spécialisé dans le livre d'enseignement. (USA)
415–419 Double page complète et photos au format original dans une brochure promotionnelle de *Compendium*, une société qui réalise aussi bien des ensembles immobiliers que des en-têtes de lettres. Le texte discute des critères de la création publicitaire de qualité. ((USA)

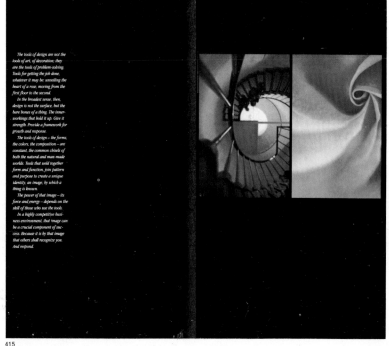

415

PHOTOGRAPHER:

415–419 Gary Brasch

DESIGNER / GESTALTER:

411, 412 Philip Gips / Diana
        Graham
413, 414 Diana Graham
415–419 Chris Hill / Mark Geer

ART DIRECTOR:

411, 412 Nicholas Pappas
413, 414 Diana Graham
415–419 Chris Hill

AGENCY / AGENTUR / AGENCE:

411–414 Gips & Balkind
415–419 Loucks Atelier

416

417

418

419

420

Corporate Publications
Firmenpublikationen
Publications d'entreprise

PHOTOGRAPHER / PHOTOGRAPH / PHOTOGRAPHE:

420 Art Kane
421 Jay Maisel
422 Tom Hollyman
423, 424 Clint Clemens

420, 421 Shots from a kit issued by the *Potlatch Corporation*, papermakers, on the subject of the presentation of annual reports. Fig. 420 is an example of the human factor in annual reports (*H. J. Heinz*), Fig. 421 refers to the presentation of industrial facilities (*Gulf Oil*). (USA)
422 From a prize-winning booklet on *Champion*, papermakers. The photograph of wood processing is entirely in brown shades. (USA)
423, 424 Cover and double spread from a handbook (*Ins and Outs*) on the production of internal and external company publications, issued by *S. D. Warren*, papermakers. Fig. 424 is a humorous listing of things to be avoided. (USA)

420, 421 Aufnahmen aus einer der Präsentation von Jahresberichten gewidmeten Mappe des Papierherstellers *Potlatch*. Abb. 420 ist ein Beispiel für den menschlichen Faktor in Geschäftsberichten (*Heinz*), Abb. 421 aus dem Bereich der Darstellung von Industrieanlagen (*Gulf Oil*). (USA)
422 Aus einer prämierten Firmenbroschüre von *Champion* (Papierhersteller). Die Aufnahme ausschliesslich in Brauntönen. (USA)
423, 424 Umschlag und Doppelseite aus einem Handbuch mit Vorschlägen für die Herstellung interner und externer Firmenpublikationen, herausgegeben von *S. D. Warren*, Papierhersteller. Abb. 424 ist eine humorvolle Aufzählung der Dinge, die man vermeiden sollte. (USA)

420, 421 Photos figurant dans un portefeuille du fabricant de papier *Potlatch* consacré à la présentation des rapports annuels. La fig. 420 exemplifie le facteur humain dans les rapports annuels (*Heinz*), la fig. 421 la projection de l'image d'une entreprise industrielle (*Gulf Oil*). (USA)
422 Brochure promotionnelle primée réalisée par le papetier *Champion*. L'installation de traitement du bois en tons uniquement bruns. (USA)
423, 424 Couverture et double page d'un manuel publié par le papetier *S. D. Warren* sur la réalisation de publications d'entreprises destinées au personnel et au grand public. La fig. 424 énumère avec humour les gaffes à ne pas faire. (USA)

422

421

ART DIRECTOR / DIRECTEUR ARTISTIQUE:

420, 421 Jack Hough
422 Philip Gips
423, 424 Robert Cipriani

AGENCY / AGENTUR / AGENCE – STUDIO:

420, 421 Jack Hough Associates, Inc.
422 Gips & Balkind & Associates
423, 424 Robert Cipriani Assoc./Gunn Assoc./Myers & Myers

DESIGNER / GESTALTER / MAQUETTISTE:

420, 421 Thomas D. Morins
422 Philip Gips
423, 424 John Gatie / Robert Cipriani

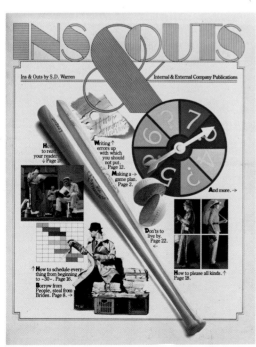

423

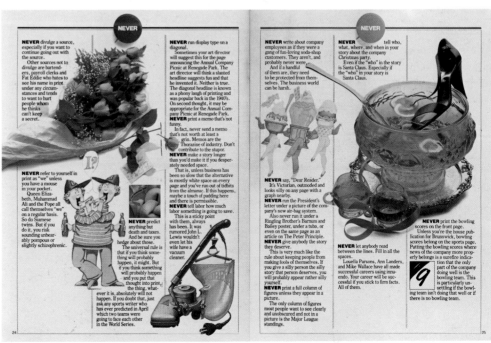

424

426

427

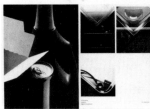

428

PHOTOGRAPHER / PHOTOGRAPH:

425 Peggy & Ronald Barnett
426 Greg Booth
427 Burt Glinn
428 Peggy & Ronald Barnett/
Greg Booth/Jerry Sarapochiello/
Ryuzo Masunaga/Roy Coggin/
John Paul Endress
429 Shigemi Kondo

DESIGNER / GESTALTER / MAQUETTISTE:

425–428 Thomas D. Morin
429 Yukihiro Hirose

ART DIRECTOR / DIRECTEUR ARTISTIQUE:

425–428 Jack Hough
429 Shigemi Kondo

AGENCY / AGENTUR / AGENCE – STUDIO:

425–428 Jack Hough Associates, Inc.
429 Studio Kondo

429

Corporate Publications / Firmenpublikationen
Publications d'entreprise

425–428 Full-page colour photograph and a fold-out from a kit issued by the papermakers Potlatch Corporation (see Figs. 420, 421). The subject is the presentation of annual reports, here subdivided into the sectors Products (Figs. 425, 428—for the *Continental Group* and others), The Industrial Landscape (Fig. 426, *Xerox*) and The Human Factor (Fig. 427, *Xerox*). (USA)
429 Double spread from *Doomo*, a joint publication by various advertising groups, here with a colour shot of Ayers Rock, Australia, known as the "navel of the earth". (JPN)

425–428 Ganzseitige Farbaufnahmen und eine auseinandergefaltete Seite aus einer Mappe des Papierkonzerns *Potlatch*. Es geht um die Präsentation von Jahresberichten, hier aufgeteilt in folgende Themen: Produktpräsentation (Abb. 425, 428 – für *Continental Group* u.a.), Darstellung von Industrieanlagen (Abb. 426, *Xerox*) und die menschlichen Aspekte (Abb. 427, *Xerox*). (USA)
429 Doppelseite aus *Doomo*, einer Gemeinschaftspublikation von Werbeschaffenden, hier mit einer Farbaufnahme des Ayers Felsens in Australien, genannt «der Nabel der Welt». (JPN)

425–428 Photos couleur pleine page et une page dépliée du portefeuille du groupe papetier *Potlatch* déjà mentionné (fig. 420, 421). Il s'agit de la présentation des rapports annuels par thèmes: présentation des produits (fig. 425, 428 – pour *Continental Group* de d'autres), images-chocs incarnant la réalité industrielle (fig. 426, *Xerox*), le facteur humain dans l'entreprise (fig. 427, *Xerox*). (USA)
429 Double page de *Doomo*, publié par un collectif de publicitaires, avec une photo couleur des célèbres Roches Ayers australiennes, appelées «le nombril de l'univers». (JPN)

171

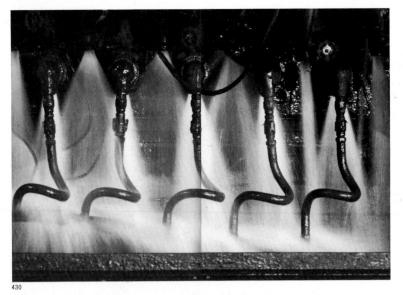

430

431

432

433

Corporate Publications
Firmenpublikationen
Publications d'entreprise

430–434 Double-spread colour photographs from a publication issued by the *Sumitomo* steel company. Fig. 430: cooling sprays; Fig. 431: steel bars, rolling along one after the other, seem to fan out from the far end of their cooling bed; Fig. 432: smokestacks rising behind tons of iron ore, brown and warm grey, blue sky; Fig. 433: steel linepipe; Fig. 434: rust-inhibiting surfaces. (JPN)
435-437 Two rectos and one verso of cover spreads from issues of the *Citroën* car company's information brochures. Fig. 437 refers to a James Bond film in which a 2 CV car appears. (FRA)

430–434 «Die Schönheit der Stahlproduktion.» Doppelseitige Farbaufnahmen aus einer Publikation des Stahlunternehmens *Sumitomo*. Abb. 430: Kühlsprays; Abb. 431: abrollende Stahlstäbe, vom äusseren Ende des Kühlbettes gesehen; Abb. 432: Eisenerz, hier in Braun und warmem Grau vor blauem Himmel; Abb. 433: Stahlrohre; Abb. 434: Rostschutz-Oberflächenmaterial mit Lichtreflexion. (JPN)
435-437 Zwei vordere und eine hintere Umschlagseite von Ausgaben einer Informationsbroschüre des Autokonzerns *Citroën*. Abb. 437 bezieht sich auf einen James-Bond-Film mit einem 2 CV. (FRA)

430–434 «La beauté de la production d'acier.» Photos couleur dans une publication de l'aciérie *Sumitomo*. Fig. 430: refroidissement par pulvérisation; fig. 431: barres d'acier émergeant du refroidisseur; fig. 432: le minerai de fer à ciel ouvert, brun et gris chaud sur bleu; fig. 433: tubes d'acier durant l'inspection; fig. 434: réflexions sur la surface antirouille. (JPN)
435-437 Deux premières pages de couverture et une dernière page de couverture de divers numéros d'une brochure d'information de *Citroën*. Fig. 437: allusion à James Bond en 2 CV. (FRA)

PHOTOGRAPHER / PHOTOGRAPH / PHOTOGRAPHE:

430–434 Nobuo Asayama
435 Jacques Rolandey
436 Marianne Haas

ART DIRECTOR / DIRECTEUR ARTISTIQUE:

430–434 Tadashi Matsuyama
435–437 Jacques Wolgensinger

AGENCY / AGENTUR / AGENCE – STUDIO:

430–434 Dentsu Advertising
435–437 Mape

434

63

435

62

436

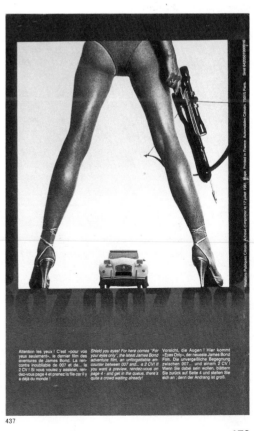

Attention les yeux ! C'est «pour vos yeux seulement», le dernier film des aventures de James Bond. La rencontre inoubliable de 007 et de... la 2 CV ! Si vous voulez y assister, rendez-vous page 4 et prenez la file car il y a déjà du monde !

Shield your eyes! For here comes "For your eyes only", the latest James Bond adventure film, an unforgettable encounter between 007 and... a 2 CV ! If you want a preview, rendez-vous on page 4 - and get in the queue, there's quite a crowd waiting already!

Vorsicht, die Augen ! Hier kommt «Eyes Only», der neueste James Bond Film. Die unvergessliche Begegnung zwischen 007... und einem 2 CV ! Wenn Sie dabei sein wollen, blättern Sie zurück auf Seite 4 und stellen Sie sich an ; denn der Andrang ist gross.

437

438

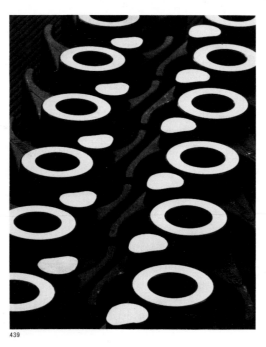

439

440

438–442 Details of the colour photographs and a complete double spread from the company brochure of Luther and Pedersen, Inc., full service machine tool distributors. (USA)
443, 444 Double spread and full-page photograph from the 1981 annual report of *Alcoa*, Aluminum Company of America. This highly-polished skin sheet at Davenport Works will be shipped to a commercial aircraft builder after this quality control check. (USA)

438–442 Details von Farbaufnahmen und eine vollständige Doppelseite aus der Firmenbroschüre von Luther and Pedersen, Inc., Auslieferer von Werkzeugmaschinen. (USA)
443, 444 Doppelseite und ganzseitige Aufnahme aus dem Jahresbericht 1981 von *Alcoa*, Aluminum Company of America. Hier ein Prüfer bei der Qualitätskontrolle eines Hochglanz-Alublechs, das für ein Linienflugzeug bestimmt ist. (USA)

438–442 Détails de photos couleur et une page double complète de la brochure promotionnelle de Luther & Pedersen, Inc., un distributeur de machines-outils. (USA)
443, 444 Double page et photo pleine page du rapport annuel pour 1981 d'Alcoa, l'Aluminium Company of America. On voit ici l'inspection d'une tôle d'alu extrapolie avant livraison à une société de construction aéronautique. (USA)

441

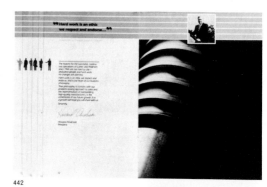

442

443

PHOTOGRAPHER / PHOTOGRAPH / PHOTOGRAPHE:

438–442 Ron Seymour
443, 444 Bob Huntzinger

DESIGNER / GESTALTER / MAQUETTISTE:

438–442 Rachel Levitan Schreiber
443, 444 John Laughlin

ART DIRECTOR / DIRECTEUR ARTISTIQUE:

438–442 Gene Rosner/Alan Brown
443, 444 Arnold Saks

AGENCY / AGENTUR / AGENCE – STUDIO:

438–442 Brown & Rosner, Inc.
443, 444 Arnold Saks Inc.

PHOTOGRAPHER / PHOTOGRAPH / PHOTOGRAPHE:

445 Al Satterwhite
446, 447 Jerry Sarapochiello
448 Rand Tapscott

DESIGNER / GESTALTER / MAQUETTISTE:

445 Al Satterwhite
446, 447 Russell Tatro
448 Tom Sizemore

ART DIRECTOR / DIRECTEUR ARTISTIQUE:

445 Al Higdon
446, 447 Jack Hough
448 Wayne Burkart

AGENCY / AGENTUR / AGENCE – STUDIO:

445 Sullivan, Higdon & Sink
446, 447 Jack Hough Associates, Inc.

445 From an annual report of the Gates Learjet Corporation, aircraft builders. (USA)
446, 447 Cover and full-page colour photograph from an annual report of the General Defense Corporation, producers of precision-machined armour piercing projectiles for the U.S. Army. (USA)
448 Double spread from a *John Deere* company publication, here with a partial view of an office building and a feature on this firm's architectural policies and traditions. (USA)

445 Aus einem Jahresbericht der Gates Learjet Corporation, Hersteller von Flugzeugen. (USA)
446, 447 Umschlag und ganzseitige Farbaufnahme aus einem Jahresbericht der General Defense Corporation, Hersteller von Waffen. (USA)
448 Doppelseite aus einer Firmenpublikation von *John Deere*, hier mit der Teilansicht eines Bürogebäudes, aus einem Beitrag über die Architektur der firmeneigenen Gebäude. (USA)

445 Rapport annuel de la Gates Learjet Corporation, un constructeur d'avions. (USA)
446, 447 Couverture et photo couleur plein page d'un rapport annuel de la General Defense Corporation, fabricant d'armements, notamment de munitions antichar. (USA)
448 Double page d'une publication promotionnelle de *John Deere*. On y voit une vue partielle d'un immeuble de bureaux en illustration d'un rapport sur l'architecture du groupe. (USA)

445

446

447

For all their similarities, John Deere buildings are far from "look-alikes." Some, in fact, are strikingly dissimilar. The West Office addition (designed by Saarinen's successor firm of Roche, Dinkeloo & Associates) continues the Cor-Ten steel motif of the Administrative Center, but its large atrium and glass gambrel roof give it a character all its own. Bold concrete pillars and a roof supported by steel cable distinguish the innovative Baltimore Region office built in 1967. The stark-white Financial Services Building, completed in 1981, is one of the first industrial structures to be sheathed in aluminum.

Precast concrete is the standard building material for John Deere factories. These utilitarian buildings would seem unpromising opportunities for design, but they are among the most contemporary and subtly designed structures in Deere's catalog. They rely on space proportions, texture, landscaping, and the interplay of light and shadow to achieve effects other buildings might gain through use of ornament. Says Eldon Hansen, Deere & Company's plant and construction engineering manager: "We want to design environments employees can relate to and take pride in, and still provide efficient working space. There is no John Deere style."

Nevertheless, the message Deere intends to convey with its buildings is the same even when the vocabulary differs. Chairman Hewitt, speaking in 1977 to the American Institute of Architects, revealed his instructions to Saarinen nearly 25 years ago. He wanted a building "in harmony with our functions and traditions," one which would be "thoroughly modern in concept but at the same time down to earth and rugged" like the people who had caused the company to flourish. He got that kind of building in the Administrative Center, and Deere's aim since then has been to continue to build buildings which, as Hewitt phrased it, "keep faith with our paternity."

Financial Services Building, Moline, Illinois

449

450

451

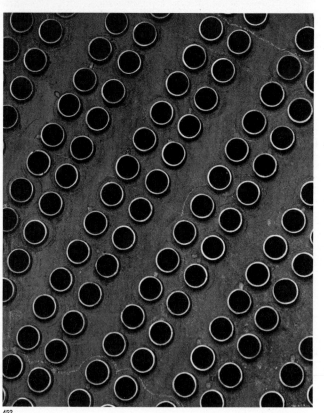

452

PHOTOGRAPHER:
449, 451, 452 Ronald W. May
450, 453 Tom Vack/
Joseph M. Essex

DESIGNER / GESTALTER:
449, 451, 452 Frank Rodriquez
450, 453 Joseph M. Essex/
Robert Petrick

ART DIRECTOR:
449, 451, 452 Frank Rodriquez
450, 453 Robert Petrick/
Joseph M. Essex

AGENCY / AGENTUR / AGENCE:
449, 451, 452 Rodriquez
Graphics
450, 453 Burson Marsteller

Corporate Publications
Firmenpublikationen
Publications d'entreprise

449, 451, 452 Cover and full-page colour photographs from an annual report of the Pacific Gas and Electric Co. Fig. 449 shows a gas/oil-fired boiler at this company's Moss Landing Power Plant. (USA)
450, 453 Full-page photographs from a linen-bound Congoleum company brochure, referring here to major lines of business such as shipbuilding, automotive and industrial products. (USA)

449, 451, 452 Umschlag und ganzseitige Farbaufnahmen aus einem Jahresbericht eines Elektrizitäts-Forschungsinstituts. Abb. 449 zeigt den Blick in einen Gas/Öl-Kessel eines Gas- und Elektrizitätswerks. (USA)
450, 453 Ganzseitige Aufnahmen aus einer in Leinen gebundenen Firmenbroschüre von *Congoleum*, hier in bezug auf die industrielle Fertigung von Rohschlüsseln und den Schiffsbau, zwei Hauptgeschäftszweige des Unternehmens. (USA)

449, 451, 452 Couverture et photos couleur pleine page d'un rapport annuel publié par un institut de recherches dans le domaine de l'électricité. 449: la vue plonge dans la chaudière fuel/gaz d'une centrale gaz/électricité. (USA)
450, 453 Photos pleine page illustrant une bochure promotionnelle reliée pleine toile de *Congoleum*. Elles se rapportent à la fabrication industrielle d'ébauches de clefs et à la construction navale, deux secteurs-clefs. (USA)

453

Oil and Gas

455

Iron and Steel

456

Corporate Publications
Firmenpublikationen
Publications d'entreprise

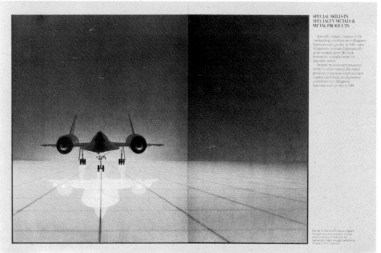

457

458

MINING/METALS

Copper prices are strong, exceeding one dollar per pound in 1979, up from 70 cents per pound not long ago. The two major consumers—the U.S. and USSR are essentially self-sufficient. The major producers—Zaire, Zambia, Chile, Peru and New Guinea—are responsible for one-third of the copper mined in the world, and consume only a small quantity. Their production supplies the major deficit areas, Japan and Western Europe.

Considerable investment in the 1980s is expected in coal, molybdenum, gold, phosphate rock and other metals and non-metals. The geographic pattern of investment for the metals industry differs markedly from that for oil and gas:

Investment* Percent of Total	% Oil & Gas Related	% Metals
United States	44	14
Canada	6	8
Latin America	10	24
Europe	12	4
Africa	7	14
Middle East	12	3
Far East/Australasia	9	33
Total	100	100

*Excluding the East Bloc

Worldwide Mineral Industry Investment by Commodity		
Projected $14 Billion Annual Investment		
A	Copper	20%
B	Iron Ore	16%
C	Lead and Zinc	4%
D	Nickel	4%
E	Uranium	6%
F	Aluminum	28%
G	Other*	22%
		100%

*Primarily coal.

Aluminum prices and operating rates are currently high, so near-term opportunities are good. Demand is growing at roughly 4 percent per year, but the industry is cyclical. Bauxite production is concentrated in Australia, Guinea, and the Caribbean, alumina production in the U.S., Australia, and Western Europe, and aluminum production in the USSR, Western Europe and North America. Almost 60% of the investment in metals in the Far East/Australasia region is expected to be in Australia.

Other major markets in the Far East include the Philippines, People's Republic of China, Malaysia and Papua New Guinea.

Developing engineering and construction projects in Latin America involve at least 10 countries. In Africa, projects are anticipated in Niger, Algeria and South Africa to highlight only a few. Fluor's prospect list for the next five years encompasses over 70 projects valued at over $45 billion.

Photo Collage Symbols:
Geostatistically-derived block model of an ore body, including drill hole positioning for core samples; three-dimensional plastic model of a copper deposit; copper smelting image; the application of microscopy for analysis of a copper ore sample; equation relating to spacing of core sample drill holes.

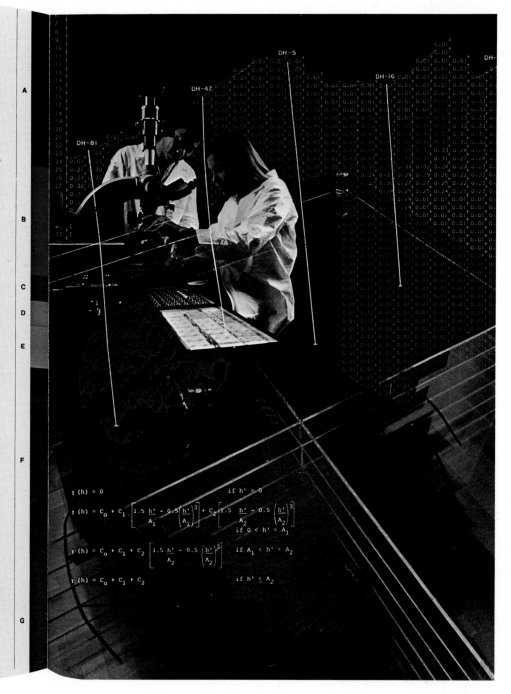

459

PHOTOGRAPHER / PHOTOGRAPH / PHOTOGRAPHE:

455, 456 Karen Coshof
457, 458 Michel Tcherevkoff
459 William James Warren

DESIGNER / GESTALTER / MAQUETTISTE:

455, 456 Peter Steiner
459 Ron & Claudia Jefferies

ART DIRECTOR / DIRECTEUR ARTISTIQUE:

455, 456 Peter Steiner
457, 458 Gabe Massimi
459 Ron & Claudia Jefferies

AGENCY / AGENTUR / AGENCE – STUDIO:

455, 456 Gottschalk & Ash Int'l
457, 458 Burton Campbell
459 The Jefferies Association

455, 456 Double spreads from an annual report of the Canadian Pacific Enterprises Ltd., Montreal. Two facets of this company's business are shown here: oil and gas, iron and steel. (USA)
457, 458 Full-colour double spreads from the *Allegheny International* annual report. Fig. 457: the SR-71 aeroplane made almost entirely of titanium; Fig. 458: tennis rackets with metal frames. (USA)
459 Full-page photograph (collage) with an unfolding text section from the annual report of the *Fluor Corporation*. This company is active worldwide in engineering and in the project planning for firms in the oil industry and those working on the extraction of mineral resources. (USA)

455, 456 Doppelseiten aus dem Jahresbericht der Canadian Pacific Enterprises Ltd., Montreal. Hier zwei Sektoren des Unternehmens, Erdöl und Gas sowie Eisen und Stahl. (USA)
457, 458 Farbige Doppelseiten aus dem Jahresbericht der *Allegheny International* in Pittsburgh. Abb. 457: SR-71, ein Flugzeug, das fast vollständig aus Titan besteht; Abb. 458: Tennisschläger als Hinweis auf die bedeutende Metallrahmenproduktion für Sportgeräte. (USA)
459 Ganzseitige Aufnahme (Collage) mit ausklappbarem Textteil aus dem Jahresbericht der *Fluor Corporation*. Der Konzern ist weltweit im Ingenieurwesen und in der Projektplanung für Unternehmen der Ölindustrie und Bodenschatzgewinnung tätig. (USA)

455, 456 Doubles pages d'un rapport annuel de Canadian Pacific Enterprises Ltd., Montréal. Référence à deux secteurs du groupe, le gaz et le pétrole, d'une part, le fer et l'acier, de l'autre. (USA)
457, 458 Doubles pages couleur d'un rapport annuel d'*Allegheny International* (Pittsburgh). Fig. 457: le SR-71, un avion presque entièrement réalisé en titane; fig. 458: raquette de tennis incarnant l'important volume de fabrication de cadres métalliques pour engins de sports. (USA)
459 Photo pleine page (collage) avec texte dépliable dans un rapport annuel de la *Fluor Corporation*, un groupe d'ingiénerie et de planning pour l'industrie pétrolière et minière dans le monde entier. (USA)

460

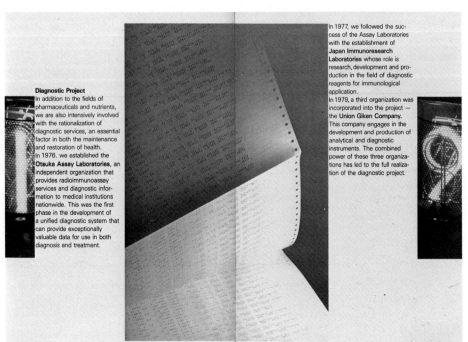

Diagnostic Project
In addition to the fields of pharmaceuticals and nutrients, we are also intensively involved with the rationalization of diagnostic services, an essential factor in both the maintenance and restoration of health.
In 1976, we established the **Otsuka Assay Laboratories**, an independent organization that provides radioimmunoassay services and diagnostic information to medical institutions nationwide. This was the first phase in the development of a unified diagnostic system that can provide exceptionally valuable data for use in both diagnosis and treatment.

In 1977, we followed the success of the Assay Laboratories with the establishment of **Japan Immunoresearch Laboratories** whose role is research, development and production of diagnostic reagents for immunological application.
In 1979, a third organization was incorporated into the project — the **Union Giken Company.** This company engages in the development and production of analytical and diagnostic instruments. The combined power of these three organizations has led to the full realization of the diagnostic project.

461

Annual Reports / Jahresberichte / Rapports annuels

460 From an annual report of the Simmering-Graz-Pauker AG, manufacturers of railway locomotives, industrial plants, etc. Shown here is a power plant in Sousse, Tunisia. (AUT)
461 Double spread from an annual report of *Otsuka Pharamaceuticals.* (JPN)
462 Cover of the ITT Research Institute's annual report. (USA)
463, 465 Black-and-white photograph from the electronic data processing sphere, taken from the Houghton Mifflin Company's annual report. (USA)
464 Cover of an annual report of *Texas Industries.* Black and white. (USA)

460 Aus einem Jahresbericht der Simmering-Graz-Pauker AG, Schienenfahrzeuge, Industrieanlagen etc. Hier ein Kraftwerk in Sousse, Tunesien. (AUT)
461 Doppelseite aus einem Jahresbericht von *Otsuka Pharmaceuticals,* die sich auf ein Diagnostik-System dieses Pharma-Konzerns bezieht. (JPN)
462 Umschlag eines Jahresberichtes des ITT Research Institute. (USA)
463, 465 Schwarzweiss-Aufnahmen aus dem Bereich der elektronischen Datenverarbeitung; aus einem Jahresbericht der Houghton Mifflin Company. (USA)
464 Umschlag eines Jahresberichtes der *Texas Industries.* (USA)

460 Rapport annuel de Simmering-Graz-Pauker AG (véhicules sur rails, usines, etc.). On voit ici une centrale électrique à Sousse (Tunisie). (AUT)
461 Double page d'un rapport annuel d'*Otsuka Pharmaceuticals.* Il s'agit d'un système de diagnostic mis au point par ce groupe pharmaceutique. (JPN)
462 Couverture d'un rapport annuel de l'ITT Research Institute. (USA)
463, 465 Photos noir et blanc illustrant le chapitre d'un rapport annuel de la Houghton Mifflin Company consacré à l'informatique. (USA)
464 Couverture noir et blanc d'un rapport annuel de *Texas Industries.* (USA)

PHOTOGRAPHER / PHOTOGRAPH / PHOTOGRAPHE:

460 Georg Riha
461 Yasuhiro Asai
462 Don Anderson
463, 465 Thomas Wedell
464 Bill Crump/Robert Latorre

DESIGNER / GESTALTER / MAQUETTISTE:

460 Wolfgang Stocker
461 Helmut Schmid
462 Gene Rosner
463, 465 Nancy Skolos
464 Alan Spaeth

ART DIRECTOR / DIRECTEUR ARTISTIQUE:

460 Christoph Schartelmüller
461 Helmut Schmid
462 Gene Rosner
463, 465 Nancy Skolos/Amanda Freymann
464 Alan Spaeth

AGENCY / AGENTUR / AGENCE – STUDIO:

460 Werbeabt. Simmering-Graz-Pauker
461 NIA
462 Brown & Rosner, Inc.
463, 465 Skolos, Wedell & Raynor
464 Robert A. Wilson Associates

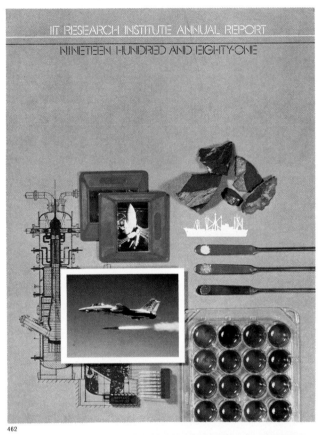

462

463

464

465

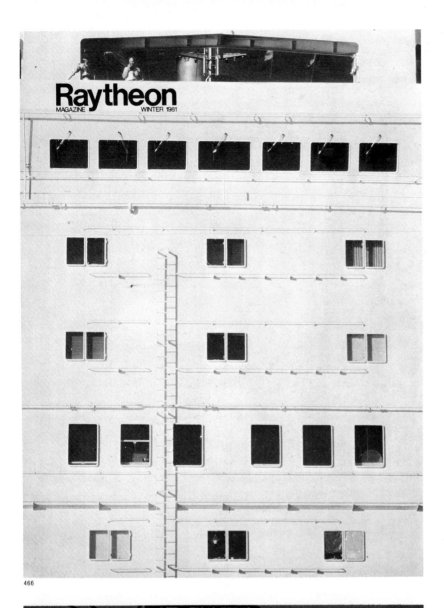

466

PHOTOGRAPHER / PHOTOGRAPH / PHOTOGRAPHE:

466 Richard Wood
467 Bruce Thomas
468, 469 Steve Fenn/ABC Photography Dept.
470, 471 Clint Clemens

DESIGNER / GESTALTER / MAQUETTISTE:

466 Barry Bomzer Associates
467 Kathleen Sullivan Kaska
468, 469 Philip Gips/Diana Graham/Gina Stone
470, 471 Wendy Hilgert

ART DIRECTOR / DIRECTEUR ARTISTIQUE:

467 Gene Rosner
468, 469 Philip Gips/Diana Graham
470, 471 Wendy Hilgert

AGENCY / AGENTUR / AGENCE – STUDIO:

467 Brown & Rosner, Inc.
468, 469 Gips & Balkind & Associates
470, 471 Ingalls Associates

468

Annual Reports
Jahresberichte
Rapports annuels

467

466 Cover of a company publication of *Raytheon*, a diversified international company in the fields of electronics, aviation, appliances, energy, construction and publishing. (USA)
467 Insulators glint in the sunlight on a transmission tower shown on the cover of an annual report of the L. E. Myers Co. Group. (USA)
468, 469 Cover and double spread referring to topical events and to music programmes, from an annual report of American Broadcasting Companies Inc. (USA)
470, 471 Cover and double spread from an annual report of the Boston Edison Company, suppliers of electric power. Objects in subdued colours. (USA)

466 Umschlag einer Firmenpublikation von *Raytheon*, eines internationalen Unternehmens, das u. a. auf dem Gebiet der Elektronik, des Geräte- und Flugzeugbaus tätig ist. (USA)
467 Im Sonnenlicht glänzende Isolatoren an einem Stromverteiler auf dem Umschlag eines Jahresberichts der L. E. Myers Co. Group, Hersteller von Hochspannungsleitungen. (USA)
468, 469 Nachrichtensendungen und Musikprogramme sind das Thema dieses Umschlags und einer Doppelseite aus dem Jahresbericht der American Broadcasting Companies. (USA)
470, 471 Umschlag und Doppelseite aus dem Jahresbericht einer Elektrizitätsgesellschaft. Objekte in matten Farbtönen. (USA)

466 Couverture d'une publication promotionnelle de *Raytheon*, un groupe diversifié international spécialisé en électronique, en appareillage, en aéronautique, etc. (USA)
467 Isolateurs resplendissant au soleil sur un pylône de ligne aérienne électrique. Couverture d'un rapport annuel du L. E. Myers Co. Group, qui fabrique ces lignes. (USA)
468, 469 Couverture et double page d'un rapport annuel d'American Broadcasting Companies sur le thème des émissions d'actualité et des programmes de musique. (USA)
470, 471 Couverture et double page d'un rapport annuel d'une compagnie d'électricité. Objets représentés en tons mats. (USA)

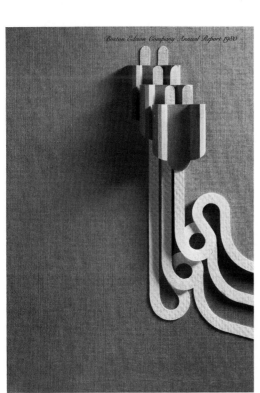
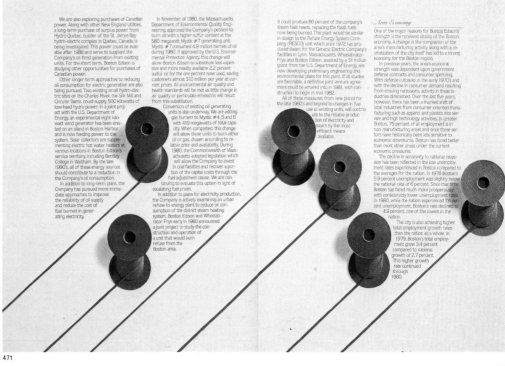

5

472

12

13

473

PHOTOGRAPHER / PHOTOGRAPH / PHOTOGRAPHE:

474 Tom Rogowski
475 S. Kercher

DESIGNER / GESTALTER / MAQUETTISTE:

472, 473 Elaine Issacson
474 Bill Sontag

ART DIRECTOR / DIRECTEUR ARTISTIQUE:

474 Bill Sontag
475 Henning Moschinski

AGENCY / AGENTUR / AGENCE – STUDIO:

472, 473 Corporate Graphics Inc.
474 Sive Associates
475 Moschinski & Partner KG

Business Review

1981 was a year of transformation for Chemed as the company streamlined its management and operational structure as well as its corporate structure, emerging as a smaller but more dynamic specialty chemical company. Although Chemed has always had a large concentration of its business in specialty chemicals, the company, in past years, also has held leading positions in certain health care fields. During 1981, Chemed contributed its non-chemical health care subsidiaries to Omnicare, Inc. Later in the year, the majority of Omnicare's common stock was sold to the public and Chemed retained a 24% equity interest in Omnicare, allowing Chemed to maintain a substantial stake in the health care field.

In recognition of the predominance of specialty chemicals as its major line of business, Chemed formed a new management group in 1981, the Specialty Chemicals Group, consisting of the Cincinnati-based DuBois Chemicals Division, the St. Louis-based Vestal Laboratories Division and the Vestal International Division, headquartered in New York. The formation of this group has allowed Chemed to streamline its management structure and achieve a higher degree of management synergy among very similar businesses.

1981 Sales by Segment

Specialty Industrial Chemicals 47%
Institutional Food Service Chemicals 30%
Water and Waste Treatment 13%
Health Care Products and Services 10%

Chemed conducted its business in 1981 through four principal operating divisions. In 1981, Chemed's largest division, DuBois Chemicals, which is comprised of the DuBois Industrial, Institutional, International and Cambridge Scientific Industries Divisions, recorded sales of $203,077,000, up 12% from 1980. The Dearborn Group recorded sales of $102,241,000 in 1981; however, these sales are no longer included in Chemed's total sales as all 1981 results have been restated to reflect the Dearborn Group as a discontinued operation. The Vestal Laboratories Division, including Vestal's international operations, advanced its sales

10% over last year to $35,311,000 in 1981. Chemed's newest operating group, the Roto-Rooter Group, including Roto-Rooter Corporation and Nurotoco, Inc., reached $12,250,000 in sales and operating revenues in 1981, increasing its contribution to Chemed's sales from $4,701,000 in 1980 (or about $9.9 million on an annual basis) from the date of its acquisition in July of that year.

The products and services of these Chemed operating divisions are classified in four major business segments. All primarily specialty chemical businesses, these segments include specialty industrial chemicals; institutional food service chemicals; water, waste treatment and air pollution control products and services (which also includes Roto-Rooter); and health care products and services. As a result of the completion of the restructuring plan and the resultant transfer of Dearborn's water and waste treatment business to Grace, specialty industrial chemicals is now Chemed's largest business segment with 47% of Chemed's total sales, followed by institutional food service chemicals contributing 30% of sales. Water and waste treatment products and services, which are marketed by all of Chemed's operating divisions, now comprise, in terms of sales, Chemed's third largest segment, with 13% of total sales. Chemed's health care segment, with 10% of sales, is Chemed's smallest segment. However, the health care segment does not include revenues generated by Omnicare, since Omnicare is accounted for on the equity basis. If a 24% share of Omnicare's revenues had been included with Chemed's health care sales, the health care segment would have contributed 23% of Chemed's total sales in 1981.

Commitment to product quality and service has made Chemed a dynamic force in the specialty chemicals field.

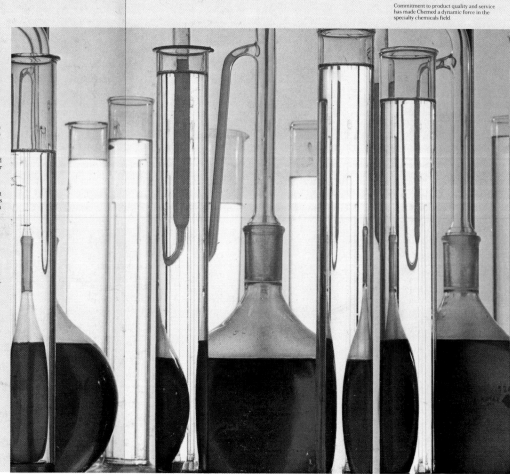

8

474

472, 473 Double spreads from a company brochure for *Pfizer*, a chemical and pharmaceutical concern. The photographs point to the various ranges of application of this firm's products. (USA)
474 Double spread from the 1981 annual report of the *Chemed Corporation*. Fluids in yellow and various shades of red. (USA)
475 Detail of a full-page photograph taken from an annual report of the *Kali-Chemie* company. The photograph refers to this company's raw material production used for first-rate optical glass. (GER)

472, 473 Doppelseiten aus einer Firmenbroschüre für *Pfizer*, einen Chemie- und Pharma-Konzern. Die Aufnahmen beziehen sich auf die verschiedenen Anwendungsbereiche der Produkte. (USA)
474 Doppelseite aus dem Jahresbericht 1981 der *Chemed Corporation*, eines Chemiekonzerns. Die Flüssigkeiten in den Reagenzgläsern in Gelb mit verschiedenen Rottönen. (USA)
475 Detail einer ganzseitigen Aufnahme aus einem Jahresbericht der *Kali-Chemie*, Hannover. Die Aufnahme bezieht sich auf die Grundstoffproduktion des Unternehmens, die für hochwertige optische Gläser benötigt wird. (GER)

472, 473 Doubles pages d'une brochure publiée par *Pfizer*, le groupe chimique et pharmaceutique. Les photos se rapportent aux domaines d'application des produits. (USA)
474 Double page tirée du rapport annuel pour 1981 de la *Chemed Corporation*, une société de produits chimiques. Les liquides contenus dans les éprouvettes sont en jaune et en divers tons de rouge. (USA)
475 Détail d'une photo pleine page illustrant un rapport annuel de *Kali-Chemie*. La photo symbolise la production des matériaux de base indispensables pour la fabrication de verres optiques de qualité. (GER)

475

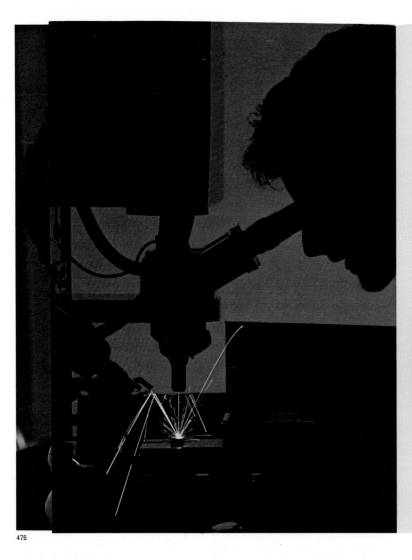

476

been expected to last five years, but in the hostile environment of the body they leaked and wore out in two years. Orthopaedic implants faced different problems: they had to withstand extremely strong forces (a force up to seven times the body's weight is exerted on the hip

Left: The titanium case which holds the intracranial implant is closed with laser-welding done under a microscope.

Below: At Case Western Reserve, a tiny device to be implanted behind the ear has been developed which measures intracranial pressure and transmits the measurements by radio frequency to a computer.

"Researchers have been working on replacements for an ever-growing list of human parts and organs."

joint as one goes upstairs, for instance) without loosening or wearing out. At the same time they, too, had to be made of materials that would not corrode or be rejected by the body.

Since the beginning of the implant era in the early 1960s, therefore, researchers have been seeking materials and power sources that would be more compatible with living tissue and would last longer. They have been trying to improve the designs of existing devices. In addition, they have been working on replacements for an ever-growing list of human parts and organs, including such vital organs as the pancreas and heart.

This search is becoming more urgent as our population grows older: the longer one lives, the greater the chance that some component of the body will fail. The average U.S. lifespan is now 73 years, 26 years more than at the turn of the century. This means a large increase in such chronic illnesses as atherosclerosis (hardening of the arteries), arthritis, heart disease, cancer and emphysema, which now account for more than 80 percent of all deaths, according to a report in *The New England Journal of Medicine*. It also means, according to Dr. Galletti, that "in the long run, we are all candidates for a prosthesis of one type or another." There will be a rising need for replacement parts—sometimes more than one per person.

Even today, it is not so unusual for a person to have both an artificial heart valve and an arterial graft, or a pacemaker and an artificial hip.

Intensive research is now going on in scores of universities and medical centers around the country to develop more sophisticated medical implants. At the University of Minnesota, for instance, Dr. Henry Buchwald has been conducting trials with a totally implanted pump which can dispense a continuous flow of drugs—insulin to diabetics, heparin (an anti-coagulant) to patients with blood-clotting disorders, or chemotherapy to cancer patients. It has already helped some patients who suffer from liver tumors by allowing the cancer-fighting chemicals to be pumped directly into the hepatic artery, which leads to the liver. The tumors are exposed to much higher—and thus more effective—doses of chemotherapy than would otherwise be possible, without causing more toxicity or side-effects. With this Infusaid* pump and a constant flow of highly concentrated anti-cancer drugs, a few patients have survived liver cancer for two years, instead of four months.

In the winter of 1980, an insulin pump of this sort was implanted for the first time below the shoulder of a 54-year-old diabetic man. Made of titanium, the pump is about the size and shape of a hockey puck and operates on a constant source of energy: body heat. Every two weeks, one of the pump's two chambers is refilled with an insulin solution by means of a syringe inserted through the skin. The insulin compresses a fluorocarbon gas in the second chamber, turning the gas into a liquid. Then the body's heat slowly changes the liquid into a gas, pumping a steady trickle of insulin into the patient's veins.

*Trademark of an unrelated company.

25

---

476 Double spread from a *Bristol-Myers* annual report containing a special report (somewhat narrower) on medical implants. (USA)
477, 478 Double spreads from *JD Journal*, house magazine of the *John Deere* company. Fig. 477 refers to a report about the popularity of slimming diets; Fig. 478: the paper war in offices. (USA)
479 Cover of the 1981 annual report of *Bristol-Myers*. (See also Fig. 476). The photograph shows a hip implant bombarded with titanium particles to improve biological fixation. (USA)
480, 481 Full-page photographs from an *American Cyanamid* annual report. Fig. 480 refers to agricultural research; Fig. 481: products manufactured by the Medical Group. (USA)

476 Doppelseite aus einem Jahresbericht von *Bristol-Myers*. Es handelt sich hier um einen Sonderbeitrag (etwas schmaler im Format) über medizinische Implantationsteile. (USA)
477, 478 Doppelseiten aus *JD Journal*, Hauszeitschrift von *John Deere*. In Abb. 477 geht es um einen Beitrag über die Popularität von Diäten, in Abb. 478 um den Papierkrieg in Büros. (USA)
479 Umschlag des Jahresberichtes 1981 von *Bristol-Myers*. (Siehe auch Abb. 476.) Die Aufnahme zeigt ein Hüftimplantationsteil, das von Titan-Partikelchen bombardiert wird. (USA)
480, 481 Ganzseitige Aufnahmen aus einem Jahresbericht der *American Cyanamid*. Abb. 480 bezieht sich auf die Landwirtschaftsforschung, Abb. 481 auf medizinische Produkte. (USA)

Have a little ice cream.
What are you afraid of?

FEAR OF FATTENING

BY JIM KROHE

477

NEVER UNDERESTIMATE THE VALUE OF A WASTEBASKET

PAPER MANIA

478

188

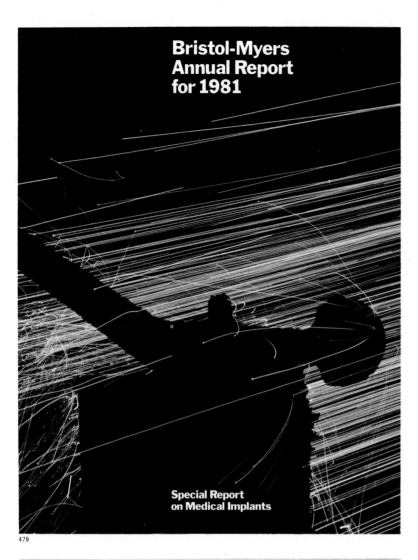

Bristol-Myers
Annual Report
for 1981

Special Report
on Medical Implants

479

Annual Reports
Jahresberichte
Rapports annuels

PHOTOGRAPHER / PHOTOGRAPH / PHOTOGRAPHE:

476, 479 Burt Glinn/Magnum
477, 478 Banner & Burns

DESIGNER / GESTALTER / MAQUETTISTE:

476, 479 Robert Jakob
477, 478 Tom Sizemore

ART DIRECTOR / DIRECTEUR ARTISTIQUE:

476, 479 Arnold Saks
477, 478 Wayne Burkart
480, 481 B. Martin Pedersen

AGENCY / AGENTUR / AGENCE – STUDIO:

476, 479 Arnold Saks Inc.
480, 481 Jonson Pedersen Hinrichs & Shakery

476 Double page d'un rapport annuel de *Bristol-Myers.* Il s'agit d'une section spéciale, au format légèrement réduit, sur les implants en médecine. (USA)
477, 478 Doubles pages de *JD Journal,* la revue d'entreprise de *John Deere.* La fig. 477 a trait à la vogue des cures d'amaigrissement, la fig. 478 à la paperasserie dans les bureaux. (USA)
479 Couverture du rapport annuel pour 1981 de *Bristol-Myers* (cf. la fig. 476). La photo montre un implant pour l'articulation de la hanche bombardé de particules de titane. (USA)
480, 481 Photos pleine page illustrant un rapport annuel d'*American Cyanamid.* La fig. 480 se réfère à la recherche agricole, la fig. 481 aux instruments médicaux. (USA)

480

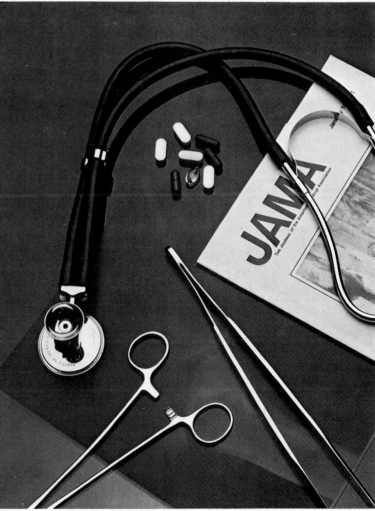

481

482–485 Cover and photograph as well as double spreads from an annual report of Transamerica Corporation. Figs. 482, 485: the pyramid-shaped headquarters of this diversified company; Fig. 483: cast-steel cylinder heads for diesel engines; Fig. 484: passenger- and freight aeroplane. (USA)
486, 487 Covers of a two-part annual report of a bank in Hongkong. Fig 486: a Cantonese opera star in full make-up balances the face of the Statue of Liberty; Fig. 487: one of the bronze lions at the bank's Head Office and one of a similar pair outside the New York Public Library. (HKG)

482–485 Umschlag und Aufnahme sowie Doppelseiten aus einem Jahresbericht der Transamerica Corporation. Abb. 482, 485: das pyramidenförmige Hauptgebäude dieses diversifizierten Konzerns; Abb. 483: Gussstahl-Zylinderköpfe für Dieselmotoren; Abb. 484: Passagier- und Frachtflugzeug. (USA)
486, 487 Umschläge eines zweiteiligen Jahresberichtes einer Bank in Hongkong. Thema war deren enge Beziehung zu New York: der Kopf eines Opernstars aus Kanton verbindet sich mit dem der Freiheitsstatue; der des Bronzelöwen vor dem Hauptsitz mit dem eines New Yorker Löwen. (HKG)

482–485 Couverture, photos et doubles pages d'un rapport annuel de la Transamerica Corporation. Fig. 482, 485: le bâtiment central de ce groupe diversifié, en forme de pyramide; 483: culasses de cylindres (acier au creuset) pour diesels; 484: avion cargo-passagers. (USA)
486, 487 Couvertures du rapport annuel en deux volumes d'une banque de Hongkong, sur le thème de la relation étroite avec New York symbolisée par le chanteur d'opéra de Canton et la statue de la Liberté, le lion devant la banque et le lion devant une bibliothèque de New York. (HKG)

PHOTOGRAPHER / PHOTOGRAPH:

482–485 Tom Tracy/John McDermott
486, 487 Ken Haas

DESIGNER / GESTALTER / MAQUETTISTE:

482–485 Linda Hinrichs/Lenore Bartz
486, 487 Henry Steiner

ART DIRECTOR / DIRECTEUR ARTISTIQUE:

482–485 Linda Hinrichs
486, 487 Henry Steiner

AGENCY / AGENTUR / AGENCE – STUDIO:

482–485 Jonson Pedersen Hinrichs &
         Shakery
486, 487 Graphic Communication Ltd.

482

483

484

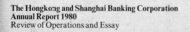

The Hongkong and Shanghai Banking Corporation
Annual Report 1980
Review of Operations and Essay

486

The Hongkong and Shanghai Banking Corporation
Annual Report 1980
Chairman's Statement, Directors Report and Accounts

487

485

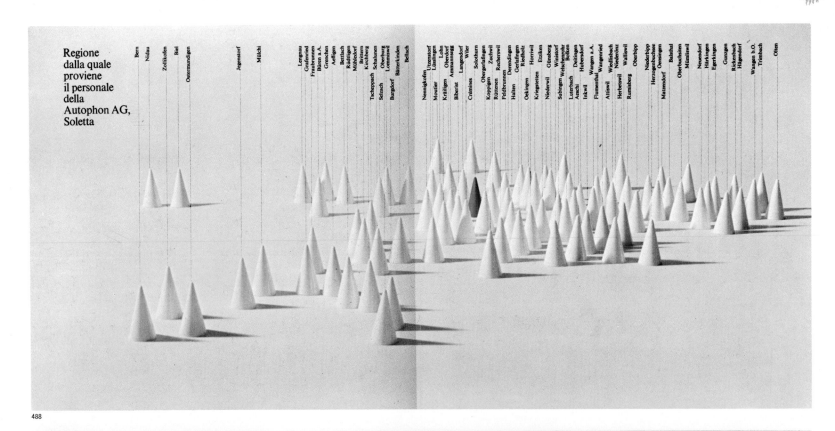

Regione dalla quale proviene il personale della Autophon AG, Soletta

488

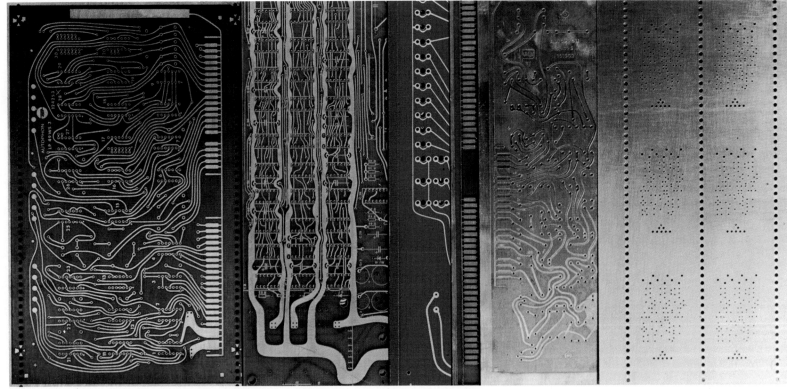

489

Corporate Publications
Firmenpublikationen
Publications d'entreprise

PHOTOGRAPHER / PHOTOGRAPH:

488, 489 Studio Visual
490–492 Roger Turqueti

DESIGNER / GESTALTER / MAQUETTISTE:

490–492 Marilyn Talarn

ART DIRECTOR / DIRECTEUR ARTISTIQUE:

488, 489 Rolf Weiersmüller
490–492 Georges Lacroix

AGENCY / AGENTUR / AGENCE – STUDIO:

488, 489 B & P Blumenstein & Plancherel
490–492 Georges Lacroix

488, 489 Double spreads from an anniversary brochure of Autophon AG, an electronics company. Fig. 489 shows the places where all the employees come from. (SWI)
490–492 Double spreads and detail of a photograph from the *Saint-Gobain* company brochure, an international group of firms of French origin. Fig. 490 shows two spheres of production of this company: fibrous cement products for the building trade, on the left; and on the right cast-iron water-pipes. Fig. 491 refers to the manufacturing of sheet glass (left) and the production of insulation material (right). (FRA)

488, 489 Doppelseiten aus einer Jubiläumsbroschüre der Autophon AG, eines Elektronik-Konzerns. Abb. 489 zeigt eine Aufstellung der Ortschaften, aus denen die Mitarbeiter kommen. (SWI)

490-492 Doppelseiten und Detail einer der Aufnahmen aus der Firmenbroschüre von *Saint-Gobain*, einer internationalen Firmengruppe französischer Herkunft. Abb. 490 zeigt zwei Produktionsbereiche des Unternehmens, links Faserzementerzeugisse für die Bauwirtschaft und rechts Rohre aus Gusseisen für Wasserleitungen. Abb. 491 bezieht sich auf die Herstellung von Flachglas (links) und die Dämmstoffproduktion (rechts). (FRA)

488, 489 Doubles pages d'une brochure de l'Autophon AG, un groupe électronique. La fig. 489 énumère les localités d'où sont issus les collaborateurs de la firme. (SWI)

490-492 Doubles pages et détail de l'une des photos qui les illustrent dans la brochure promotionnelle de *Saint-Gobain*, un groupe international d'origine française. La fig. 490 montre deux secteurs de produits du groupe, à gauche les produits en fibres de ciment pour le bâtiment, à droite les tubes en fonte pour conduites d'eau. La fig. 491 se réfère à la production de verre plat (à gauche) et de matériaux isolants (à droite). (FRA)

490

491

492

493

"Our biggest challenge in Europe is producing—18 times a year—eight separate versions of the campaign literature, error free and on time."

Wilfried Wagner was born in Germany and spent his youth in Hamburg. Following apprenticeship and technical schooling at the Academy of Graphic Arts in Munich, he joined Avon 13 years ago as a Print Production Specialist.

As Director of Print Production for Avon Overseas Limited (AOL), Avon's European Marketing Center in London, he oversees a group of graphic arts professionals who produce 93 million campaign brochures in eight languages every year.

"When I was at school, the idea of setting common standards for print production throughout Europe was strictly a theoretical goal. Today those standards are a reality, and I'm very proud that Avon has contributed greatly to this movement.

"Our biggest challenge in Europe is producing—18 times a year—eight separate versions of the campaign literature, error free and on time," he says. "Our unique demands forced us to take the lead in encouraging our printers to adopt common standards.

"What standardization does is make us completely independent of any specific vendor. This way we can buy printing of a defined quality anywhere in Europe simply by looking at a printer's equipment list."

Wilfried is very proud of his group of specialists at AOL and puts great emphasis on team effort.

"What we have here is a team of highly skilled people who really know their particular disciplines," he says. "This is critical in dealing with printers, because we have always believed that we, as the buyer, should know as much about printing as the printers themselves."

Wilfried values the freedom his group has been given by Avon management to adopt the latest in printing technology.

"There is a lot of trust in the ability of teams like ours to keep abreast of new developments and bring them into the system.

"Our printing needs are so complex as anyone's," he adds. "And when any new technology becomes feasible, you can be sure that Avon will be among the first to adopt it."

494

Born and raised in Denver, Colorado, Donna Brooks attended Tennessee State University and California State University at Hayward.

"In school, I majored in elementary education. My father, who was a very strong figure in my life, had wanted me to teach. But I realized that I really wanted to pursue a career in business instead. So prior to leaving school, I studied different industries, and the cosmetics field appealed to me the most," she says.

After completing her education, she joined another direct seller of cosmetics in the Denver area, and was later transferred to Atlanta. "I recruited and trained the largest sales force the company had in Georgia," she says. "But I wanted to be with number one, and everyone knows that in the cosmetics business, Avon is it!"

Hired as a District Manager by Avon in 1974, she was assigned to an inner-city market in Atlanta. In 1977, after a brief period as an Operations Supervisor at the Atlanta Branch—and time off to have her second daughter—Donna was offered a promotion to Division

Manager covering North Florida.

"I love a challenge, and that certainly was one. I was to be the first black female Division Manager at the Atlanta Branch—and the area that I was offered in North Florida was not your most progressive when it came to racial attitudes. But I had studied the market and the growth potential, and I felt it was worth it, so I accepted."

Donna's division was later expanded to include parts of southern Georgia. Today, it extends from north of Savannah, Georgia to south of Jacksonville, Florida.

"I have real Avon country," she notes. "It's very rural, mostly farmers growing peppers, onions, peanuts and soybeans. And there are coastal areas where you find shrimpers and fish camps. I even have Representatives who visit their customers by boat."

Consistently among the top Division Managers in sales performance at the Atlanta Branch, she says, "In 1978, I led the Branch with over a $2 million sales increase. I haven't been number one since then—but I'm going to do it again!"

"I have real Avon country. It's very rural, mostly farmers growing peppers, onions, peanuts and soybeans. And there are coastal areas where you find shrimpers and fish camps."

495

Annual Reports
Jahresberichte
Rapports annuels

PepsiCo Worldwide

Symbolizing PepsiCo's
growing presence in
Europe, a bright new
truck services soft
drink vending machines
in a medieval village
one-half hour from
Frankfurt, Germany – a
less developed but high-
potential market.

Within 100 meters of
Magellan's landfall,
Mountain Dew and
Pepsi-Cola are carried
ashore from shallow-
draft outriggers; daily
deliveries are scheduled
for dawn and sunset
on the island of Cebu in
East Central Philippines.

496

497

493 Doppelseite aus dem Jahresbericht 1980 für ein auf dem Immobilienmarkt tätiges Investment-Unternehmen. Das rechts sichtbar werdende Gelb gehört zur nächsten Seite. (USA)
494, 495 Doppelseiten mit Farbaufnahmen aus einem Jahresbericht für *Avon.* Der Textteil besteht ausschliesslich aus Porträts einiger Mitarbeiter. (USA)
496, 497 Aus dem Jahresbericht 1980 für PepsiCo, Inc. Die Aufnahmen dokumentieren *Pepsis* Präsenz in aller Welt – hier ein Ort in Deutschland und eine philippinische Insel. (USA)
498 Vollständiger Umschlag eines Jahresberichtes für Marsh & McLennan Companies, Inc., Versicherungen und Anlageberatungen. Leuchtende Körnchen auf nassem Strandsand und Seestern. (USA)

493 Double page du rapport annuel pour 1980 d'une société d'investissements immobiliers. Le jaune qui apparaît sur la droite fait déjà partie de la page suivante. (USA)
494, 495 Doubles pages illustrées en couleur d'un rapport annuel d'*Avon.* Le texte dresse le portrait de divers collaborateurs de la société. (USA)
496, 497 Rapport de la PepsiCo, Inc. pour 1980. Les photos documentent la présence de *Pepsi* dans le monde entier – ici, dans une localité allemande et une île des Philippines. (USA)
498 Couverture complète d'un rapport annuel de Marsh & McLennan Companies, Inc. (assurances et conseils en investissements). Grains lumineux sur sable humide; étoile de mer. (USA)

PHOTOGRAPHER / PHOTOGRAPH / PHOTOGRAPHE:

493 Jeff Smith
494, 495 Burt Glinn/Peggy Barnett
496, 497 Charles Harbutt
498 Cheryl Rossum

DESIGNER / GESTALTER / MAQUETTISTE:

493 Patty Nalle
494, 495 Ingo Scharrenbroich
496, 497 Stan Eisenmann
498 Karen Katinas

ART DIRECTOR / DIRECTEUR ARTISTIQUE:

493 Arnold Wechsler
494, 495 Arnold Saks
496, 497 Stan Eisenman

AGENCY / AGENTUR / AGENCE – STUDIO:

493 Mayo-Infurna Design Inc.
494, 495 Arnold Saks Inc.
496, 497 Eisenman & Enock Inc.

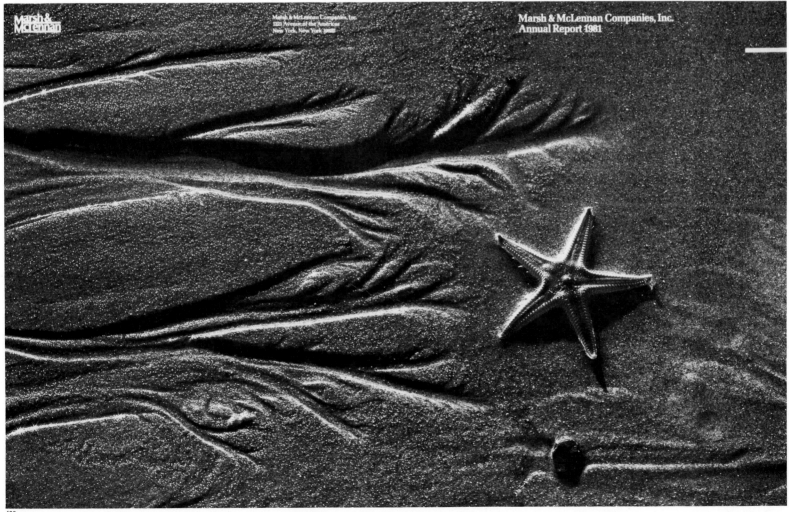

Marsh & McLennan Companies, Inc.
1221 Avenue of the Americas
New York, New York 10020

Marsh & McLennan Companies, Inc.
Annual Report 1981

498

salesperson and customer is certainly no exception. If selling is an art, it is the art of one person communicating those intangibles to another person, while at the same time discussing the relative merits of items like paper, plywood, and packaging.

The 2500 men and women who sell Champion's wide variety of products daily represent the company's face, voice, and handshake to its thousands of customers. Their

have the products we manufacture and market.

In style and temperament the men and women who sell Champion are as different from each other as the geographical regions in which they live and work. They come from diverse backgrounds and varied life experiences. But in listening to them speak about their jobs, recurrent themes emerge which suggest a basic unity in their character.

Champions Sell. It happens
every working day — in mills and offices, automobiles and telephone booths, on superhighways and country roads, in big cities and small towns — all across America. It begins with intangibles: an expression on a face, a tone in a voice, the strength of a handshake. Trust is the basis for all human relationships, and the one between

by Stuart I. Frolick

pushing a little bit harder than their competition.

But they didn't do it alone. Champion's outside sales representatives are backed up by mill representatives and inside sales teams described by one salesman as "second to none." These support groups of sales service personnel and secretaries complete dozens of tasks — from follow-up calls, correspondence, and appointment scheduling to sending out the bills. In short, they assist in much of

501

PHOTOGRAPHER / PHOTOGRAPH:

499 Al Kahn
500, 501 Guy Powers
502, 503 Simpson Kalisher
504, 505 Farrell Grehan
506, 507 Herman van Haasteren

DESIGNER / GESTALTER / MAQUETTISTE:

499–501 Al Kahn
502–505 Richard Hess
506, 507 Hans Versteeg

ART DIRECTOR / DIRECTEUR ARTISTIQUE:

499–501 Al Kahn
502–505 Richard Hess

AGENCY / AGENTUR / AGENCE – STUDIO:

499–501 Al Kahn Group
506, 507 Dots Design

499–501 Full-page photographs and a complete double spread from a company brochure of The Al Kahn Group advertising agency. Fig. 499 is an example of this agency's work in the field of corporate identity programmes; Fig. 500 underlines the survival chances of corporations able to solve intricate identity and marketing problems in the 80's; Fig. 501 documents the commissions obtained in the marketing sphere. (USA)
502–505 Double spreads from a feature in the *Champion International* house magazine in which representatives of this paper company in various regions are introduced to the reader. (USA)
506, 507 Double spreads with black-and-white photographs from the house magazine ("Prikkel") of the paper wholesalers Proost en Brandt N.V., here using the slogan "Are you superstitious?" Fig. 506: "Woe betide the one who opens his umbrella indoors"; Fig. 507: "He who cracks a mirror has seven years' bad luck." (NLD)

499–501 Ganzseitige Aufnahmen und eine vollständige Doppelseite aus einer Firmenbroschüre der Werbeagentur Al Kahn Group. Abb. 499 ist ein Beispiel für die Arbeit der Agentur auf dem Gebiet der Corporate-Identity-Programme; Abb. 501 dokumentiert die Aufträge im Marketing-Bereich, während Abb. 500 unterstreichen soll, wie wichtig diese Dinge für ein Unternehmen sind: «Lassen Sie Ihr Licht nicht verlöschen.» (USA)
502–505 Doppelseiten aus einem Beitrag in der Hauszeitschrift von *Champion International*, in dem die Vertreter des Papierkonzerns in den verschiedenen Regionen vorgestellt werden. (USA)
506, 507 Doppelseiten mit Schwarzweiss-Aufnahmen aus der Hauszeitschrift («Prikkel») des Papiergrosshändlers Proost en Brandt N.V., hier unter dem Motto «Sind sie abergläubisch?». Illustriert sind folgende Sprichworte: Abb. 506: «Wehe dem, der seinen Schirm im Hause aufspannt»; Abb. 507: «Wer einen Spiegel zerbricht, hat sieben Jahre Pech.» (NLD)

499–501 Photos pleine page et double page complète d'une brochure de l'agence publicitaire Al Kahn Group. La fig. 499 représente un exemple de travail dans le domaine des programmes d'identité globale d'entreprise; la fig. 501 se réfère aux commandes de marketing; la fig. 500 souligne tout le bénéfice que les clients retirent de cette double approche; «ils seront la lumière des années 80. Ne laissez pas la vôtre s'éteindre.» (USA)
502–505 Doubles pages d'un article de la revue d'entreprise de *Champion International* mettant en vedette les représentants régionaux du groupe papetier. (USA)
506, 507 Doubles pages illustrées de photos noir et blanc de la revue d'entreprise «Prikkel» du grossiste en papier Proost en Brandt N.V., sous le slogan «Etes-vous superstitieux?» Fig. 506: «Gare à qui ouvre son parapluie sous son toit»; fig. 507: «Qui brise un miroir connaîtra sept années de malchance.» (NLD)

506

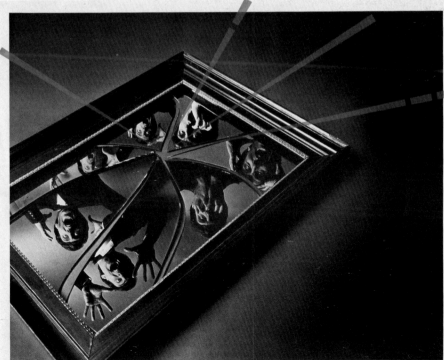

507

4

Record Covers

Calendars

Schallplatten-Umschläge

Kalender

Pochettes de disques

Calendriers

Record Covers
Schallplattenhüllen
Pochettes de disques

508

509

512

513

508 Cover of an RCA record featuring Pete Wyoming. In full colour. (GER)
509 Black-and-white cover for a CBS record of Ramsey Lewis singing popular songs. (USA)
510 Record cover of a Dave Davies album, member of the Kinks group. (USA)
511 Cover of a record featuring the guitarist Eric Gale. (USA)
512 For a Shaun Cassidy album, issued by *Warner Brothers*. Full-colour shot. (USA)
513 Cover in subdued shades of green and red for a rock-pop record issued by *Asylum Records*. (USA)
514 Cover of a Bruce Cockburn record issued by RCA. (USA)
515 For a record by W. Michels. Recto in black and white, verso in full colour. (GER)

508 Hülle für eine RCA-Schallplatte mit Aufnahmen von Pete Wyoming. In Farbe. (GER)
509 Schwarzweisse Hülle für eine CBS-Platte mit bekannten Songs von Ramsey Lewis. (USA)
510 Schallplattenhülle für Aufnahmen von Dave Davies, Mitglied der Gruppe Kinks. (USA)
511 «Ein Hauch von Seide.» Hülle für eine Platte des Gitarristen Eric Gale. (USA)
512 Für eine Schallplatte von Shaun Cassidy mit dem Titel «Wespe». Aufnahme in Farbe. (USA)
513 Hülle in gedämpften Grün- und Rottönen für eine Rock-Pop-Platte von *Asylum Records*. (USA)
514 Hülle für eine Schallplatte mit Aufnahmen von Bruce Cockburn, herausgegeben von RCA. (USA)
515 Für eine Platte von W. Michels. Vorderseite in Schwarzweiss, Rückseite in Farbe. (GER)

508 Pochette d'un disque RCA dont la vedette est Pete Wyoming. En couleur. (GER)
509 Pochette noir et blanc d'un disque CBS avec des enregistrements de Ramsey Lewis. (USA)
510 Pochette d'un disque de Dave Davies, membre du groupe Kinks. (USA)
511 «Un soupçon de soie.» Pochette d'un disque du guitariste Eric Gale. (USA)
512 Pour un disque de Shaun Cassidy intitulé «Guêpe». Photo couleur. (USA)
513 Pochette aux tons verts et rouges mats pour un disque rock-pop d'*Asylum Records*. (USA)
514 Pochette d'un disque RCA avec des enregistrements de Bruce Cockburn. (USA)
515 Pour un disque de W. Michels. Recto noir et blanc, verso couleur. (GER)

510

511

514

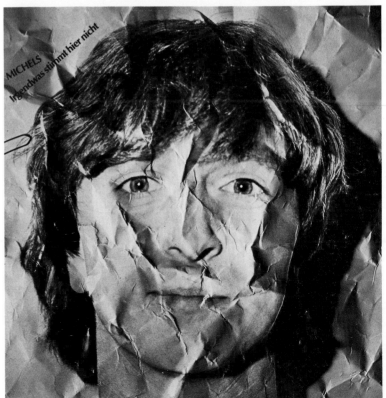

515

516

517

Record Covers
Schallplattenhüllen
Pochettes de disques

518

519

PHOTOGRAPHER:

516 Jim Shea
517 Welden Andersen
518 Steve Sakai
519 Bob Seidemann
520 Michael von Gimbut
521 David Kennedy
522, 523 Buddy Endress
524 Elliot Gilbert
525 Jacques Schumacher/
        Bert Brüggemann

DESIGNER / GESTALTER:

516 Ron Coro/
        Denise Minobe
517, 519 Tony Lane
518 Hans Inauen/Rod Dyer
520 Roland Schmidt
521 John Berg
522, 523 Paula Scher
524 Johnny Lee
525 Fact Design

520

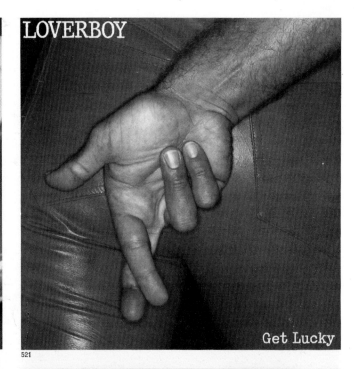

521

522

523

ART DIRECTOR:

516, 524 Ron Coro
517, 519 Tony Lane
518 George Osaki
520, 525 Stefan Böhle
521 John Berg
522, 523 Paula Scher

PUBLISHER:

516, 524 Elektra/Asylum/
        Nonesuch Records
517, 519, 521–523 CBS
        Records
518 MCA Records, Inc.
520 RCA Schallplatten
525 Polydor International

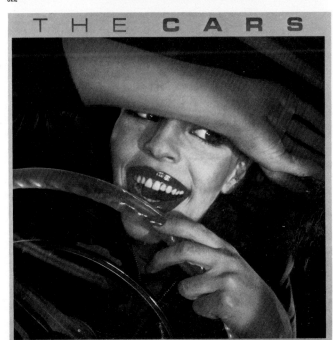

524

525

203

527

526

526, 527 Photograph and opened page of a Stephenson Inc. agenda. (USA)
528, 531, 532 Double spread and examples of unusually presented foodstuffs, taken from a Saga Corporation agenda. (USA)
529, 530 The calendar for *Knipping*, Gummersbach, screw manufacturers, offers "a programme to your taste" and shows screws photographically conjuncted with food – here a carrot and sweets. (GER)

526, 527 Aufnahme und aufgeschlagene Seite aus einer Agenda von Stephenson Inc. (USA)
528, 531, 532 Doppelseite und Beispiele von ungewöhnlich präsentierten Nahrungsmitteln, aus einer Agenda der Saga Corporation. (USA)
529, 530 «Ein Programm nach Ihrem Geschmack.» Aufnahmen aus einem Kalender des Schraubenherstellers *Knipping*, in dem alle Arten von Schrauben in Verbindung mit Nahrungs- und Genussmitteln präsentiert werden. (GER)

526, 527 Photo et page ouverte d'un agenda de Stephenson, Inc. (USA)
528, 531, 532 Double page et exemples d'aliments présentés de manière insolite. Agenda de la Saga Corporation. (USA)
529, 530 «Un programme à votre goût.» Photos d'un calendrier de la visserie *Knipping* où toutes sortes de vis sont présentées en association avec des produits alimentaires et des produits de consommation de luxe. (GER)

PHOTOGRAPHER / PHOTOGRAPH / PHOTOGRAPHE:

526, 527 Alfredo DaSilva
528, 531, 532 Bret Lopez
529, 530 Wolfgang Weiss

DESIGNER / GESTALTER / MAQUETTISTE:

526, 527 Jack Beveridge
528, 531, 532 Julie Riefler
529, 530 Wolfgang Weiss

AGENCY / AGENTUR / AGENCE – STUDIO:

526, 527 Beveridge & Associates Inc.
528, 531, 532 Bright & Associates
529, 530 Appelwerbung

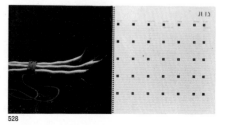

528

Calendars
Kalender
Calendriers

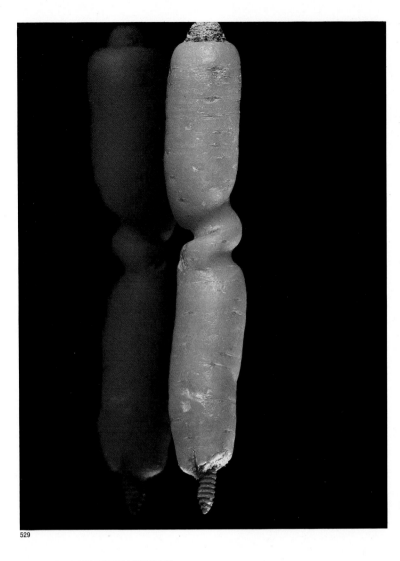

529

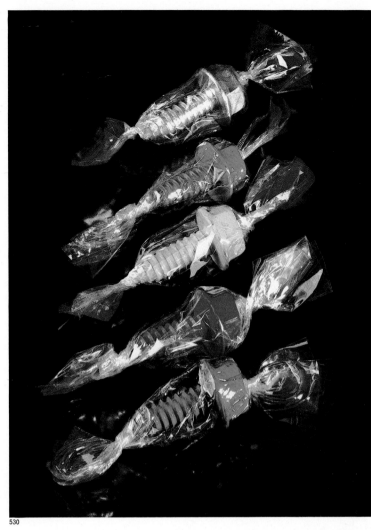

530

ART DIRECTOR / DIRECTEUR ARTISTIQUE:

526, 527 Jack Beveridge
528, 531, 532 Keith Bright

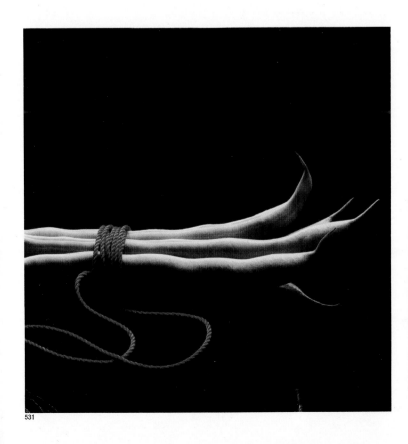

531

532

533

533 From the *AEG-Telefunken* calendar for 1982 consisting of aerial shots taken by the Swiss photographer Georg Gerster. Shown here is a photograph of Mount Olga, a red massif situated in Northern Territory, Australia. (GER)
534, 536 Photograph and complete sheet from the *AEG-Telefunken* wall calendar for 1982 (see also Fig. 533). This hundred metres high equestrian figure is cut in the turf near Osmington in the county of Dorset, England. (GER)
535 One of twelve photographs from a calendar for *Suntory Whisky.* Taken in strong, dazzling light, this woman's figure appears almost black with contrasting yellow glass. (JPN)

533 Beispiel aus dem *AEG-Telefunken*-Kalender 1982, der aus Luftaufnahmen des Schweizer Photographen Georg Gerster besteht. Hier eine Aufnahme des Mount Olga, ein Bergmassiv aus rotem Gestein im Northern Territory, Australien. (GER)
534, 536 Aufnahme und vollständiges Blatt aus dem *AEG-Telefunken*-Kalender für das Jahr 1982 (siehe auch Abb. 533). Dieses 100 m hohe, in das Gras geschnittene Reiterbild befindet sich bei Osmington, Dorset, England. (GER)
535 Eine von zwölf Aufnahmen aus einem Kalender für *Suntory Whisky.* Im starken Gegenlicht aufgenommene, fast schwarz wirkende Frauengestalt mit gelbem Glas. (JPN)

533 Photos tirées du calendrier d'*AEG-Telefunken* pour 1982 illustré de vues aériennes réalisées par le photographe suisse Georg Gerster. On voit ici le Mont Olga, un massif rocheux rougeâtre du Territoire du Nord australien. (GER)
534, 536 Photo et feuillet complet du calendrier d'*AEG-Telefunken* pour 1982 (cf. aussi la fig. 533). Cette figure équestre haute de 100 m taillée dans le gazon se trouve près d'Osmington, dans le Dorset, en Angleterre. (GER)
535 L'une des douze photos illustrant un calendrier réalisé pour *Suntory Whisky.* Personnage féminin pris à contre-jour, la lumière violente le faisant apparaître noir. Verre jaune. (JPN)

Calendars
Kalender
Calendriers

534

535

536

PHOTOGRAPHER / PHOTOGRAPH / PHOTOGRAPHE:

533, 534, 536 Georg Gerster
535 Jerry Friedman

DESIGNER / GESTALTER / MAQUETTISTE:

533, 534, 536 Werner E. Müller
535 Jerry Friedman

ART DIRECTOR / DIRECTEUR ARTISTIQUE:

535 Jerry Friedman

Calendars
Kalender
Calendriers

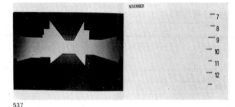

537

538

537–539 A complete double spread, cover illustration and photograph from an agenda for 1983 consisting of photographs by the New York photographer Jay Maisel, entitled *America, America*. A colour photograph is devoted to each week. The photograph for the cover was taken in Kansas (Fig. 538) and the one in Fig. 539 was taken in New York. (USA)

540–542 Two motifs and one complete sheet from the 1982 calendar of Brillant Offset GmbH & Co., Hamburg. The title of the calendar is *Segelflieger* (Gliders). The photographs were obtained with the aid of sophisticated technical equipment and at the cost of considerable effort on the part of the glider pilots in Germany, Austria and the USA. (GER)

537–539 Eine vollständige Doppelseite, Umschlagillustration und Aufnahme aus einer Agenda für das Jahr 1983 mit Aufnahmen des New Yorker Photographen Jay Maisel, unter dem Titel *America, America*. Jede Woche wird von einer Farbaufnahme begleitet. Das Photo für den Umschlag wurde in Kansas aufgenommen (Abb. 538), jenes in Abb. 539 in New York. (USA)

540–542 Zwei Motive und ein vollständiges Blatt aus dem Kalender 1982 der Brillant Offset GmbH & Co., Hamburg. Der Titel des Kalenders ist *Segelflieger*. Die Luftaufnahmen entstanden unter ungewöhnlichem technischem und fliegerischem Aufwand in Deutschland, Österreich und den USA und wurden durch H.-W. Grosse, K. Hillenbrand, K. Hollighaus, T. Schirzinger und die Publikationen *Geo* und *Zeit* ermöglicht. (GER)

539

540

541

PHOTOGRAPHER / PHOTOGRAPH:

537–539 Jay Maisel
540–542 Gert Wagner

DESIGNER / GESTALTER / MAQUETTISTE:

540–542 Eike Göpffarth

ART DIRECTOR / DIRECTEUR ARTISTIQUE:

537–539 Linda Simmons

537–539 Double page complète, illustration de couverture et photo d'un agenda pour 1983 illustré par le photographe newyorkais Jay Maisel sous le titre de *America, America*, à raison d'une photo par semaine de l'agenda. L'illustration de couverture a pour thème le Kansas (fig. 538), celle de la fig. 539 provient de New York. (USA)
540–542 Deux sujets et un feuillet complet du calendrier de Brillant Offset GmbH & Co., Hambourg, intitulé *Planeurs*. Les photos, réalisées au prix de véritables prouesses aériennes et techniques en Allemagne, Autriche et aux Etats-Unis, sont dues à H.-W. Grosse, K. Hillenbrand, K. Hollighaus, T. Schirzinger, avec le concours des publications *Geo* et *Zeit*. (GER)

542

543

544

Calendars
Kalender
Calendriers

PHOTOGRAPHER / PHOTOGRAPH / PHOTOGRAPHE:

543–547 Uwe Loesch
548, 549 Siegfried Himmer

DESIGNER / GESTALTER / MAQUETTISTE:

548, 549 Klaus Winterhager

545

546

547

543-547 Photographs and complete sheet from the calendar *In Sight 82* of the Uwe Loetsch advertising studio. Fig. 543: Potters Fields, London, for February, mainly in brown-grey; Fig. 544: Earls Court, London, for March, mainly in various blue shades; Figs. 545, 546: Brooklyn Bridge, New York, for January, blue with pink; Fig. 547: Queensboro Bridge, New York, for May, blue sky. (GER)
548, 549 Complete sheet for December, and colour photograph, from the 1982 calendar issued by W. Brügmann & Sohn, Dortmund, makers of wood and plastic products. All twelve of the large-format sheets show scenes from virgin forests photographed by Siegfried Himmer. (GER)

543-547 Aufnahmen und vollständiges Blatt aus dem Kalender *In Sight 82* des Werbestudios Uwe Loetsch. Abb. 543: Potters Fields, London, für Februar, vorwiegend in Braungrau; Abb. 544: Earls Court, London, für März, mit verschiedenen Blautönen; Abb. 545, 546: Brooklyn Bridge, New York, für Januar, Blau mit Rosa; Abb. 547: Queensboro Bridge, New York, für Mai, blauer Himmel. (GER)
548, 549 Vollständiges Dezemberblatt und entsprechendes Farbphoto aus dem Kalender 1982 der Unternehmensgruppe *Brügmann*, Dortmund, Hersteller von Holz- und Kunststoffprodukten. Alle zwölf grossformatigen Blätter zeigen Aufnahmen, die Siegfried Himmer im Urwald machte. (GER)

543-547 Photos et feuillet complet du calendrier *In Sight 82* du studio publicitaire Uwe Loetsch. Fig. 543: Potters Field, Londres – février, tons gris brun prédominants; fig. 544: Earls Court, Londres – mars, avec divers bleus; fig. 545, 546: Brooklyn Bridge, New York – janvier, bleu et rose; fig. 547: Queensboro Bridge, New York – mai, ciel bleu. (GER)
548, 549 Feuillet complet pour décembre et photo couleur l'illustrant dans le calendrier pour 1982 du groupe d'entreprises *Brügmann* de Dortmund, qui fabrique des produits bois et plastique. Siegfried Himmer a photographié la forêt vierge pour ces 12 feuillets grand format. (GER)

ART DIRECTOR / DIRECTEUR ARTISTIQUE:

543-547 Uwe Loesch
548, 549 Siegfried Himmer

AGENCY / AGENTUR / AGENCE – STUDIO:

543-547 Arbeitsgemeinschaft für visuelle und
          verbale Kommunikation Uwe Loesch

548

549

550

551

552

PHOTOGRAPHER / PHOTOGRAPH / PHOTOGRAPHE:

550, 551 Pete Turner
552, 553 Evert van Kuik

DESIGNER / GESTALTER / MAQUETTISTE:

552, 553 Peter Jan Schuin

ART DIRECTOR / DIRECTEUR ARTISTIQUE:

550, 551 Olaf Leu
552, 553 Peter Jan Schuin

AGENCY / AGENTUR / AGENCE – STUDIO:

550, 551 Olaf Leu Design & Partner
552, 553 Peter Jan Schuin

550, 551 Two motifs from the calendar of Druckfarbenfabrik Gebr. Schmidt GmbH, Frankfurt, printing ink manufacturers. The title of this 1982 calendar is *Color Space*, and the pictures are Pete Turners's personal visions inspired by space travel—this New York photographer using his medium as a design tool to present aspects of the universe. (GER)
552, 553 Complete sheet and motif in actual size from the 1982 calendar made for *Lutkie Combinatie*. (NLD)

550, 551 Zwei Motive aus dem Wandkalender der Druckfarbenfabrik Gebr. Schmidt GmbH, Frankfurt, für das Jahr 1982. Der Titel des Kalenders ist *Color Space*, und die Aufnahmen stammen von dem New Yorker Photographen Pete Turner, der damit seine persönlichen Visionen von den «Welten im Weltraum» präsentiert. (GER)
552, 553 Vollständiges Blatt und Motiv in Originalgrösse aus dem Kalender 1982 für *Lutkie Combinatie*. (NLD)

550, 551 Deux sujets du calendrier mural pour 1982 de la fabrique d'encres d'imprimerie Gebr. Schmidt GmbH de Francfort, publié sous le titre *Color Space* (Espace couleur). Les illustrations sont du photographe newyorkais Pete Turner, qui y présente sa vision personnelle des «mondes dans l'espace». (GER)
552, 553 Feuillet complet et sujet au format original tirés du calendrier pour 1982 de *Lutkie Combinatie*. (NLD)

553

Calendars
Kalender
Calendriers

554, 555 Complete sheet and photograph in actual size from a Stephenson Inc. calendar. (USA)
556 Another motif from the 1981 calendar of Stephenson Inc. (see Figs. 554, 555). The "Still Life" photographed by Alfredo da Silva was reflected off a silver mylar film, which was then manipulated until the desired level of distortion of elements was achieved. (USA)
557–559 Complete sheet and two motifs from a calendar for the Japanese company Matsushita Electric Industrial Co., Ltd. The photographs are in full colour. (JPN)

554, 555 Vollständiges Blatt und Aufnahme («Mond über Golden Gate») in Originalgrösse aus einer Agenda für Stephenson Inc. (USA)
556 Ein weiteres Motiv aus der Agenda 1981 der Stephenson Inc. (s. Abb. 554, 555). Alfredo da Silva photographierte das Stilleben nicht direkt, sondern dessen Reflexion von einem «Mylar»-Silberfilm, der entsprechend der gewünschten Deformation der Elemente manipuliert wurde. (USA)
557–559 Vollständiges Blatt und zwei Motive aus einem Wandkalender für die japanische Firma Matsushita Electric Industrial Co., Ltd. Farbaufnahmen. (JPN)

554, 555 Feuillet complet et photo («La Lune au-dessus de la Golden Gate») au format original figurant dans un agenda réalisé pour Stephenson, Inc. (USA)
556 Un autre sujet tiré de l'agenda de Stephenson, Inc. (cf. les fig. 554, 555). Alfredo da Silva n'a pas photographié directement cette nature morte, mais la réflexion du sujet sur un film argent Mylar manipulé en fonction de la déformation recherchée des éléments. (USA)
557–559 Feuillet complet et deux sujets d'un calendrier mural de la société japonaise Matsushita Electric Industrial Co., Ltd. Photos couleur. (JPN)

554

557

PHOTOGRAPHER / PHOTOGRAPH:

554, 555 Roger Miller
556 Alfredo DaSilva
557–559 Takakiyo Okamoto

DESIGNER:

554–556 Jack Beveridge
557–559 Hideki Katsura

ART DIRECTOR / DIRECTEUR ARTISTIQUE:

554–556 Jack Beveridge
557–559 Hideki Bamba/
    Yoshihiro Thujitani

555

558

559

AGENCY / AGENTUR / AGENCE – STUDIO:

554–556 Beveridge & Associates, Inc.
557–559 Pana Co., Ltd.

566

561

562

560, 561 Motif and complete sheet from the 1983 calendar of the *American President Lines* shipping company. The photograph refers to Galileo Galilei and the time when the telescope (reconstructed by Galileo Galilei one year after it had been invented in Holland) was the sailor's only aid as opposed to today's computerized electronic systems. (USA)
562, 563 Complete sheet and one of the twelve motifs used in the 1982 *Porsche* calendar. Each of the photographs shows a *Porsche* car in a typical European landscape, here Piazza del Campo in Siena, Italy. (GER)

560, 561 Motiv und vollständiges Blatt aus einem Wandkalender der Reederei *American President Lines* für 1983. Die Aufnahme bezieht sich auf Galileo Galilei und jene Zeit, als das Fernrohr (von Galileo Galilei ein Jahr nach dessen Erfindung in Holland nachgebaut) das einzige Hilfsmittel der Seefahrer war, im Gegensatz zu der heutigen elektronischen Ausrüstung. (USA)
562, 563 Vollständiges Blatt und eines der zwölf im *Porsche*-Kalender 1982 verwendeten Motive. Jede der Aufnahmen zeigt einen *Porsche* in einer typisch europäischen Landschaft, hier Piazza del Campo in Siena, Italien. (GER)

560, 561 Sujet et feuillet complet du calendrier mural pour 1983 de l'armateur *American President Lines*. La photo se rapporte à Galilée et à l'époque où la longue-vue (réalisée par Galilée un an après qu'elle eut été inventée en Hollande) constituait le seul instrument d'orientation des marins contrairement à l'équipement électronique actuel. (USA)
562, 563 Feuillet complet et l'un des 12 sujets du calendrier *Porsche* pour 1982. Les photos montrent des *Porsche* dans des sites européens caractéristiques, ici la Piazza del Campo de Sienne (Italie). (GER)

PHOTOGRAPHER / PHOTOGRAPH:

560, 561 Terry Heffernan/Light Language
562, 563 Karen Ostertag

DESIGNER / GESTALTER / MAQUETTISTE:

560, 561 Kit Hinrichs
562, 563 Werbeagentur Strenger GmbH

AGENCY / AGENTUR / AGENCE – STUDIO:

560, 561 Jonson Pedersen Hinrichs & Shakery
562, 563 Werbeagentur Strenger GmbH

Calendars
Kalender
Calendriers

563

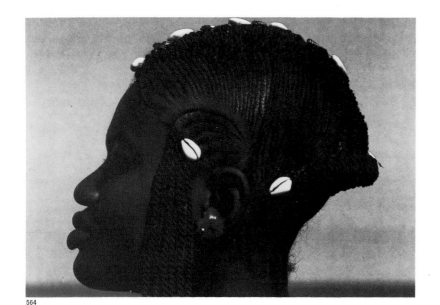

564

PHOTOGRAPHER / PHOTOGRAPH / PHOTOGRAPHE:

564 Guido Mangold
565 Hiroji Kubota
566 Hans-Jürgen Burkard
567, 568 Peter Johnson

DESIGNER / GESTALTER / MAQUETTISTE:

564–568 Franz Braun / Erwin Ehret

565

566

**Calendars
Kalender
Calendriers**

567

564-568 Motifs from the 1982 calendar issued by the geographic magazine *Geo*, with a complete specimen sheet for May (Fig. 567). The pictures reproduced here are a girl of the Wolof tribe (but with Ashanti features) living in Sene-gambia, who has decorated her hair with shells and golden ornaments (Fig. 564); the conical mountains of Guilin in Southern China (Fig. 565); chapels, cells and stables of the longdeserted monastery of Korama cut in the curious tufa hills of Cappadocia, Turkey (Fig. 566); and stones of many provenances found in a depression in the Namib Desert, South West Africa (Figs. 567, 568). (GER)

564-568 Motive und ein vollständiges Blatt aus dem von der Zeitschrift *Geo* (Gruner + Jahr AG, Hamburg) herausgegebenen Kalender für 1982. Die hier abgebildeten Aufnahmen zeigen eine Frau aus dem Wolof-Stamm (aber mit klassischen Zügen der Ashanti), der in Senegambia lebt; in ihrer Frisur sind Muscheln und Goldornamente verflochten (Abb. 564); die Kegelberge von Guilin in Südchina (Abb. 565); die Kapellen, Zellen und Stallungen des in die Tuffkegel Kappadokiens (Türkei) gehauenen und seit 100 Jahren verlassenen byzantinischen Klosters Korama (Abb. 566); Flusskiesel unterschiedlicher Herkunft, die von den Regenfluten in eine Senke der südwestafrikanischen Namib-Wüste geschwemmt wurden (Abb. 567, 568). (GER)

564-568 Motifs du calendrier publié par le magazine géographique *Geo*, avec un feuillet type complet, celui du mois de mai (fig. 567). Les sujets des photos: une jeune fille ouolof (mais aux traits achanti) de Sénégambie, à la chevelure décorée de coquillages et d'ornements dorés (fig. 564); les montagnes aiguës de Guilin, Chine du Sud (fig. 565); les chapelles, cellules et étables du monastère rupestre désaffecté de Korama en Cappadoce (Turquie), creusé à même de tuf (fig. 566); des pierres de diverse origine trouvées dans une dépression du désert de Namib dans le Sud-Ouest africain (fig. 567, 568). (GER)

568

569   570

569–571 Complete sheet and two of twelve motifs from the calendar issued by the Smiling Advertising Team Studio 6, Lausanne, Switzerland, and entitled *The Best of the World's Sport Photography '82.* Fig. 571 is a black-and-white photograph from this 1983 calendar. (SWI)

572–574 Two motifs and a complete sheet from the 1983 calendar issued by *Nikon* and Vontobel, lithographers, with shots taken by various photographers—here for August and July. (SWI)

572

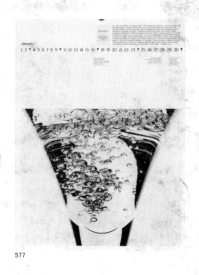

576

577

PHOTOGRAPHER / PHOTOGRAPH / PHOTOGRAPHE:

575, 576 Jordi Gomez
577–580 Peter Hendrie

DESIGNER / GESTALTER / MAQUETTISTE:

575, 576 Yves Zimmermann
577–580 Kan Cato

ART DIRECTOR / DIRECTEUR ARTISTIQUE:

577–580 Ken Cato

AGENCY / AGENTUR / AGENCE – STUDIO:

575, 576 Diseño Integral
577–580 Cato Hibberd Design Pty Ltd

578

575, 576 Detail of the photograph and complete sheet from the 1982 calendar issued by *Cromoherma*, offset printers and lithographers. (SPA)
577–580 Complete sheet and three of twelve colour photographs from the 1982 Australian Classic Wine Calendar, which contains information about certain wines as well as about wine exhibitions and winetasting. The examples shown here are shots of white wine; photographs in various yellow and brown shades. (AUS)

575, 576 Detail der Aufnahme und vollständiges Blatt aus dem Wandkalender des Offset-Druckers und Lithographen *Cromoherma* für das Jahr 1982. (SPA)
577–580 Vollständiges Blatt und drei von zwölf Farbaufnahmen aus einem Wandkalender, der dem australischen Wein gewidmet ist. Er enthält Informationen über bestimmte Weine sowie über Weinausstellungen und Degustationen. Die hier gezeigten Beispiele sind Aufnahmen von Weissweinen, in verschiedenen Gelb- und Brauntönen. (AUS)

575, 576 Détail de la photo et feuillet où elle figure dans le calendrier mural pour 1982 de l'imprimerie offset et de l'atelier de lithographie *Cromoherma*. (SPA)
577–580 Feuillet complet et trois des douze photos couleur d'un calendrier mural consacré aux vins d'Australie. On y trouve des renseignements sur les divers crus, les expositions vinicoles et les séances de dégustation. Les exemples montrés ici sont relatifs à des vins blancs aux divers tons jaunes et bruns. (AUS)

579

580

Paper / Papier: Papierfabrik Biberist–Biber art paper, super white, glaced,
130 gm² and Biber Offset SK3, pure white, machine-finished, 140 gm² /
Biber-Kunstdruck ultra weiss, glaciert, 130 mg²
und Biber-Offset SK3, hochweiss, maschinenglatt, 140 gm²

Printed by / gedruckt von: Sigg Söhne AG, Winterthur
(Colour pages and dust jacket / Farbseiten und Schutzumschlag),
Merkur AG, Langenthal (black and white / schwarzweiss)

Typesetting / Lichtsatz: Sauerländer AG, Aarau (Univers,
MONOTYPE-Lasercomp)

Binding / Einband: Buchbinderei Schumacher AG, Bern / Schmitten

Glossy lamination / Glanzfoliierung: Durolit AG, Pfäffikon SZ